Haunting and the Educa

Bold Visions in Educational Research

Volume 43

Scope:

Bold Visions in Educational Research is international in scope and includes books from two areas: *teaching and learning to teach* and *research methods in education*. Each area contains multi-authored handbooks of approximately 200,000 words and monographs (authored and edited collections) of approximately 130,000 words. All books are scholarly, written to engage specified readers and catalyze changes in policies and practices. Defining characteristics of books in the series are their explicit uses of theory and associated methodologies to address important problems. We invite books from across a theoretical and methodological spectrum from scholars employing quantitative, statistical, experimental, ethnographic, semiotic, hermeneutic, historical, ethnomethodological, phenomenological, case studies, action, cultural studies, content analysis, rhetorical, deconstructive, critical, literary, aesthetic and other research methods.

Books on *teaching and learning to teach* focus on any of the curriculum areas (e.g., literacy, science, mathematics, social science), in and out of school settings, and points along the age continuum (pre K to adult). The purpose of books on *research methods in education* is **not** to present generalized and abstract procedures but to show how research is undertaken, highlighting the particulars that pertain to a study. Each book brings to the foreground those details that must be considered at every step on the way to doing a good study. The goal is **not** to show how generalizable methods are but to present rich descriptions to show how research is enacted. The books focus on methodology, within a context of substantive results so that methods, theory, and the processes leading to empirical analyses and outcomes are juxtaposed. In this way method is not reified, but is explored within well-described contexts and the emergent research outcomes. Three illustrative examples of books are those that allow proponents of particular perspectives to interact and debate, comprehensive handbooks where leading scholars explore particular genres of inquiry in detail, and introductory texts to particular educational research methods/issues of interest to novice researchers.

Haunting and the Educational Imagination

Barbara Regenspan
Colgate University, New York, USA

SENSE PUBLISHERS
ROTTERDAM / BOSTON / TAIPEI

A C.I.P. record for this book is available from the Library of Congress.

ISBN 978-94-6209-816-9 (paperback)
ISBN 978-94-6209-817-6 (hardback)
ISBN 978-94-6209-818-3 (e-book)

Published by: Sense Publishers,
P.O. Box 21858, 3001 AW Rotterdam, The Netherlands
https://www.sensepublishers.com/

Cover design by Madison Kuhn

Printed on acid-free paper

This book is dedicated to my sister-in-law, Susan Milligan, whose commitment to making the appreciation and creation of jazz music central to preschool curriculum in the current neoliberal era makes her a teacher-heroine.

I also want to honor seven people who died during the years I was writing the manuscript, and whose inspiration for my life has been immeasurable: the poet Seamus Heaney; musician Dave Brubeck; Rochester, New York-based psychotherapist Armin Klein; Ithaca-based therapist Carole McCarthy; educational philosopher/theorists Jean Anyon and Sara Ruddick, and beloved model for my life's work, Maxine Greene.

CONTENTS

ACKNOWLEDGMENTS

This book evolved from reflections on numerous classes; conversations with colleagues, students, friends, and family members; dreams; conference presentations; and writing workshop sessions, both formal and informal. I cannot thank all of the people who, through their participation in my life, contributed to its conception and creation, but I teach in a department whose members make me want to come to work each day, and who equally stimulate my thinking and warm my heart. To Kay Johnston, John Palmer, Sheila Clonan, Melissa Kagle, Mark Stern, Anna Rios, Susan Woolley, Jo Anne Pagano (now retired), and for a term as visitor, Janie Ward, I owe special thanks. The work of a number of them is featured in this book. Tony Hoagland has been a terrific source of inspiration and comfort throughout the writing of this book, and he also approved the poem at the end, as did my poet friend and colleague, Peter Balakian.

Colgate University has been very generous to me and has provided me with a wonderful work environment for more than eight years. I am grateful to all of its administrators, faculty, and staff.

The actual earliest writing of this book was supported by numerous formal and informal writing support groups convened by writer-friends, including my beloved Binghamton University colleagues Judy Kugelmass and Sue Crowley; my former Colgate colleague Nisha Thapliyal; Patricia Lewis and Diana Gordon of the Patchwork Farm writing retreats; Irene Zahava of Zee's Writing Studio in Ithaca, New York; workshops at the Rowe Retreat Center led by poets Tony Hoagland and Marie Howe; The Colgate Writers Conference of summer, 2010, led by my generous colleague and friend Peter Balakian; leaders of Amherst Writers and Artists' group sessions; and the Friday morning writers' group led by Ellen Watson, (translator of the Brazilian poet, Adelia Prado) of the Smith College Poetry Center. Emerging individual chapters were critiqued by my dear friend Cathy Currier.

Other early readers were Hamilton Central School's editor extraordinaire, Donna Moren, and former MAT student Christina Alexander. More recently, my friend, psychologist Jonathan Hartshorne, and my own beloved student teaching supervisor (and later, principal), Florence Seldin, read, appreciated, and reflected with me on Chapter 6. Friend and colleague Celia Oyler at Teachers' College has been a source of detailed feedback, inspiration, encouragement, and faith. Wendy Kohli welcomed a read of the entire manuscript at the point her reading would be most helpful to me. Mark Stern, who gave me not only numerous suggestions of resources, but also the framing of this book—the concept of hauntagogy—read and offered useful feedback on Chapter 3, which features his own dissertation research. Deborah Britzman's support for my use of her theory in an earlier iteration of Chapter 6 brought much-needed encouragement during a challenging time in my envisioning of the book. That early iteration of Chapter 6 was based on my teaching of an article by my colleague and friend at Colgate, Emilio Spadola, and Emilio's very personal reception of my writing about his conversion to Islam led me to a slight softening of tone that I know improved the entire manuscript. Former colleague from Binghamton and friend Joe DeVitis offered mixed feedback of an earlier draft of the manuscript that helped me refocus some earlier content and tighten the connections between and among the chapters. Friend and colleague Paula Salvio introduced me to the work of Bill Readings and supplied greatly appreciated encouragement. Neighbor and freelance editor Chelly Crouch read and gave insightful feedback on four chapters.

The charge to write presidential addresses for the annual conference of NYSFEA kept me especially inspired, and the dedicated core members of that organization have provided me with a loving and critical environment to develop my ideas. To Sue Books, Jane Fowler Morse, Mark Garrison, Richard Ognibene, David McGough, Shawgi Tel, Rachel Bailey-Jones, Arlene Leach-Bizari, Leigh M. O'Brien, David Granger, Brian Morgan, Linda Steet, Joyce Lehman, and the late Norm Bauer: I feel deep gratitude.

Ellen Boesenberg, Denise Yull, Kjersti Van Slyke, Barrel Gueye, Annette Passapera, Laura Lamash, Rebecca Hemzik, Joan Koster, and Elizabeth Bloom are former doctoral students from Binghamton University whose work has profoundly influenced my own thinking. Elizabeth, now president of NYSFEA, continues to inspire me as a leader among teacher educators in the movement to oppose the current neoliberal standardization and testing debacle as it plays out in New York State.

In early summer 2012, a wonderful Colgate undergraduate student, Diana Stephens, who was an advisee of mine in educational studies and had taken my curriculum theory course, and the Democracy and Education seminar explored in Chapter 2, served as my research assistant. Diana sorted through more than one hundred computer files of my writing, assigning each of them to a folder correlated with my description of intentions for the chapters that developed into this book. Diana had an ability to reinforce correlations between and among ideas that I had not yet fully articulated.

During the summer and fall terms of 2013, two other exceptional students, both in the MAT secondary English program I lead, read the chapters of the first draft and commented on its strengths and problems from the perspectives of their own wonderful minds and deep hearts. Jennifer McDowall, returning to graduate school after significant life experience in both theater and work in the corporate world and step-mother of three high school-age children, had been a stellar student in my Philosophies of Education the previous term. Her comments on my manuscript helped me reframe the introduction, reorder the chapters, and refine the wording of other chapters. She not only introduced me to the essay by Louise Glück that helped shape the epilogue of this book, but she also moved me to appreciate its specific haunting focus in an essay she wrote in our course. Mary Dinapoli is the second MAT student who served as an editor, and it is difficult to imagine having brought the book to completion without her. Wise beyond her years, she is also a truly gifted editor who sat across from me at my kitchen table and challenged me on unclear ideas and too-long sentences. Mary is also well-schooled in post-modern social and literary criticism, and her insights into my occasionally rigid structuralist allegiances were invaluable. She developed an identification with my book project that was genuinely moving to me; our wrangling over ideas and wording represented the capacity of a teacher-student relationship to become genuinely peerful. Finally, Tom Wiley, current MAT student teacher in English, both amplified and interpreted the astute revision requests of the anonymous and encouraging reviewer assigned by my co-editor at Sense, Carolyne Ali-Khan. Tom had the uncanny ability to raise a question about my intentions in a passage of text that immediately alerted me to what was wrong with it. We have tentative plans to write about how and what we learned not only as a result of this collaborative process, but also from his being a student in two classes of mine, one of which was more successful than the other. Tom also proved to be a gifted manuscript formatter.

I must thank other sustaining friends, colleagues, cooperating teachers, and family members who influenced this book in different ways: Kay Embrey, Deb Margolin, Barbara Neman, Rebecca Younes, Betsey Fernbach, Noa Dauber, Tasha Kimball, Joseph and Barbara Blumenthal, Maudemarie Clark, Nancy Ries, Larry Klein, Alan Cooper, Helen Kebabian, Jill Harsin, Rich Regen and Eileen Larence, Georgia Frank, Beverly Rainforth, Ulla Grappard, Dai Yamamoto, Kira Stevens, Jessica Kaplan and Mark Fowler, Judith Spiegel, Ardyth and Gil Gillespie, Arthur Godin and Joanna Green, Ruth Hartshorne, Heather Dunshee, Rachel Milligan, Dan Ferat, Terry and Susan Milligan, Deb Dushko, Rich Bernstein, Pat Stringham, Kathy Sabino, Holly White, Donna Moren, Brian Rose, Harry Jarcho, Dena, Liz, and Isaac Bodian, Rick Hanson, Mike Levy, Wendy Everard, Christie Brenneck, Jane Pinchin, Madeleine Grumet, and David and Marcia Radin of the Ithaca Zen Center.

Joe Greenberg, former principal, and Diane Carruthers, current principal, of the Lehman Alternative Community in Ithaca have welcomed and continue to welcome me and my students into their public school that models the social justice focus so central to our programs at Colgate. The visionary leadership of Project Looksharp by Chris Sperry and Cyndy Scheibe keeps alive the critical media literacy focus that has been a compelling influence on my own teaching and thinking. Similarly, the inspirational work of Melissa Davies at Colgate in the development and teaching of Visual Thinking Strategies, including direct work with my students, has provided me with another model for curriculum-making.

My decision to recently rework the first chapter of this book is a tribute to the boldness, irreverance and intellectual flexibility of the students in my spring term, 2014 Child and Adolescent Growth course, a course I was teaching for the first time. It was especially the unwillingness of Melissa Melendez to see her family and neighbourhood obliterated by the values of ego psychology that turned the course on its head and guided all of us on one wild ride!

I want to also thank the students on Colgate's 2012 Manchester Study Group, whose work with me that term in the UK inspired my decision to reframe Chapter 6 around my teaching of *This Side of Brightness*. Jessica Aquino from the study group created a wonderful cover design for this book, as did Madi Kuhn from my Fall 2013 first-year seminar on The Challenges of Modernity. Wendy Hernandez and Katya Meltaus gave me permission to include in the book their especially helpful contributions to class discussion in Curriculum Theory, and Moana Fogg allowed me to use both her exceptional student teaching experience and her special project/masters thesis. Amy Brown worked with me to come to a deeper understanding of the works of Deborah Britzman in a non-credit study group we convened just for the fun of it. Without Kate Maffei's excellent work organizing this year's NYSFEA conference, I could never have completed my book in time. I owe a great debt to too many other beloved students to name.

I have Michel Lokhorst and Ken Tobin to thank for the contract from Sense which came at a time when I feared I would have to reshape my manuscript so that it conformed to an already established genre. I remain so grateful to them that they believed in the integrity of what I created. Carolyne Ali-Khan, my co-editor at Sense, has conveyed that same quality of respect for my vision, and has been a pleasure to work with. She has shepherded this book through to completion with a mindfulness I have rarely experienced in someone whom I had not known personally. She took great pains to interpret for me the reviewer's intentions in a way that kept me fully invested in the significant editing process after I thought the book was finished. My deep thanks go to Rebecca Costello, an extremely kind and gifted copy-editor at Colgate who handled the first preparation of this manuscript for publication in record time.

My family has sustained me throughout the writing of this long-in-gestation project, but has also contributed significantly to my thinking. As a community organizer, my loving daughter Sarah knows the griefs and joys of deep commitment to social justice. As a web developer, Ben regularly shoots me sources and inspiration. More significantly, my children are exactly the ones I needed to help me sort out my own complex personhood and to grow my capacity to love and be loved. I am extremely grateful for their willingness to allow stories of their growing up to be included in my book.

Finally, I am married to the most widely literate person I know, a man whose intellectual curiosity, deep spirituality, musicality, fabulous humor, and unfailing love and honesty have given me much of the joy of my adult life. David is also a great editor who knows every idea in this book, but I am stubborn, so he deserves no blame.

INTRODUCTION

LOCATING PRESENT ABSENCES

As an educational philosopher who learned from John Dewey to equate life and education, I write letters to editors and websites as a part of my job description. At the beginning of the Iraq War, I wrote a letter to the editor of Binghamton, New York's *Democrat & Chronicle* newspaper asking what it meant for our supposedly "safer" Western young people to learn that the death of Iraqi children in this war was publicly classified and legitimated as "collateral damage." I proposed an inquiry into the concept of "collateral damage" as school curriculum, certain from my knowledge of child and adolescent development that without the opportunity to unpeel the layers of oppressive assumptions whereby the killing of certain children could be legitimized, our supposedly safer young people would need to emotionally detach from Iraqi children in order to feel safe themselves. Clearly such detachment would bode poorly for sane political directions for this generation, facing global warming and the realization that we can no longer afford empire-building as a "growth" strategy. Western children's alliance with their peers around the globe was certainly more likely to promote such a dialogue about the global future. Further, I suggested that the phrase "downsizing to protect the health of the economy," quoted from a local manager explaining a recent round of layoffs in that same issue of the *Democrat & Chronicle*, might be introduced in that curricular unit plan as well. I did not use the term "haunted discourse" at the time, suggesting in my letter that both of these conceptions left unexamined—that dead children of certain ethnic or nationality groups represented legitimate collateral damage, and that creating unemployment brought health to the economy—would "haunt" the educations of our young people.

By haunting I refer to the distorting *present absences* in the curriculum of both schooling and the less formal education the society offers young people. They receive this less formal education through the media and their everyday experience, both of which are increasingly shaped by market relations. What can be bought and sold, for how much, and to whom has been negotiated through violent suppression of some groups by others throughout history. Such violent negotiations have determined, for instance, who will select those whose lives can be dismissed as collateral damage. This intentional violence and its impact are unacknowledged in the curriculum, but profoundly present in the form of ideological obfuscations like individualism, patriotism, and related, American exceptionalism, and the presentation of militarization as ordinary. Such ideological obfuscations, in turn, mask classism, white supremacy, sexism, and homophobia, which exist as a ghostly presence in the curriculum. Added to these unacknowledged oppressions is a more recent obsession with the accountability of all but the capitalist class. In public schools, standards and testing dominate the curriculum, producing the distorted perception that only what is testable is important. Exploration of qualities like our knowledge of our interdependence as human beings, for instance, falls out of the curriculum, along with conceptions of the value of emotions, once understood to be an aspect of thinking. Indeed, the understanding of the legitimate presence of emotionality in thinking was famously re-illuminated in the field of educational philosophy by Elliot Eisner, author of the classic *The Educational Imagination*, intentionally inscribed in the title of my book (Eisner, 1979/2002).

In both normalizing the obliteration of an Iraqi child's life as collateral damage, and in the normalizing of an intentional process of making people unemployed as promotion of economic health, we experience the phenomenon of market relations defining human relations. The insurance of profit to Haliburton, Bechtel, and Blackwater corporations as well as swift marketization of Iraqi society in the name of "democracy promotion" was reason enough to fight an illegal war on pretences known to be false, a war that would kill Iraqi children as collateral damage. My intention as a teacher and teacher educator writing that letter was to state the obvious—to recognize that our lives, and the curriculum of public schooling as representative of the values expressed by those lives, are haunted by market relations. Further, the assumption of the normalcy of these relations translates into uses of language that are fundamentally mis-educative, identified with what I am calling *haunted discourse*. A hope I continue to nurture and explore repeatedly in this book is that a growing chorus of people are noticing the devastating threat not only to the *lives* of socially marginalized children but to the ordinary child and adolescent *development* of all young people in the internalization of market relations as normalcy—indeed, increasingly as education. I identify with the pedagogical practices that seek to reclaim from their straitjacketing in market relations, which my colleague, Mark Stern, has named hauntagogy. "Haunting plus pedagogy = *hauntagogy*" (Stern, 2012). Hauntagogy, then, refers to teaching which privileges broadened conceptions of knowledge and thinking that make social injustice and the complexity of human life visible. It is a process that unearths both happy and unhappy ghosts, delivering them into the curriculum of life and schooling in the hopes that they will inspire enlivening artistic and intellectual expression and citizen activism.

I had intuited that haunted sites, places in the curriculum where masked discourses bury unpleasant or inconvenient knowledge, are markers for clues about what sociologist Avery Gordon names a *something-to-be-done*. Now, with access to Gordon's magnificent book, *Ghostly Matters: Haunting and the Sociological Imagination* (Gordon, 2008), I have become more intentional about the unearthing of haunted sites and their intimation of a something-to-be-done as the practice of teacher education. This book is my record of that project to date. As a Deweyan teacher educator in the educational studies department of Colgate University, I work from John Dewey's partly idealistic assumption that education is life, as stated above. Then, life (as education) is the project of enhancing personal growth in the context of fueling the nurturing capacities of communities, with communities understood to circumscribe each individual growth project.

I bring complications to this book, however. My framing draws from Dewey, but is fueled by other scholarly literature, much of which respects (with significant reservations) both Marx and Freud. I invoke material and spiritually inspired psychological thought in an effort to revive what I appreciate to be Dewey's combined material and psychological direction for contemporary teacher education. Further, writing as a curriculum theorist who equates education and life, my book will sometimes conflate a something-to-be-done in relation to curriculum for the classroom, with a broader political response, perhaps implicating policy change or movement building, to address a social problem. I make no apologies for this complication; the interplay between the school classroom as laboratory and the life of the broader culture that includes its laboratories is precisely the paradigm to which we must rededicate ourselves. Such a paradigm is especially important in the contemporary neoliberal era, with its agenda for schooling that negates such a holistic perspective at every turn. Indeed, the neoliberal agenda is precisely the effort to impose the dominance of market relations on knowledge, such that market relations permeate all consciousness. Certainly many teachers and parents organizing against the current neoliberal reform agenda, especially its pervasive high-stakes tests, recognize that these "reforms" are related to other social problems arising from the normalization of market relations as human relations. Broader teacher and parent activism is an anticipated response to the unearthing of haunted sites in schools; although such activism is extremely important, it is not a direct focus of this book, nor are specific prescriptions for broader social change.

AUTOETHNOGRAPHY INTRODUCES RUDDICK'S MATERNAL STORIES AND BECKER'S *DENIAL OF DEATH*

The data I interpret in this book are grounded in the specific, coherent wisdom of autoethnography, "an approach to research and writing that seeks to describe and systematically analyze in writing (*graphy*) personal experience (*auto*) in order to understand cultural experience (*ethno*)" (Ellis, Adams, & Bochner, 2011). As someone with a long history of reclaiming stories as more than data, I join, in the words of Carolyn Ellis, "scholars across a wide spectrum of disciplines [who have begun] to consider what social sciences would become if they were closer to literature than to physics, if they proffered stories rather than theories, and if they were self-consciously value-centered rather than pretending to be value free" (Bochner, 1994). Avery Gordon contributes to this revisioning of the social sciences her conception of complex personhood, which disrupts any tendency to assume that "systematic analysis" will compensate for the fact of human irrationality:

> Complex personhood means that all people (albeit in specific forms whose specificity is sometimes everything) remember and forget, are beset by contradiction, and recognize and misrecognize themselves and others. Complex personhood means that people suffer graciously and selfishly too, get stuck in the symptoms of their troubles, and also transform themselves. (p. 4)

Searching for a paradigm to consider the realities of children's lives I was then observing for my dissertation in the early 1990s, I encountered in Sara Ruddick another feminist philosopher seeking to complicate notions of personhood. Ruddick proposed a conception of *maternal storytelling* that offered a political bridge to my preoccupation with what I named the *visceral* in human experience: "As she pieces her children's days together, a mother creates for herself and her children the confidence that the children have a life, very much their own and inextricably connected with others" (p. 98).

For Ruddick, a mother's stories reflect the balance between that aspect of her child's life that represents a separate quest, indeed, a separating quest, and the marginalized other growth project of learning to appreciate and face the reality of one's inextricable connections to others. Given the compelling feminist perspective of Madeleine Grumet and other educators and researchers that the prototype for teaching (by either women or men) is mothering (1988), Ruddick's formulation appears to capture the empowering balance of attention required in maternal work, which also characterizes the work of autoethnography. (Grumet's clarity that the late nineteenth to early twentieth century sentimentalizing of children coincided with their actual political disempowerment remains timely; contemporary neoliberal educational reforms touting the importance of our young people as critical thinkers while serving them up to the non-sustainable global economy appears to represent a parallel and haunting hypocrisy.)

Further, because they extrapolate social wisdom from personal experience, Ruddick's *maternal stories* must address the project of refusing to bifurcate the political and the personal. This project of conceiving of the personal as political is natural to myself and my peers who entered the field of educational studies after engaging in the political activity of the late 1960s and 1970s, political activity that was meant to be socially and personally transformative. We were educated by both the emerging feminisms of the 1970s and discourses that respected, while evolving continuing critique of, both Marx and Freud, typical of the work of Ernest Becker (who won the Pulitzer Prize in 1974 for *The Denial of Death*). Becker's thesis legitimized two important arguments that are not only contested but also invalidated in the public mind by contemporary market relations. The first is that it's not primarily sexual desire that colors and distorts what Avery Gordon describes as *complex personhood*, but rather our universal fear of death. Our behavior as human beings is perennially distorted by the anxiety engendered by this fear, but contemporary market relations both exploit and exacerbate such anxiety by making it less available to depth-enhancing self-reflection. We are flooded with new iterations of technological possibilities, each bringing with it an illusion of personal renewal. There is a sense of endless postponements of death; such a false perception of immortality marks another haunted site. The death-denying individual as a consumer of technology brings us to the second focus of Becker's argument. It is only the individual's attention to the needs of others that provides a genuine solution to unmanageable levels of anxiety. (Becker, 1973).

RECLAIMING THE ECONOMICS OF MARX AND FREUD

An important part of this project, then, is the reclaiming of Marx and Freud, especially in conversation with one another. The knowledge both invoked and generated in the pursuit of a collectively sustainable life for us humans is the major focus of my field of educational studies. Both Marx and Freud offer the current neoliberal moment a challenge to its ahistorical claims, to its socio-cultural blindness, to its insistence that all fields of human endeavor can be rationalized according to dollar value and accreditation based on conformity to dollar-valuing systems. Both Marx and Freud offer methods of deconstruction for the purpose of finding how and where power hides, and how it asserts itself, often from its hiding places, even as it can negate personal and/or collective agency. For Freud, individual and collective history accretes a certain kind of depth, requiring of individuals that we re-evaluate our pasts in order to act with increased awareness. This increasing awareness then guides a more thoughtful and compassionate dispersal of the libido or life force.

For Marx, the accretion of history that shapes us requires examination of its patterns; we must understand how power is lost to us when we forfeit awareness of our collective interests. These two theorists offer roadmaps for the reclaiming of power to avert totalitarianism both within and without us through redistribution of that power which both conceive as economic. Freud recognizes investment in the "economics of libido" that are individual, producing the less or more aware complex personhood recognized by Avery Gordon. He requires of us that we agree to study/*learn* ourselves so that we distribute our life force as thoughtfully and compassionately as possible, given that the unconscious will always make self-awareness a partial project only. Freud argues for the necessity of redistributing the accessible resources within, not as solution, but as strategy for navigating a potentially meaningful life. Marx hopes for the same, although his roadmap has the intention of leveling the playing field (Scialabba, 2011, p. 14) so that each individual's more thoughtful distribution of life force becomes possible. Marx's intention is to prevent the inequitable accretions of power that block individual access to an appropriate share of the world's resources, including education, for the enactment of the project of living. As social philosopher George Scialabba notes, "Like Freud, Marx sought only to deliver mankind from needless misery to inevitable unhappiness" (p. 14).

Both theorists recognize human interdependence, and both view its denial as perilous. Both ascribe to the leanest of aphorisms, "Know thyself," and "Only connect," and both point to avenues for alliance with the others on whom one's life is dependent. In this regard Freud is more focused on obstacles to both self-knowledge and alliance with others, with his astute observation of the "narcissism of minor difference" actually deepening our awareness of the internalized challenges to finding allies and building alliances (Freud, 1930/1962, p. 72). Marx, in turn, supports our understanding of how the external economy can overwhelm the "economics of libido," can overwhelm the intentional apportioning of individual life force into expression as passion for others, for art, for industry, for development of intellect and (from my perspective), for meditation. Both explain how the resources of the self can be made invisible to the self. Marx offers a critique of the evolution of the market relations of capitalism that have represented a kind of collective unconscious that he seeks to make conscious. Freud's psychoanalysis seeks to make possible the unearthing of the typically invisible depths of knowledge about self and other, much of it learned when the infant had no choice to refuse its lessons. Both underappreciated the power of the system being interpreted by the other: for Freud, there was an undervaluing of the external elements in the politics of totalitarianism. He could not consider that the domination of the super-ego might be determined by the very powerful socioeconomic historical forces, which, once internalized, actually constructed it. Related, he did not appropriately credit the power of the broadly social to shape the individual psychologies/complex personhoods of human beings (Gordon, 1997). For Marx, there was an attachment to rationalism and determinism that blinded him to the power of complex personhoods to derail the project intended to level the playing field. Then, too, that project's prescriptive certainties in turn defied the mutability of both complex personhood and the playing field.

THE ART OF TEACHING AND EISNER'S *EDUCATIONAL IMAGINATION*

As noted above, this book, including its title, is also indebted to Elliot Eisner, who recognized that teaching was an art as opposed to a conventionally construed science. Beginning with *The Educational Imagination*, he famously elaborated particular qualities of its artfulness in numerous works that helped shape my own teaching and capacity to evaluate the work of my student teachers. Eisner's conception of *educational connoisseurship* is indebted to the four qualities he identifies in "The Art of Teaching," a chapter that is required reading for all of our student teachers at Colgate, which for me describes the possibilities of redrafting a symphony in every lesson we teach; the movements are as applicable to the college classroom as to elementary, middle and high school. Teaching is an art because:

> [It] can be performed with such skill and grace that, for the student as well as the teacher, the experience can be justifiably characterized as aesthetic ...: teachers, like painters, composers, actresses, and dancers, make judgements that unfold during the course of action...; the teacher's activity is not dominated by prescriptions or routines but is influenced by qualities and contingencies that are unpredicted ...; [and] the ends [teaching] achieves are often created in process. (pp. 154, 155)

In the qualitative research he prescribes for the assessment of effective and inspiring teaching, Eisner supplies the interpretation of "objectivity" he acknowledges as valid, asserting that "... objectivity is a function of intersubjective agreement among a community of believers" (p. 237). Here he affirms his allegiance to the radical indeterminacy of the Deweyan project of democratic education. With regard to curriculum ideology, Eisner distinguishes from Deweyan progressivism the "cognitive pluralism" for which he advocates (pp. 79-83). Yet I believe that the "mind-body in wholeness of operation" featured in Dewey's later conception of life as education and education as life points to similar absences in the curriculum so worrisome to Eisner that he coined a new term: the "null curriculum" (p. 97). Eisner argues that what schools do not teach is as significant or even more significant than what they do teach or attempt to teach, inviting my conception of haunting with its focus on unappreciated absences. However, the null curriculum is not the same thing as the haunted curriculum, as Eisner does not theorize as product of market relations his recognition of a splitting off of feeling from thinking. Nor does he suggest political reasons for the typical school curriculum's lack of cognitive pluralism. What he does do is recognize the need for a vastly expanded understanding of literacy, arguing persuasively, as introduced earlier, that schools as currently constituted promote a constrained conception of *thought*:

> Aside from the problems inherent in the reification of distinctions among thinking, feeling, and acting, cognition itself has come to mean thinking with words or numbers by using logical procedures for their organization and manipulation, and not thinking in its broadest sense ... Yet, in the literature of education the term [cognition] has been impoverished, and in the process what we consider to be thinking has also been diminished. (p. 98)

Eisner was clearly concerned that the educational connoisseurship he prized was already being marginalized by instrumental evaluation of teaching at the time he first crafted his book. I'd argue that his unwillingness to assert that internalized (capitalist) market relations were responsible for the exclusion of affect, the body, and the arts from typical curriculum and teaching in schools, has returned to haunt his work. The marginalization of the arts in particular has never been so extreme as in the present. The practices of hauntagogy are now required to affirm Eisner's own now classic contention that "the cultivation of imagination is not a utopian aspiration" (p. 100).

RECLAIMING THE PERSONAL AS POLITICAL: AVERY GORDON AND MAXINE GREENE

In my own first book, *Parallel Practices: Social Justice–Focused Teacher Education and the Elementary School Classroom*, I described my methodology as teacher educator self-study, a methodology then validated by the research of Mary Lynn Hamilton and Stefinee Pinegar. I began the introduction: "I have long believed the truism that no matter what the subject matter you intend to teach others, you can really only teach who you are. What I learned writing *Parallel Practices* is that it is also the case that you can only *write* who you are" (Regenspan 2002, p. 1). Although I *did* articulate that belief, I did not at the time appreciate the possibility of systematic parallels of life experience and political reality illuminating both. In other words, I was not prepared to answer the question, "Exactly how is the personal political?" an inquiry pursued with, I hope, poetic zest in this book. For those who would charge that autoethnography is the ultimate narcissism, I reply that denial of the reality that all social research is, at least in part, product of the complex personhood of the researcher, is the ultimate narcissism. For a social science researcher who believes, as Dewey did, that life is education and education is life, denial of the very socially constructed being from whose processing the research emanates, is to suggest some divine objectivity. Such objectivity would represent abstraction from all contexts that influence personhood, and therefore, a denial of the socially constructed nature of reality that includes the collectivity of complex persons.

Although Gordon's book has more in common with literary criticism than autoethnography, her characters certainly play out the reality that the personal is political. In the foreword of *Ghostly Matters: Haunting and the Sociological Imagination,* Janice Radway captures my understanding of the author's achievement:

> What Gordon traces is the intricate process by which the reductive and universalizing powers of the market are lived at the level of the conceptual and the intellectual and how the resulting divide between the general and the particular, between the social and the individual, constrains our ability to recognize and to redress the profound human costs of a system that is utterly dependent on the repression of a knowledge of social injustice. (Gordon, 2008, p. ix)

Gordon's work, then, implicates the taken-for-grantedness of market relations; the result of such taken-for-grantedness is that the need to generate *private* profit obscures all questions of whom and whose resources will be devalued or altogether erased as the markets rationalize the transfer (theft?) of their value to private others. Yet, I can convey what I understand to be unique to Gordon's argument by applying it to my initial collateral damage example: the reality that these same market relations determine that (conventional, but even progressive conventional) social science research will unwittingly validate and normalize the metric by which an Iraqi child becomes collateral damage. Radway writes of the divide effected in our consciousness (by market relations internalized) "between the general and the particular, the social and the individual." I understand now that grieving for the particular individual Iraqi child (killed as "collateral damage") is constrained to the private sphere of her family, while the very public (general and social) grieving that would be so educative for us teachers and our students is conflated with research about war and collateral damage presented with the best of intentions at sociology conferences. We made the war that turned that child into collateral damage, and our grief for her must haunt us *or we haven't learned anything.* Yet her life-and-death experience is removed from our education, even if we attend the sociology conference, where she has been reduced to data.

Gordon's inquiry not only relies on imaginative literature to contest this process that objectifies and sequesters *what we need to learn*, but also confirms the reality that imaginative literature is most likely to offer us the opportunity to grieve for an Iraqi child not our own. Through such grieving we assess the "debilitating costs we must redress" more effectively than we might *in theory*. Perhaps more clearly than those who write about imaginative literature from within the humanities, Gordon recognizes that imaginative literature thrives on its ability to bring together in the same context "the general and the particular, the social and the individual." Readers observe simultaneously the two realities that make life complicated according to Gordon: the reality that power takes multiple, often contorted, and sometimes-invisible forms, and the reality of complex personhood—that as individuals, we are neither consistently rational nor consistently self-preserving. These two realities inevitably rub up against one another, complicating both our lives and our capacities to interpret them, as well as our abilities to come together as Maxine Greene, my mentor in philosophy of education, proposes, in order to enact the *dialectic of freedom* (1988). Greene defined the process of this enactment as the coming together of individuals with the intention to overcome social obstacles to our flourishing; the context for such flourishing was recognition of our obligations to one another in some community. Writers were heavily included in her narrative, as she interpreted their response to collective human struggles. Greene identified the unpredictable course of that dialectic for the U.S. experience of late modernity as represented in a combination of historical accounts and selections from imaginative literature.

This book is also powered by my belief that my own enactment of the dialectic of freedom has directed the practices that have proven most promising in my teaching of philosophical, political, and curricular foundations of education, as well as my direct supervision of student teachers. I support my students to unearth the ghosts in both the curriculum they will reinterpret and re-present and in the complex personhoods of all of us who commit to teaching. As teachers and prospective teachers, we represent the collective power to include the previously excluded and marginalized from the curriculum of public schooling and life.

CHALLENGES OF THE CONTEMPORARY NEOLIBERAL ERA

Gordon's endeavor to understand how knowledge of social injustice is effectively repressed in this neoliberal era speaks poignantly to the work of educational studies more generally as we examine, for instance, how triumphalist rhetoric of educational reform initiatives like "No Child Left Behind" and "Race to the Top" coexist with the defunding of public education. The annual, typically local budget-cutting cycle makes the firing of teachers and elimination of particularly arts-based programs in schools a taken-for-granted aspect of all of our lives, ruled as they are by market relations. These relations are not static and their increasing tendency is to privilege short-term profit over any long-term consideration of a public good. I interpret that consideration of a public good like social reconstructionist education (education rooted in consideration of how to reconstruct our disappointingly inequitable and violent social worlds, certainly the ultimate goal of hauntagogy), is now part of what Bill Readings identifies as a "waste economy" (p. 175). Readings considers this "waste economy" as represented in colleges and universities in the teaching of cultural studies, closely related to my field of educational studies, where what is un-cynically privileged is attention to "our unknowable obligations to others." The charge of "wastefulness" is levelled both ironically and not ironically. In the context of the contemporary corporate university of excellence, "excellence" refers to the capacity of both the individual and the corporation to garner excellent returns on one's investment. Here Readings captures the most disconcerting aspect of our work educating future teachers: we Deweyans want to make what Readings identifies as "thought" the point and product of a college education. Yet Readings insists that we make peace with our place in the waste economy—we must understand that from the corporate university's perspective, such thought is part of a waste economy whose purpose is to afford the corporate university a kind of moral cover while business as usual supports the construction of enhanced sports facilities, the growth of economics departments that trivialize fundamental critique of capitalism, and capital projects that conform to the demands of wealthy donors. Readings conveys that any thought inspired by these projects is incidental to their major function: to perpetuate the corporate university serving the needs of the corporate class. Returning to the premise of this paragraph and to Gordon's book, these needs include the repression of knowledge of social injustice.

Those of us in teacher education have a privileged and ironic vantage point from which to appreciate Readings's charge of thought occupying a waste economy, as the public schools which should be laying the groundwork for the generation of thought at universities are continually assaulted with charges of wastefulness, even as their budgets are eviscerated. So caught in the conceptual divides described by Janice Radway, the public schools have become almost everybody's scapegoats. In response to such scapegoating, their collective despair and loss of confidence provokes intensified "accountability" measures representing collusion with cynical would-be destroyers. In turn, this collusion creates such irrational functioning that the "effects" on student learning of the newest neoliberal reform, "The Common Core," are being evaluated before classroom teachers can study the content and intentions of these reforms. And the job security of these teachers on whom we rely to help shape the practice of our students in their classrooms is already dependent on their adherence to its prescriptions. Further, as I write this introduction, I learn that a cooperating teacher who lovingly supported one of my most gifted MAT student teachers in English last year is now, on account of a recent round of budget cuts, the only English teacher in her entire high school, and that her teaching load is clearly illegal. Yet, the front page of the AFT (American Federation of Teachers) quarterly journal sitting on my desk argues for "Letting the Text Take Center Stage" in the context of its elaboration: "How the Common Core State Standards Will Transform English Language Arts Instruction" (Shanahan, 2013). The article is sponsored by a powerful union, yet it advocates magical thinking related to the neoliberal standards that replace the genuine thought supplied by well-paid, well-educated and plentiful teachers who are respected for their creativity. Guided by such magical thinking, the teacher will harness the controlling power of the more complex texts whose place in the curriculum is now being mandated by the Common Core standards, in order to shepherd increasing numbers of students into more sophisticated literacy. We might view such an unrealistic projection of the magical power of (fewer) teachers and (more demanding) texts disciplined by standards as another haunted site.

In this era of triumphalist rhetoric for such reformist educational initiatives including the new edTPA standards, my current student teachers are struggling to stage videotaped lessons that marginalize our program's social justice focus so that they can successfully package evidence of immediate student learning for their corporate evaluators. Our social justice focus requires time for thought that is squeezed out of the curriculum by these invasive neoliberal policies characterized by thoughtlessness. Most maddening is the reality that the thoughtlessness of such policies is widely recognized yet they continue to deform contemporary teaching. Indeed, "No Child Left Behind" and "Race to the Top" have been appropriately invalidated by parodies rolled out almost simultaneously with the policies themselves: "No Billionaire Left Behind" and "Race to the Bottom," the latter of which now appears in credible, even mainstream literature, without quotation marks. The "reductive and universalizing powers of the market" impose a haunting presence that can be comical.

The hope for Gordon's project of locating something(s)-to-be-done is found in the fact that all knowledge is haunted almost literally, by the specters of the socially disappeared and enslaved. There is no way for knowledge to have escaped distortion, having been produced under the market conditions that have made some people invisible, made some disappear, literally, and ruined the lives of others. The distortion has the potential to announce itself as a haunted site, so our hope, as teachers and teacher educators, is to do our research and teaching in such a way that the haunted sites become appreciable to our readers and students.

My investment in this writing project emerges from an increasing sense of clarity that our global human culture is out of sync with the reasonable humane goals of promoting greater democracy, social and environmental sustainability that includes an end to war, and the related nurture of soulful citizens, which are all grounded in John Dewey's conception of *what education is for*. Meanwhile, the real-world costs of repressing social justice are increasingly apparent. It is not a secret that Wall Street has quietly refunded itself since the near economic collapse from which the world reels; yet recent college graduates, those ostensibly poised with fresh research to solve social problems, face the prospect of massive unemployment and underemployment. Worse, the wars that enrich private mercenary armies continue despite a chorus of expert opinion that the destruction they have wreaked is nearly unmitigated, despite mounting death tolls, continuous refugee crises, and devastation of artificial and natural environments to which, it seems, until recently, few but immediate sufferers have paid attention, let alone had their attention recorded for public reckoning. Certainly my students, except for a few each term, have not paid much attention at all—and no wonder. An important element of this global agenda is the creation of continual distractions from thought in the form of the glut of branded technology mentioned earlier; even our colleges are branded, yet investment in green building and vehicles, as well as alternative energy generally, is minimal.

Without major structural supports for a revolutionary turnaround towards the reasonable humane goals above, pursuit of which I am collectively naming (borrowed from Alain Badiou, without carrying over his formerly Maoist politics) the *global egalitarian project* (cited in Peterson, 2010, p. 162), I am exploring the possibility of keeping these humane goals alive in teacher education. Despite what I see as Badiou's over-determinism, his project aligns with Avery Gordon's conception of something-to-be-done. It's precisely this notion that "something has to happen" that makes Badiou and Gordon so relevant to teacher education, as they both recognize the need for direction regarding the real, vulnerable "text" that is the world we must navigate with and for our students. Further, I am reporting on my own efforts in this direction not out of an illusion that my work is unique, but rather, inspired by a Kierkegaardian belief that the only objectivity that is useful grows out of subjective commitment.

In effect, I am writing a rationale for continuing to work as an educational studies professor and teacher educator who has no faith in violent revolution, while nurturing a vision for greater democracy, including an end to poverty and war, and reversal of the current devastation of our natural environment. Further, I am interested in broadening the scope of teacher education and the definition of "teacher," as I consistently announce to all of my students in both educational studies and liberal arts core curriculum courses. By virtue of their commitment to the global egalitarian project, all of my students are teachers. I understand that there will be charges of vagueness about the unwieldy term "global egalitarian project," invoked repeatedly on the pages that follow. I defend my vagueness, though, because the project to which I commit is indeterminate, as is the dialectic of freedom, and specific action in its pursuit will need to be negotiated in complicated and sometimes contradictory circumstances. Nonetheless, I advocate for the pursuit of a socially and environmentally sustainable world in which all human beings have the potential to develop our possibilities as gifts to our communities. This project will require reasonable security about both basic material needs and a publicly afforded education that encourages a playful spirit towards ideas. For me, such a commitment means that we allow a belief in the project to affect significant choices about our behavior and therefore allow the commitment to help direct our lives.

I write this book inspired by hopeful signs of wake-up calls in both the Arab Spring and the Occupy movements. I also link my project of identifying haunted sites to the reporting in *Harper's Magazine* of Jeff Madrick (2013), who offers evidence that Occupy was destroyed less by internal dissension and more by systematic government surveillance and manipulation. I find it haunting that it is so easy to normalize the view that internal dissension killed this movement, when we are so aware of both the illegal spying operations by the NSA, and the continued virtually unchecked rapaciousness of Wall Street. Still, global demonstrations against the evisceration of government support for safety nets and a reasonable minimum wage offer hope of a reawakening consciousness on the part of working people. In this regard the recent limited success of fast-food workers in New York City has been especially inspiring, as has the refusal of a broad enough public to support military strikes against Syria. Although I am not systematically involved in movement building as was the case in my past, I respond to current crises as time and energy allow. For instance, I organized a local vigil against the bombing of Syria, and continue to work with colleagues to help organize the annual conference of the increasingly activist New York State Foundations of Education Association. This year the conference explored inequitable distribution of resources for public schools and teacher organizing against neoliberal policies of excessive standardization and testing. A poetry craft workshop modeled the inspiring and playful curriculum often displaced by the current obsession with "accountability" and testing in the public schools. Much of my energy is invested in the development of strategies to defeat the distraction of my students chronicled in this book. The neoliberal assaults on public education are closely related to the cynical teacher education accreditation movements that literally, at this moment, compromise this focus of mine. Teacher educators like myself are now required to support my students to produce data about our work together for Pearson, a multinational corporation authorized by the state to collect what I view as artificial evidence for a tautological project of accountability.

Without oversimplification here, I note that the Philadelphia Public Schools were able to open this academic year only after firing more than five hundred teachers in order to cut costs, and that billions of dollars were cut from the federal food stamps program during the same time period. In the meantime, I am invited to a special conference for teacher educators about poverty. Presentations will address evidence that children living in poverty perform more poorly in school than children from financially secure homes. I try to articulate my distress to one of the organizers of this conference. Is there new knowledge here? Will we now re-craft research agendas that re-bury the ghosts? Will we pretend we didn't realize that public schools cannot be "held accountable" for the repair of a society that defunds these same schools and the food budgets of its most vulnerable families?

I know that we in educational studies are not alone in raising these questions and strategizing to make thought possible. Increasing mainstream public attention to certain kinds of costs, including the budget cuts related to public education, represents a hopeful sign. Martha Nussbaum (2009), a recent Colgate commencement speaker, continues to draw attention to how these cuts are destroying art and music programs in favor of a pitifully depleted instrumentalist (test-driven as opposed thoughtful/substantive) curriculum in all but the best-funded public schools, and eliminating teaching positions in the name of fiscal responsibility. Mainstream newspapers report that there are big city high schools offering no physics classes, no chemistry classes. Districts have ended the school term early. Teachers—with the blessings of their administrators—are refusing to sponsor student teachers; with job security and/or pay now partly or significantly attached to student performance on high stakes standardized tests, teachers feel understandably threatened by the necessarily uncertain performances of neophytes. Thus the often-promising and necessary experimentation of student teachers, the best results of which can inspire the future work of all practicing teachers, is lost. Another perspective from which to consider these enormous social costs: how will we race anywhere, having created quite reasonable resistance to the once honored work in elementary and high schools of preparing the next generation of teachers and reaping the imaginative ideas of the most serious among them?

The current neoliberal agenda denies the hauntedness that Janice Radway captures in that complex one-sentence navigation of how knowledge of social injustice is effectively repressed in this era; in doing so she unwittingly explains how a conference *establishing* [emphasis added] the link between poverty and poor school performance can be launched without irony in 2013. Avery Gordon's book is a literary elaboration of how comparable occasionally naïve, but typically deadly contortions of separatedness between "the individual and the social, the general and the particular" play out in the interdisciplinary world of actual life stories, to which few but relatively marginalized journalists, writers and poets are attending.

My work is to move beyond deconstruction in order to make the intimated socially reconstructive work in our haunted reality appealing to my students who will be formal or informal teachers. In order for this reconstructive work to be appealing, my students need to believe and teach that putting our life energy behind what Bill Readings names "our unknowable obligations to others," that is—choosing to allow the dialectic of freedom to move our lives along—is actually likely to create gratifying experience for us because it returns to us our stolen agency. I am arguing that the work of educational studies is the work of defeating the hold of what Readings names *subjective autonomy* on our students' sense of self. His conception of subjective autonomy combines both personal and political expressions of narcissism, as well as false claims of an immutable self. Yet, Readings adds a further element to his critique, which causes me to attach it to my own theorizing about human development. He perceives as a moral reality precisely what subjective autonomy denies: the fact that we can neither measure nor know the extent of our obligations towards others (Readings, 1996). Suggested in his work is the probability of the reality that these "unknowable obligations" are all the immutable humanity we have. Further, I believe that this central knowledge of our "unknowable obligations" answers Elliot Eisner's charge of the null curriculum, the missing curriculum of affect and action (as an inextricable aspect of *thinking*) in typical schooling. Paradoxically perhaps, part of our work involves using the terrific intellectual resources available to us at colleges and universities to convince our students that subjective autonomy is a fundamentally anti-intellectual, even vapid perspective, because in denying their obligations to face honestly and challenge the non-sustainable global culture in which they live, they deny the importance of the past on the construction of the collective present. They also deny the creation of our individual complex personhoods as responsive to what came before in our family and community histories. Such denials reduce the content of their liberal arts education to cocktail party chatter. Also paradoxically, we must help our students detach from their narcissistic view of their own excellence, the pursuit of which is attached by mission statement to both their identities and the elite colleges and universities in which we teach that seek to attract them.

In public schools this same neoliberal construction of selfhood as subjective autonomy promotes a closed, testable curriculum that will determine who deserves what in a society that has few publicly available resources to offer, and will allow increasingly privatized wealth to accrete to the very few who rarely attend public schools in the first place. My students increasingly identify with these few when they enter college; their education needs to introduce them to the possibility of their unknowable obligations propelling wide awake lives immersed in the potentially enlivening terrain of the global egalitarian project.

My experience in social justice-focused teacher education has convinced me that this project is viable in the present, and furthermore, that its pursuit is the only project of integrity that is thinkable to me. I have experienced my contemporary students identifying with what Badiou so appropriately names "the suffocating reality principle whose distillate is the economy" (as cited in Peterson, 2010, p. 162), and a number of them have pledged to not be defeated by it. Many of them are energized by increasing awareness of their unknowable obligations to others, as I have been. Such awareness appears to answer both their desire for meaningful lives and for confirmation that something is lacking in the mainstream student culture that frequently leaves them feeling alienated.

As an educational researcher clearly proud to invoke John Dewey's influence on my thinking, my contention is that the project of bringing awareness to sites of haunting could represent promising education in this baffling contemporary era, particularly for people who are or will be teachers. This is so whether we pursue that work in formal employment by colleges, school districts, museums, writing programs, theater programs, and after-school and recreation programs, or whether we pursue it simply as citizens committed to the global egalitarian project. I believe that hauntagogy also revives Dewey's relevance for the current era and corrects for the excessive edge of his inspiring idealism: his failing was too much optimism, too much faith in the rationality of his democratic project, with too little understanding of how subtly forces of domination can accrete and subvert, as well as a related incapacity to figure in complex personhood. For these shortcomings, the scholarly literature of my field that is more respectful of both Marx and Freud provides useful correctives.

Related to Dewey's assumption of well-behavedness is the recognition that the social imagination he took for granted is initially foreign to our students who aged in classrooms very different than that of social reconstructionist childhood educator Mary Cowhey (featured in Chapter 1). Cowhey decouples deserved delight in human ingenuity as a motor of civilization from its typical connection to projects of colonization, enslavement and imperialism. She creates a model of early education that respects and grows the social imagination of her young students. My experience reinforces that we can do similar work in our efforts to decouple the confidence to *play with ideas* from its context in the unearned privilege accrued to many of our students by the accidents that positioned them at birth as "affluent professionals" or "executive elites" (Anyon, 1981). Our students gain self-knowledge when they begin to understand how their own attitudes reinforce an inequitable and relatively non-productive economic system. Many learn to question the legitimacy of the "loser" status of those who serve capitalism's increasingly rapacious need for a reserve army of labor. (The reserve army of labor is the expanding class of people who are meant to be unemployed.) I observe that as my students become increasingly angry about the purposeful maintenance of a reserve army of labor, they come to understand how this social class can be reproduced in underfunded and under-stimulating public schools. By forming attachments to characters in thoughtfully selected imaginative literature and historical accounts, students empathize with different experiences of oppression. They observe, for instance, that the unconscionable levels of human misery that fuelled the industrial revolution are being reproduced in much of contemporary "development" across the globe.

Additional hope for this project is reflected in the fact that the re-infusion of imagination into student consciousness is a project supported by much contemporary research in both the social sciences and the humanities. In *The Postmodern Marx,* political economist Terrell Carver (1998) provides one particularly potent example in his recovery of Marx's invocation of images of horror to describe the workings of capitalism. Carver calls our attention to Marx's identification of capitalism with the metaphor of the vampire in *Capital* (see Chapter 7 for a more detailed consideration of Carver's work). Here he gratifies my own belief that metaphor—and, by association, poetry—is a most underestimated teacher and teaching tool of our era. Related to such connection-making is the work of psychoanalytic educational philosopher Deborah Britzman, whose proposal of *wild* education (2011, p. 9) makes available to our students exploration of how the family romance leaves all of us challenged by the presence of transference relations, causing "new experiences [to] conjure old ones" (1996, p. 117). (See Chapter 6 for a richer sense of wild education.) Again, along these lines of imaginative thinking based on dialogue between Marx and Freud, it was my stumbling upon interpretation of Alain Badiou's writing in the work of educational philosopher Thomas E. Peterson, while tracing references to Badiou in the work of Britzman, that made possible the contribution of that French anti-capitalist philosopher to the literal framing of this book. Indeed, Badiou's conception of a "suffocating reality principle whose distillate is the economy" supports the deconstruction of psychology as, at least in part, politics internalized; this conception, in turn, continues to offer a framework for my own pedagogy increasingly conforming to what my colleague, Mark Stern, has named hauntagogy. Moved to recognize the impact of inequitable systems of distribution of wealth and services on the creation of the values that nurtured and/or failed to nurture them in their families and communities of origin, they may find further opportunities for self-education in the effort to love the characters in carefully selected imaginative literature; such self-education represents a something-to-be-done unearthed by our hauntagogy.

At the same time that I pursue this direction in my teaching, I am aware that my own devotion of an increasing percentage of my energies to spiritual goals and processes of education must figure in as well. I use the term "spiritual" broadly, wishing to invoke updated conceptions of John Dewey's "mind-body in unified wholeness of operation" (see fuller context in Chapter 1), as opposed to more constrained association with traditional religious practices, for which I also have respect, however. Here, too, my process is at least partly inspired by my autobiography. My writing reflects my experience that "teaching against the grain" (Cochran-Smith, 1991) increasingly requires practices of personal spiritual maintenance in order to fend off too-weighty discouragement.

Indeed, young people, such as my students, are generally more able to discuss the reality of death and its place in making meaning of our lives than many adults who treat it as unnatural. Related, I am aware of not wanting to cut myself off from the increasing numbers of students in my classes who have committed or recommitted to traditional religious practices. This is especially the case as the majority of non-fundamentalists among these students are likely, more so than their unaffiliated peers, to have committed to the global egalitarian project.

I also write also out of a new willingness to face the possibility that the damage to our natural and social environments is too great to reverse for human civilization as we know it. In this case, a certain degree of abandon is warranted, as it is a time to release anything held back on account of worries about propriety, fears of being misunderstood or representing oneself as an unserious teacher-writer-researcher. Matthew Crawford names his related project for our students "unselfing." He urges them to examine the narcissism that allies them to the bureaucratic work opportunities being sold to them—work that is likely to be ungratifying. His revaluation of work characterized as craft (Crawford, 2009), invites openness to grounding our daily lives in certain related time-honored values. In this context I think about the useful awareness of the relative unimportance of our individual existences, even as we necessarily hold on for dear life.

INTENTIONS OF THE FOLLOWING CHAPTERS

Related to my own effort to hold on for dear life, I offer the chapters of this book. In Chapter 1, "On Haunted Contradictions of Development: Ben, the Bat, Mary Cowhey, and *The Communist Manifesto*," I examine the developmental context of the story of my (then) five-year-old son's assertion in the early 1990s, "Do not pull out this plug." This story is contrasted with the *developmental* implications of an assurance of Colgate's director of career services in the fall of 2008: despite the ongoing Wall Street crash and near-global economic collapse, students aspiring to Wall Street internships and jobs should remain confident that financial industry recruiters would continue to target the Colgate campus and provide opportunities (Neefus, 2008). Here I examine how market relations challenge not only the University's legitimacy relative to its age-old justification as promoter of thinking, but also the primacy of personal agency in child development and indeed, human development. I am guided by Deweyan philosophy, aspects of which have been helpfully reconceived by recently deceased Sara Ruddick in *Maternal Thinking Towards a Politics of Peace* and by Mary Cowhey in her ingenious early elementary social reconstructionist curriculum as documented in *Black Ants and Buddhists*.

Chapter 2, "Social Action as Curriculum: Unearthing a *Something-to-be-done* in the Current Era," records the demise of my Social Action as Curriculum course, my earlier conception of the activism that I believed was a necessary part of the curriculum of teacher education, the same conception that engendered my first book, mailed to my editor on September 11, 2001. I record how, while processing my disappointment about what I experienced as insurmountable obstacles to continuing this commitment in the haunted politics of 9/11's aftermath, I began developing new practices that potentially address similar long-term intentions of Social Action as Curriculum. Some of these examples of new practices are featured in my examination of a recently taught Democracy and Education seminar in which students presented to a school board how patterns of class conflict threatened the viability of parent involvement efforts in their district.

Chapter 3, "Failed Lesson: The Unteachability of the Mayors' Anti-war Resolution," offers a story about my unsuccessful efforts to teach the curiously buried 2011 *New York Times Article,* "Mayor's anti-war resolution" (Cooper, 2011). Aspects of my frustration are illuminated by two other stories, the first featuring the marginalization of psychoanalyst Sabina Spielrein through sexism, then her inspired teaching, and finally her tragic murder. I explore how the thought of Spielrein distracts Avery Gordon from her academic presentation at a sociology conference, and the implications of that distraction for the work we do in the related field of educational studies. The second story concerns the decision of the photographer Alfredo Jaar to bury photographs of the Rwandan genocide rather than subjecting them to the failed education of an audience who would grossly misunderstand their hauntedness, the subject of my colleague Mark Stern's dissertation. Jaar's exhibition begs the critical question: Can the inaccessibility of hauntedness in certain contexts make lessons unteachable? And with regard to this inaccessibility, did Freud steer us wrong by underestimating the extent to which psychic pain and manifestations of the uncanny are caused by actual social oppressions, as opposed to intrapsychic phenomena?

Chapter 4, "Why is Dave Brubeck Crying?" opens with examination of the classroom use of a five-minute film clip featuring recently deceased jazz pianist Dave Brubeck from the Ken Burns Jazz series (Burns, 2001), in order to explore the reality that affect can sometimes signal the presence of a haunted site. In this case, a visibly emotional Brubeck offers insight about the presentation of World War II as a struggle for freedom masking the haunted politics of white supremacy/racism in the United States after that war against fascism/racism in Europe. I also re-examine my teaching of Barbara Kingsolver's young adult novel *Animal Dreams*; I consider the substance of social reconstructionist teaching, teaching that is overtly committed to pursuit of the global egalitarian project through the valuing of peoples' history, affect, and marginalized community knowledge, including the hauntingly absent-from-the-curriculum tools of community organizing. Finally, educational philosopher Wendy Kohli's classic insights about useful attention to feelings as support for the global egalitarian project (which I share) are contrasted with concerns about affect theory as a growing academic discipline influencing educational studies.

Chapter 5, "Why is Sarah Crying?" contrasts an aspect of the education I believe I offered my daughter, perhaps out of a lack of confidence and a certain amount of shame, with the education I believe was typical for many of my students, which was more instrumental and less socially critical. I am arguing that while I was able to help shape my own daughter's identification with the project of Deweyan democracy—the global egalitarian project (though probably out of a hauntedness within), my more-privileged students were encouraged to tightly identify with their families of origin, and to prize what Bill Readings characterizes as a misconception: their own subjective autonomy. This distorted sense of self has implications for my students who will be teachers, and for all of them if we agree to consider everybody a potential teacher. In the context of the often fine work I continue to observe as part of my supervision of student teachers, more recently I have seen only three social studies students break out of the limiting liberal conception (upheld by a belief in autonomous subjects), "there's two sides to every story" (cited in Peterson, 2010, p. 162) in their work in the classroom with young people; all three of them had non-dominant culture identities. I am arguing that identity politics, for all of its shortcomings, must be cautiously defended at this time, and that affirmative action remains particularly important in teacher education. Yet my identification with my own non-white and non-upper middle class students raises some unanswered questions about my motivation to teach.

Chapter 6, "*Wild* Education: Teaching *This Side of Brightness*" features my increasing confidence that Deborah Britzman's concept of "wild education" has much to offer education committed to the global egalitarian project as we deal with the struggle to deepen the thinking-feeling of our students of this era. As a psychoanalytic conception of education, *wild*ness illuminates some of what interrupts the neat transmission of knowledge, belief in which we continue to delude ourselves. A story about my teaching of Colum McCann's novel *This Side of Brightness* explores complexities of wildness, and hopefully justifies my willingness to allow it to help shape my classes. As one iteration of the teaching of this book happened while I was leading a Colgate study group in Manchester, U.K., I consider other factors that enhance a teacher's access to resources for wild education including the site of schooling being a city whose preservation of artifacts of the industrial revolution can inspire poetry: "Everything is cobbled on the rubble of ancient cities."

Chapter 7, "On Personal and Political Ghost Stories: *Hauntagogy*, Nurturance, and Investment in the Pretend," features parallel ghost stories intended to reclaim the application to our work of the now-buried conception the *personal is political*, complicated by the reality of adultism. My husband, David, shares a ghost story that eventually leads to his own partial emancipation. Featuring the responses of two different mothers to the existential questions that inspire children, I consider the possibility that hauntagogy might unearth wisdom about school curriculum that prizes the individual creative energies of young people in the interest of the public good. The pursuit of the public good, then, is a force to counteract the universal oppression of adultism, an oppression whose impact in this era is terrifically exacerbated by internalized market relations. Finally, my colleague Melissa Kagle reinforces for myself and for her students the Up'ik (Native Alaskan) cultural awareness preserved linguistically in the root for "pretend," appearing in a diverse array of words, that all divorce of us human beings from direct visceral experience of which we can make collective spiritual and political sense carries potential danger.

In the epilogue, I begin to very briefly rationalize my current passion for poetry and poetry craft both in my private life and in the classroom. I also allow that poetry makes space for the contention that doubts are inevitable; in this case there is even the possibility of a doubt about my commitment to the global egalitarian project. I close with a poem of mine in order to suggest the way poetry honors wild education while potentially transmitting "hole-piercing" knowledge. Finally, I leave it for my readers to respond (or not) to the question about whether "this book is something anybody needs."

CHAPTER 1

ON HAUNTED CONTRADICTIONS OF DEVELOPMENT

Ben, the Bat, Mary Cowhey, and The Communist Manifesto

> We can never settle our obligations to other people. There is no emancipation from our bonds to other people, since an exhaustive knowledge of the nature of those bonds is simply not available to us.
>
> —Bill Readings, *The University in Ruins*

In my recent teaching of educational studies courses, I came to an awareness that is the focus of this chapter. I now understand that the most important work I can do in my college teaching is to normalize our unknowable obligations to one another and to link those obligations to a structural critique of social inequality as the basis for interdisciplinary education that informs a life of meaning. The chapter begins with the rationale for a thinking trajectory that connects our very agency as human beings with awareness of our bonds to others. This trajectory rests on the expansive humanism of John Dewey and his contemporary heirs in philosophies of education and social reconstructionist childhood education but has important implications for what we do in universities as well.

Following this theoretical introduction, I offer two stories set in early childhood that are intended to model the basis for enlivening education in active response to the social challenges that present themselves in daily life. The first story is set in my family life at the time my children were young. It features my son Ben's creation and posting on the ceiling of a warning sign as the last phase of a collective response to the intrusion of a bat in our kitchen. The second features a parallel story set in the social reconstructionist early elementary classroom of Mary Cowhey. Her students are responding to the intrusion of black ants in their classroom, and the curriculum she co-creates with them around this intrusion leads to the study of world religions, a rule about not stepping on the words of your peers, and later, an examination of how Bartoleme de las Casas changed his mind about his acceptance of the exploitation of the Taino people. After theorizing the differences between the necessarily limited nature of Ben's agency in the family story, versus the social expansiveness Dewey called "conjoint communicated experience" featured in the story from Cowhey's classroom, I narrate an anecdote from my own college classroom. This story features my teaching of *The Communist Manifesto* at the time of the near-global economic collapse of 2008, when an article in the Colgate Maroon News assures our students that Colgate will protect its Wall Street internships. The chapter is framed by the oppositional quality of the early childhood stories versus the story about teaching *The*

Communist Manifesto to my college students while the global economy is collapsing. While the young children in the family and early elementary classroom stories appear to delight in their own agency, the college students appear to be unsettled, and perhaps even wryly amused by my implication that their agency has been stolen from them. Both the childhood stories and the anecdote from my college teaching are glued together by theory from John Dewey, Maxine Greene, Avery Gordon, Ernest Becker, and Bill Readings. Even as it serves the function of making meaning of the stories, this theory trajectory, a continuation of the one that introduces the chapter, is intended to model "thought." Bill Readings conceives of thought as the appropriate goal for teaching in college, even though it is currently situated in the waste economy of universities. In contrast to all of this thoughtfulness, I interpret that the promise in the Maroon News article offers thought's opposite: reinforcement of the belief in subjective autonomy that takes the form of reserved seats for my students in the now-ghostly economy of calculation. Finally, I narrate the results of giving my college students clay so that they can enact the pinch pot lesson. This lesson represents my effort to pull them back into the social reconstructionist education characterizing the waste economy of the university. Yet that waste economy appears to make a home for delight that provokes thought in my students, similar to the experience of Mary Cowhey's six and seven-year-olds.

STRUCTURAL CRITIQUE INFORMS A LIFE OF MEANING

An education in structural social critique can begin early, when it is conveyed to children in the context of the challenges that make life worth living. We human animals are important because we are members of a vast human community to whom we have incalculable obligations. Further, we have allies in the community of all living things who are counting on us to pursue a sustainable vision for the future. An obstacle we face as we pursue this vision is the reality of social inequality, which structures a human society in which some people are unfairly advantaged, while others lack what they need in order to develop their full humanity. Our obligations to others implicate us in the work of better balancing the distribution of opportunities, goods, and services we all need.

Unfortunately, as I realized this year while teaching Child and Adolescent Development for the first time in my career, research from ego psychology and its offshoots, including developmental psychology, have significantly constructed the field of child and adolescent development. The result is a narrowing of our focus so that we tend to examine individualistic challenges of being human *as* characteristic of child and adolescent development. Further, these individualistic challenges tend to be identified and reified based on a very limited sample of human children and adolescents, and typically these informants are upper middle class and white. In normalizing the individualistic growth challenges of young people from the upper middle class, especially in this neoliberal era driven by market relations, we normalize what Bill Readings terms "subjective autonomy." Subjective autonomy is the illusion of an autonomous self whose goals focus on personal achievement and success narrowly construed within market relations, where what sells and earns profit is what counts. This powerful illusion then helps determine the policies and practices of not only public school K-12 education, but also of contemporary higher education, which Readings, not quite parodying its own advertising, refers to as "the contemporary corporate university of excellence." Structural critique, by contrast, educates the learner in the systemically perpetuated social inequalities that partly account for our "unknowable obligations to one another." Such a focus, in turn, provokes what Readings's and social re-constructionist educators construe as "thought," precisely because the thinking that matters to social re-constructionists is focused on the potential for a sustainable, even flourishing natural and social environmental future for all humanity. In this chapter, then, I use what I have come to realize through this recent teaching experience of Child and Adolescent Growth in order to do inductive reasoning about the limitations of education more broadly. I also seek to redress those limitations.

The contemporary university of excellence remains solvent on the basis of the majority of its students and their families accepting the illusion of subjective autonomy as the terms of their growth and development. Investment in their subjective autonomy counteracts investment in thought, although thought certainly continues to happen at colleges and universities, and even morally justifies the institutions' existence. Indeed, it is the prizing of thought that attracts most faculty to the work, even when the contemporary emphasis on measurability and accountability of educational outcomes, increasingly correlated to salaries of graduates, constrains their work. (The neoliberal accountability reforms in teacher education and public schooling are especially constraining, although they are not specifically considered in Readings's book, *The University in Ruins*.)

Succinctly put, Readings interprets that the dominant conception of subjective autonomy marginalizes thought, which is dependent on acceptance of the reality of our unknowable obligations to one another. Although these obligations are made visible by the existence of social inequalities and environmental non-sustainability, which challenge the future of humanity, there is an intimation in Readings's book that they are also a fundamental aspect of being human. Some of these obligations are products of geographic and historical circumstances resulting from empire building and the subjugation of some groups for the immediate advantage of others. Bill Readings does not use his intellectual energy specifically accounting for all of these obligations, however. Some of the obligations would seem to flow from what Avery Gordon calls "complex personhood," and the sometime human irrationality conveyed by this term. I find some humor in Gordon's conception, related to an apparent unwillingness of an otherwise fabulously broad and deep intellectual to pin it down, which seems to parallel Readings's unwillingness to absolutely account for our unknowable obligations to one another. He accepts them as the fact of our existence, as do social reconstructionist educators like John Dewey, and now, Mary Cowhey, whose work will be examined later in this chapter.

I believe this vagueness derives from the inability of academics to embrace spirituality given our traditional trappedness in both rationality and positivism. Romanticism occasionally provides an escape from both of these traps, but there is another possibility more appealing to social scientists: those anxious to avoid charges of non-scholarliness associated with consideration of spiritual realities that are not adequately captured by the study of religions can invent new terms. Readings offers "our unknowable obligations to others" and Avery Gordon conceives "complex personhood" through the work of Patricia Williams. (Similarly, Sara Ruddick invented "maternal thinking towards a politics of peace" in her book of that same name.) I, personally, delight in the intimation from these authors of our social construction complicated by spiritual conceptions of what it means to be human, even if the authors themselves avoid overt conceptions of spirituality in their writing.

As a social reconstructionist teacher myself, a challenge of my work is not immediately overburdening my students with the weight of so much unaccustomed responsibility for themselves and their world, given that most of them have been schooled in subjective autonomy. Yet, what I have come to recognize is that it is impossible to protect students from such responsibility without protecting them from their own enlivening agency, necessarily all mixed up with their complex personhoods. Further, the challenge of my teaching is their recognition of this agency, which exists as a buried, haunted site within them as individuals, and as a collective haunted site in both typical (and increasingly neoliberal) K-12 education and higher education. In this chapter, I hope to illuminate aspects of the identification, even excavation, of these haunted sites.

BEN, THE BAT, AND JOHN DEWEY'S EDUCATIONAL PHILOSOPHY

"*DO NOT PULL OUT THIS PLUG.*" I still have the sentence strip featuring my son Ben's wobbly five-year-old handwriting. Rescued from the ceiling of our kitchen in Geneva, New York, on moving day twenty-two years ago, it is kept in a safe place because I am the mother of its author as well as a teacher educator whose focus is critical literacies. While my daughter, Sarah, played with the (pretend) reading of arbitrarily selected letters scrawled on all available paper, Ben used letters only to spell his name and then to write the few three-letter words he could read in kindergarten. As will be explored in Chapter 5, Sarah covered papers with capital letters from age three, and experienced real grief the first time I didn't make up an interesting sentence, but phonetically decoded "XOTRST" in response to her demand: "This time, really *read* what I wrote." No such visible emotional or interactive process attended Ben's acquisition of literacy. There appeared to be little transition from his early name-writing to that summer evening after his kindergarten year when he wrote "DO NOT PULL OUT THIS PLUG" with the help of his seven-year-old friend, Alexandra. The writing was his idea, occasioned by the sudden appearance of a bat that emerged from a hole in the kitchen ceiling—a hole we thought had once held a screwed-in hanging plant, and was apparently connected to the outdoors through a space under the roof. An exterminator friend was consulted by phone. It was only after we had successfully shooed the bat out the front door with a badminton racket and observed the children as they plugged the hole with steel wool and Play-Doh that Ben had announced our need for a sign.

Ben situated this project of response to the challenge to our family and friends represented by the intrusion of the bat in a literacy act—just as a Deweyan teacher would do. Dewey prized both in the classroom as in life outside of it—the negotiation of citizens, each situated in one or more communities where they were able to use the material reality locally available, in order to move along the ever-democratizing process of life. Here Ben worked to fulfill a recognized need for a sign that would warn potential plug-removers of the plug's immediate importance. (Alexandra dictated the correctly spelled words in response to Ben's effort to sound them out aloud to her as he transcribed them onto a strip of unrolled adding machine paper.) The experience required Ben to enact what Patrick Finn (1999) refers to as the early stages of empowering literacy: Ben recognized his ability to use language to interact meaningfully with the community of those who preferred not having a bat in the kitchen, and to the community of bats for whom our kitchen was not an appropriate living environment. Alexandra loaned her higher level of decoding skills to the experience in which she, too, was delightedly invested. And Ben won the appreciation of an older and much-admired child for having initiated an engaging and "real life" activity that did not require his direct interaction with a creepy animal.

I offer the bat story as autobiographically inspired introduction to an inquiry about an orientation to human life that I proposed in my earlier scholarship and named *viscerality*. By *viscerality* I referred to materiality as characterized by our living blood and guts, so elemental as to be unaccountable in market relations—even defying market relations in representation of *what we are really made of*. I had always been committed to keeping viscerality front and center in the curriculum of my field of social justice-focused teacher education, but could never exactly rationalize the choice. My conscious intention had been to use the alignments between Dewey's critique of the division of labor in his earlier scholarship and his advocacy for primary school curriculum that does not separate doing from thinking.

MIND BODY IN WHOLENESS OF OPERATION

My discovery of Dewey's later-in-life explicit focus on "mind body in wholeness of operation" provided a more direct rationale for my own concept of *viscerality*, however. In his collaboration with F.M. Alexander, inventor of the Alexander Technique, John Dewey had explicitly advocated for Alexander's practice of a kind of passive yoga connected with breath awareness. Dewey's intimation was that the division of labor was literally internalized as faulty breathing, which, over time, made people sick. His writing in support of Alexander's philosophy and method uncannily foreshadowed the infusion of eastern modes of thought and body-mind practice into western rationalist thinking less than two decades after

Dewey's death. He describes the problem of the mind-body duality both in his introduction to Alexander's book, and in a lecture to the New York Academy of Medicine in 1928:

> The division in question is so deep-seated that it has affected even our language. We have no word by which to name mind-body in a unified wholeness of operation. For if we said "human life" few would recognize that it is precisely the unity of mind and body in action to which we were referring. (Dewey, 1928)

Four years later, Dewey introduces Alexander's book with his assessment of its political significance:

> Thus the question of integration of mind-body in action is the most practical of all questions we can ask of our civilization. It is not just a speculative question, it is a demand—a demand that the labor of multitudes now too predominantly physical in character be inspirited by purpose and emotion and informed by knowledge and understanding. It is a demand that what now pass for highly intellectual and spiritual functions shall be integrated with the ultimate conditions and means of all achievement, namely the physical, and thereby accomplish something beyond themselves. Until this integration is effected in the only place where it can be carried out, in action itself, we shall continue to live in a society in which a soulless and heartless materialism is compensated for by soulful but futile idealism and spiritualism. (Dewey, 1932)

I had proposed *viscerality*, the stuff of Dewey's "human life," as an appropriate foundation for a social justice-focused teacher education curriculum, paralleling the work we want our students to be doing in their own future classrooms. In this book, I am interested in establishing that Dewey's "mind-body in action" has special relevance for very contemporary teacher education, as we identify the haunted space occupied by neoliberal policies that further enlarge the separation between mind and body. This separation occurs through a disrespect of agency (the potential for self-directed action related to membership in some community) in growing the humanity of young people. I believe that both Readings and Gordon offer important direction as we seek to revalue such agency. Avery Gordon's conception of a something-to-be-done, a possible pro-social, pro-democracy action dependent on recognition of haunting, might conform to the curriculum of thought Readings proposes. I conceive in "something-to-be-done" a parallel curriculum for all education and for the quality of critical and enlivening work we hope our students will do in their classrooms, should they choose to become teachers in the more formal sense. This curriculum for our prospective teachers' future classrooms then parallels the work that students who are not slated to teach in the formal sense can enact in the world, as they choose alternative routes (alternative to teaching) towards the development of their humanity.

Now I seek to complicate Dewey's critique by establishing the parallels between Cowhey's social reconstructionist work with children in public school, and Readings's proposal that "thinking" be substituted for the university's current mission of "excellence." Both Dewey's early critique of the division of labor and the famous conception of a dialectic of freedom from my mentor in educational philosophy, Maxine Greene, intimate a universal human spirit that asserts the integration of body and mind through purposeful action. Yet, this conception is, as suggested earlier, peculiarly marginalized in the contemporary theory in critical educational studies. The often compelling post-structuralist theory that dominates the field tends to highlight difference and identity struggles over the doings of everybody's spiritualized body. This choice to highlight difference over universality is understandable. It is motivated by the need to show how difference is constructed as wrong or inadequate when dominant social groups are in charge of the construction. Still, a focus on difference tends to invalidate any conception of a universal and/or essential truth about what it means to be human, and to obscure the meaning of Alain Badiou's charge that we (and our students) are currently possessed by "a suffocating reality principle whose distillate is the economy." I believe that Badiou's identification of this suffocating reality principle brings much-needed attention to the inquiry, "What, precisely, is being suffocated?"

Interestingly, Dewey has maintained an honored place in most progressive education circles, despite his early collusion with the racism of the Woodrow Wilson administration and his general unawareness of sexism. Close study of parts of his challenging *Democracy and Education* continues to captivate my educational studies and teacher education students with its elegant conception of education *in* and *as* democracy. Dewey's conception of democracy promotes a universal account of what it means to be a human being that is rooted in agency exercised with awareness of human interdependence. Agency is simply the very responsiveness to the needs that present themselves as we live our lives with this awareness. Schooling, then, represents the possibility for the education of that responsiveness beyond what is available in one's necessarily limited community of origin. As will be explored later in this chapter, with expanded implications in Chapter 2, Ben's agency was exercised in one such limited community of origin when he carried out his intentions with, for instance, none of the complications to democratic negotiation represented by people who speak languages other than English.

My assessment of our debt to Dewey is also connected to his unwillingness to promote education that is overtly ideological. Dewey's intention to avoid direct teaching of what he construed as ideology has allowed me to find in his work support for a perspective that is increasingly available to me as I age and identify the holes in all ideological perspectives. His Chicago Lab School curriculum and the philosophy he develops to rationalize it in *The School and Society; The Child and the Curriculum* appears to derive from his conception of how the human spirit is distorted by the (dehumanizing) division of labor, and not from what we would typically construe as political ideology. Perhaps, though, we need to acknowledge the usefulness of how what we conceive of as pre-modern thinking *must* live on in the modern, and even in the postmodern. Such acknowledgement might allow us to examine with our students the construction of the overtly ideological, as in teaching *The Communist Manifesto*. We might even discuss with them whether overtly ideological teaching might be necessary in our contemporary haunted work. When Dewey goes on to critique the inequitable distribution of wealth and power, which both emerges from and perpetuates the distortion of our beings represented by the division of labor, he appears to be engaging in more modernly construed political philosophy or ideology. Thankfully, in the era of the *first* robber barons, he helped develop language to rebalance and redirect attention towards a positive foundation for our own pro-democratic pedagogy. In doing so, he reminded us that critique alone does not make a social justice-focused teacher.

Dewey's specific identification of mind-body in his lesser-known writing inspired me to reread Ernest Becker's Pulitzer Prize-winning *The Denial of Death* (1973), which, in turn, invoked a recollection of the bat story. I remembered how periodically I used to look up to check on Ben's sign during the months it coexisted with that plug in the kitchen ceiling. Indeed, my association was triggered by Becker's theme, intended as a corrective to Freud's emphasis on sex: that the paradox of human life is that we creatures with bodies that fail us and eventually die have to live with consciousness of that reality every day. Becker's theme invited me to reconsider another wonder of literacy related to Ben's advocacy for the two communities of potential residents of our home: we creatures who know that we will die make symbols that might last forever. I imagined Ben's sign outliving the bat, outliving me, and outliving Ben, its warning intended to preserve the health of both bats and residents, potentially in motion even after we were all dead. I believe it is important to consider such a spiritual conception of literacy, as it supports both Dewey's, and now Readings's assumption that the social imagination is propelled by awareness of our obligations to others; Readings supports the consciousness that we can't know those obligations in part because they include people who are dead. Such a consciousness offers openings to levels of awareness that extend beyond the limitations of our individual existences, and offers a framework of understanding different from the political one. Again, "everything cobbles itself on the rubble of ancient cities" is grandly metaphoric.

Influenced by Freud, my own formulation, "everything cobbles itself on the rubble of ancient cities," is an attempt to express the depth and weight of the fabric of our indebtedness (neither necessarily positive nor negative) to others who came before us. Deborah Britzman reminds us, "[Hannah] Arendt will place development within the fact of our natality, our beginnings as met by the reception from those already here" (2009). With my students, I use phrases like "our global and historic parents" to convey this combined spiritual and political conception of our social construction.

SOM JET'S STORY: MARY COWHEY'S CONTEMPORARY SOCIAL RECONSTRUCTIONIST EDUCATION

In *Black Ants and Buddhists*, seven-year-old Som Jet, originally without allies, wants to stop his peers from stomping on the ants that have appeared in Cowhey's classroom. Through this story Cowhey introduces us to the possibility of the teacher negotiating the curriculum even with very young students. When unattended juice spills end up attracting ants, a classmate of Som Jet's garners support for the position that "we can kill ants if we want to." Another peer, Sovan, astutely notes that the classroom rules "be kind" and "work hard" don't cover the killing of ants. Cowhey reframes the inquiry: "'If there is even one person in our class who would feel very upset about us killing even one ant, would it be kind for us to go ahead and kill that ant anyway?' she asks. And then, 'Could a person work hard if he felt very sad or upset?'" (2006, p. 3)

Ultimately, compassion in the "Peace Class" is systematically affirmed through the knowledge supplied by thoughtfully selected literature, guest speakers who are community members, and social action in the community that presents itself not as "service learning," but rather as a logical extension of the curriculum. Cowhey's expansion of the curriculum parallels the sense of an expanded fabric of connections and obligation. From a Deweyan perspective, the curriculum is a controlled arena for life to play out, and human life requires assumption of our obligations to others in order to be human in character. The speakers who explain and represent Buddhist, Muslim, and Hindu beliefs against the killing of living things educate the heart-fed mind or mindful heart of this classroom community. These obligations make it wrong to step on ants in the same way that it's not okay "to step on other people's words." Cowhey negotiates this other rule, too, with the students, responsive to the new immigrant English language learners; students with different English capabilities are taught to respect other people's needs for the time and space to complete a sentence without interruption.

The negotiation around Som Jet's need for change based on his moral belief system generates a curriculum that is continually reshaped as the children consider the latest implications for the functioning of their classroom community. The recognition that ants must be kept out of the classroom invites the children to propose a more intentional clean-up protocol after lunch; the revised clean-up process then requires a spontaneous demonstration by Ms. Cowhey of wringing out sponges. Two children also offer to become more responsible about taking home their lunchboxes everyday so as not to attract ants. Cowhey continues to nurture the intellectual and cultural growth of the children, even as they work towards a long-term solution of their immediate problem. She reports to the children of her attendance of a community *iftar* at Smith College following Ramadan. There, the Muslim chaplain has informed her that, "in Islam, we should not kill the ants because all life is created by Allah" (p. 5). In her reporting to the children of the Muslim chaplain's information, Cowhey widens the common ground of the classroom both spiritually and intellectually. This common ground then inspires Cowhey's invitation to her student, Krish, and his family (who have recently arrived to the area from India) to attend Cowhey's family Thanksgiving. At the dinner table, Krish's father, Ranjit, informs both Krish and Cowhey that Hindus should not kill black ants because they are living things. When Krish and Cowhey bring this knowledge back into the classroom, the rapidly expanding curriculum—generated by the intrusion of ants—then prompts a classroom visit from the

Buddhist husband of a retired neighborhood teacher who explains the Wheel of Dharma and the Noble Eightfold Path. This new community player, Dr. Unno, clarifies that, "Right conduct includes the commitment not to harm living things" (pp. 6-7). Dr. Unno leads the children in a popular lyrical adaptation of a Buddhist meditation, introducing another text for their examination.

CONNECTIONS BETWEEN BEN AND SOM JET'S STORY

My Ben's early world was comprised of the people and animals who live in and visit his house. Mary Cowhey expands that community to the classroom and its environs, where a boy like Ben would learn how many world religions oppose the harming of an ant (or bat). It's a simple associative leap from such knowledge to the awareness that you can't "step on the words" of a classmate who is still thinking in a first language other than English, a classmate who consequently needs more time to formulate her responses. Further, just as some of the families speak a language other than English at home, another classmate's family would run out of food before the next pay check if it were not for the assistance of the Northampton Survival Center and its community garden. This knowledge necessitates collaboration with the center as part of the Peace Class's commitment to the health of an ever-widening community into which the children are drawn. The case for this collaboration is made especially compelling after the children learn from their beloved teacher that she, too, relied on the Northampton Survival Center to feed her own child earlier in her life. "It is not enough to be compassionate. You must act!" is a theme articulated repeatedly in the Peace Classroom.

Ben's concerns about the bats and the people who prefer not living with them would find a home here, where his sense of obligation to others would undoubtedly expand, given the social justice focus of the classroom. Yet, perhaps even more significant is the opportunity for a child to experience the shifts in consciousness of others in the classroom community, to observe the process of people being influenced by others and changing their minds. Such a process must be navigated by a leader who respects the dialectic of individual and group development. This leadership of a community of young people is precisely what can happen in public schools, whose mission, in turn, gives public schools their reason for being. And that work is parallel to Readings's conception of "placing thoughts side by side" as driving the genuinely useful mission of colleges and universities.

In the parallel stories of Ben in my family life and Som Jet in Mary Cowhey's teaching life, we also observe the ways in which the responsible actions of the children emerge from their delight about the activation of their own social imaginations. The Deweyan understanding that the point of education is access to culture beyond the local—to knowledge expanded by broader contexts of inquiry—is made concrete in the work of Cowhey, where individual students are empowered to contribute to an ever wider understanding of the potential of democratic community negotiation. As Ben's mother, I could not enact the same process, however expansive the private community of our lives. I could not enact for him a collectively negotiated curriculum where the Deweyan understanding of living in community is literally what ignites the imagination. (From this igniting of social imagination comes the ability to negotiate with difference and with people different from ourselves.) I could give Ben a broadening context, but it was limited by the necessarily limited nature of my own personal identifications and associations. Not so with the navigations of Cowhey's curriculum, which mirror the obligations of my secondary English and History student teachers to navigate and articulate for their students broad tensions in practice. Clearly such tensions, both tensions in the practice of democracy in the society, as well as those in the practice of schooling, become more significant as the complexity of the curriculum grows in range and depth.

Demonstrating a necessary degree of faith in her young students' abilities to engage with an ever-widening community, fueled by the Deweyan principle that imagination is the specific quality by which young people address social challenges, Cowhey develops an activist curriculum that challenges stereotypes about poverty and contests the normalcy of wars. When her student teacher marvels at Cowhey's ability to respond to the fears of a child who learned of the 2004 deadly Bezlan elementary school hostage crisis and explosion in Northern Caucasus (near Chechnya), Cowhey coaches her in a practice of self-reflective inquiry. "When our government begins a pre-emptive war with a military campaign described as 'shock and awe,' your children [meaning those in that prospective teacher's future classroom] might feel …" (p. 183). Her student teacher must learn how the social imagination of children is premised on their potential identification with all others.

In my curriculum theory class at Colgate, my students are in a similar position and are learning to recognize the hauntedness of a public proclamation that we would shock and awe others with our bombs. Everything we do in teacher education must be part of their preparation to identify with every child they will teach, including some new immigrants who personally had, or whose countrymen had our bombs dropped on their relatives and homes. How can it be that we allowed our government to pursue another war guaranteed to produce more desperate refugee crises in the name of all of us individual potential Deweyan teachers? The abstraction of children into collateral damage dissolves when we see our responsibility to these children in very concrete terms. They will be the children in our classrooms.

Cowhey's work removes the stigma of both poverty and activism, in part by claiming both as part of her own developmental growth. She recounts stories about the struggles and even the idiosyncratic joys of living at or below the minimum wage. Here she deftly straddles the question of the extent to which the agency of human beings is nullified when they are positioned as oppressed victims. We must raise this question in our educational studies' classrooms, where the critical theory we teach our college students can unwittingly lead to reinforcement of rescue fantasies, or perhaps worse, a sense of hopelessness about their potential to contribute to positive social change. Related, she prepares our students to question the naming of "losers" in the popular vernacular, a practice that derives from, identifies with, and justifies market relations. Our students, too, are audience for the personal stories she tells her first and second graders. They learn, for instance, that as a teenager, Ms. Cowhey lived outdoors alone in a tent one summer, then went to college on a full scholarship, left school to become a community organizer, and eventually returned to earn her degree and become a teacher. Such stories reinforce the compelling nature of human agency and complex personhood. They also offer depth to the inquiry about how human beings strategize in unique ways to answer needs common to all of us. Related, from these stories emanate the quality of good-natured wide awakeness that characterizes the spirit of her curriculum and provokes us to consider why that spirit is so generally lacking in our own college classrooms. A new focus for the primary school language arts curriculum emerges as students in Cowhey's classroom create their own posters and letters to elicit donations to be sheltered under the school's Giving Tree. Instead of proving their competence on tests, the children prove their competence through genuine communicative skill that brings results for their neighbors. This curriculum expands in interdisciplinarity as the children are required to use their math skills to categorize, weigh, graph, and inventory donations, which they themselves then collect and transport in a caravan of baby carriages to the Northampton Survival Center. With such a comprehensive curriculum in place, it is not surprising that families show up at the closed school on the unexpected snow day to rescue the pies the children had baked the previous day; the local homeless people's coalition awaits both the children and their Thanksgiving dessert. Again, Cowhey teaches a vocabulary of acting as opposed to rescuing: "You know what the Dalai Lama says, Ms. Cowhey: 'It is not enough to be compassionate. You must act!'" exclaims six-year-old Jack during the spontaneous field trip to reclaim and deliver the pies. Children begin to learn about the social construction of poverty; their actions take the focus on our unknowable obligations to others, which propel our social imaginations, the very mechanism of growth.

Cowhey has many allies in her process of reaching for and connecting with the best possible humanity of all members of the community, the very process John Dewey, perhaps optimistically, calls "human life." She introduces community members as her allies in the teaching of her students; this is the work of *non*-neoliberal public education, its continual "piercing a hole in knowledge," its expansion of the available and usefully engaged community as the work of the curriculum. The education of Cowhey's students grows progressively as the community in the classroom announces its ability to absorb new layers of intellectual and spiritual complexity. For instance, her students not only learn that Bartolome de Las Casas documented the Spanish invasion of the Caribbean, but that he also gave up his plantation worked by Taino slaves when his own methodically collected data convinced him that the exploitation of the Taino people and its related cruelty were wrong and specifically un-Christian. So although her young students learn the heartbreaking reality of how European contact decimated native families, they also experience the model of a human being re-evaluating his behavior and learning from some of his worst mistakes. This complex historical figure, de Las Casas, is then positioned as an ally to the children in their own growth projects. Here's where the equally spiritual and political element of human agency emerges and unleashes its potential to unearth haunting, as de Las Casas did.

Cowhey further attests, "I can respect Columbus for his awesome navigation and sailing ability" (p. 143). She recognizes that students need to appreciate "the sophisticated understanding of mathematics, geography, weather, wind, and ocean currents" that sailing and navigation represent, as specific collective manifestations of human agency. At the same time, she discusses with the children the limitations of her own knowledge base, modeling for them that the sharing of intellectual curiosity, as opposed to the teacher's greater expertise, is perhaps the more important foundation of the student-teacher relationship. And perhaps most significant for social justice-focused teacher education, she further explains, "I also read my students *Captain Pinkney's Journey* about an African American sailor's autobiography of circumnavigating the globe alone in 1992. I use this book to help children grow accustomed to tracing routes on maps and globes, noting continents and oceans and looking for the ocean and wind currents along his route" (p. 143). Cowhey strategizes about how to inspire her classroom community with the historical record of human ingenuity and technological development. The historical record can reinforce the motivational impetus for achievement and quest, while decoupling (both achievement and quest) from the racist and classist colonial and imperialist projects in which they are typically situated. Such decoupling for our youngest formal learners builds the foundation for their later receptivity to my student teachers' work with them as high schoolers. My student teachers in secondary classrooms need to support their students' appreciation for the artistic and scientific cultural achievements of the West (as well as the global East and South), contextualized, as they typically were, in the dehumanizing market relations of conquest and colonization.

Cowhey offers us the bridge between the structuralist practice of identifying the weight, deeply embedded, of oppressive power relations, and the post-structuralist recognition that we, as individuals, and our students, and their students, remake the world with every gesture, every action, every word we utter. The discouragement we teacher educators feel about the project of remaking the world cannot be imported into teacher education, because remaking the world is the point of their work. Maxine Greene expresses this idea eloquently: "But we are educators, and education has to do with new beginnings and reaching toward what is not yet" (1982, p. 4). Much of what we have to offer both Ben and Som Jet is Maxine Greene's faith in new beginnings and reaching toward what is not yet.

SOCIAL RECONSTRUCTIONIST EDUCATION ADDRESSES MAXINE GREENE'S "GRACE UNREALIZED"

The writing of Maxine Greene, my beloved mentor in educational philosophy, represents a precursor of cultural studies in educational studies. Greene, who died as I was completing the editing of my manuscript for this book, devoted her long career to the possibility that all levels of formal education might contest the U.S.

conception of freedom as freedom from obligations to others. Writing as if in response to Maxine Greene from her location as a sociologist as astute in history as in literary criticism, Avery Gordon, in her haunting treatment of Toni Morrison's *Beloved* asserts: "Reconstruction ratified a prevailing but limited notion of freedom as the freedom to own property, to sell one's labor, and to not be owned as property" (p. 173). Greene's dialectic of freedom drives the existential motor for an education in specific enlightened moments of history and literature when this limited conception of freedom was contested. Now Greene writes as though in response to the painful histories of oppression captured by Gordon, locating moments when people came together to challenge what she termed in earlier lyrical writing the "grace unrealized" (1982) in this limited notion of freedom, especially the unfulfilled promise of the possible U.S. multicultural and democratic experiment. Although Greene focuses her teaching for "grace unrealized" in the college-level teacher education/educational philosophies and curriculum theory classroom, her goals and even process play out in Mary Cowhey's work with young children, as narrated in *Black Ants and Buddhists*. Especially moving are the intimations of "grace realized" in the ingenuous identifications of her young students with the authors, philosophers, and historical actors they are educated to perceive as allies. These allies include Gandhi, whom one student identifies as "Ms. Cowhey's friend." I have witnessed the tears of more than one college student who has tried to express in class how she was moved by this belief of a young child that her teacher was friends with Gandhi. At her best, Maxine Greene achieves a similar kind of intimacy between our students in educational studies with the historical and literary figures who have seized the dialectic of freedom during nineteenth and twentieth-century history as she narrates it.

Similarly, Bill Readings identifies the potentially realizable grace in the ruins of the contemporary corporate university, where what he names a waste economy preserves acknowledgment of our unknowable obligations to others as foundation of a thoughtful social education/cultural studies curriculum. To create a conversation for our students between and among Mary Cowhey, Maxine Greene, Avery Gordon, Ernest Becker, and Bill Readings is to open to our students the idea that haunting recognition could be a key to grace unrealized in their own lives, should they choose to identify with the global egalitarian project.

TEACHING THE COMMUNIST MANIFESTO WHILE THE GLOBAL ECONOMY COLLAPSES

I continue to teach at an elite private college, Colgate University, an institution that has been very good to me, and to which I feel a large measure of complicated loyalty. I know that what Readings names the "waste economy" in which I participate as an educational studies professor is only marginally different in other elite (and non-elite) institutions of higher education. Indeed, Colgate has been more generous than average in continuing to fund both Master of Arts in Teaching, (MAT) and now Ninth Term Teacher Education Programs, which many elite colleges have eliminated. As well, I would argue that Colgate's mandated core curriculum can (and often does) represent a mandated refuge for thought (as Readings conceives of *thought*). It was in the mandated core curriculum course called The Challenges of Modernity that I had the opportunity to teach *The Communist Manifesto* while the global economy was collapsing.

I estimate that approximately one-fifth to one-quarter of Colgate students enroll with the goal of earning large salaries and bonuses in Wall Street firms. Indeed, even as the economic meltdown of 2008 was publicly recognized as a financial industry collapse, largely caused by short-sighted financial industry greed, a comment by the director of career services appeared in an article written by the senior editor of the student newspaper, the *Colgate Maroon-News.* The director of career services intended to assure students and their parents that Colgate's career development office was doing everything possible to ensure the continuation of our pool of Wall Street internships (Neefus, 2008). Of perhaps equal interest was the article's title, "Economic Downturn Hits Hard for Colgate Students," and the fact that an interview with FOX Business anchor Liz Claman was the only source for the one-sided information it provided about the crisis.

We were studying *The Communist Manifesto* for the third class period on the day the article appeared. I projected the *Maroon-News* article on the screen at the front of my classroom and gave the students time to read it. Then, with a smile on my face, I asked my students if they saw any indication in the comment by the director of career services that she intended for the prospective Wall Street interns among them to use their current education (our study of Marx and Engels's manifesto) to prepare for those internships. Their laughter, perhaps expressing a combination of discomfort, amusement, and even delight in the awareness that learning is complicated, left me hopeful.

I interpret that in its still-relevant critique of market relations, Marx and Engels set the stage for an examination of haunted sites, offering us the opportunity to re-enliven the potential for Readings's notion of thought in the college classroom. By contrast, the comment by the director of career services, in addition to the apparent legitimacy ascribed to FOX News as the singular source provided for knowledge about a momentous global event, certainly has the intention of shutting down thought. Very specifically, after the laughter subsided, my students did interpret that the *Maroon-News* article would appear to make irrelevant our lively process of navigating the tensions generated in class discussion of *The Communist Manifesto.* In this prominent article in their campus newspaper, the students are literally being told by the university official perhaps mostly explicitly associated with their future life trajectories that Colgate's historic Wall Street internships will be preserved just when it has become clear to some of them (my students) that Marx and Engels's writing offers a valuable and devastating critique of how these Wall Street firms have functioned within market relations to collapse the global economy. Here the process of the marginalization of thought by the work of market relations (in normalizing subjective autonomy, because all that matters in the context of the article is the future ability of these students to earn huge salaries) is beautifully illustrated.

Returning to my college classroom story, in which I appreciated the laughter of my students (without fixing its meaning), I now had the obligation to determine how to use the critique of Marx and Engels in the same way Cowhey used the story of Bill Pinckney's adventures with her six-and seven-year-olds. She was able to decouple the intellectual curiosity and remarkable human ingenuity characterizing global navigation from its typical context in inhumane imperialism and colonization. I had to similarly decouple the broadly humanistic social critique supplied by Marx and Engels from its context in the theory of (appropriately reviled) totalitarian revolutionary communism. Our curriculum needed to ignite their buried social imaginations—to represent a gradual broadening out of the context of their own lives from my students' typical situatedness in the assumptions of subjective autonomy. Further, I had to assume for many of them a narcissistic identification with their own "excellence," affirmed in the heady world of those Wall Street internships, associated as they were with money and power, access to which an "excellent" Colgate education is intended to guarantee. Yet, recommitment to promotion of these internships without thought is a feature of the culture of the corporate university of "excellence," which, paradoxically and hauntingly, relies on the (unvoiced) characterization of thought as wasteful, useful for cocktail party chatter only.

I take Readings's lead in asserting that the promotion of Colgate's Wall Street internships, the focus of my teaching story, is a part of the "restricted economy of calculation," (p. 175) which is no longer compatible with what he (and I) call *thought*. Thought is premised on an understanding of our obligations to one another as human beings, and we humans are now no longer part of national cultures guided by high-minded humanistic principles, if they ever were. Rather, we are all circumscribed in the "restricted economy of calculation" from whose "suffocating reality principle" thought maps the only escape. Such thinking on my part represents the specific operation of deconstruction we need to model for our students who will be teachers in classrooms or in whatever potential communities they will situate themselves.

How, then, can we use the teaching of *The Communist Manifesto* to help our young adult students begin to understand the extent to which human ingenuity and technological development are largely wasted in the context of the contemporary non-sustainable capitalist economy, where rapidly increasing concentration of wealth so constrains the already "restricted economy of calculation" (Readings, p. 175)—that the capacity for genuine productivity is strangled?

MY PINCH POT LESSON FINDS A NEW USE

Directions: Use the wire provided to cut for yourself from the block of clay a ball a bit smaller than a baseball. Then consider the following: we are an early human community, which has just discovered or uncovered or developed the first semi-permanent container known to our group. Make a pinch pot with your ball of clay. In your small group, predict any possible

> *positive and negative effects on our community of the introduction of this new technology, the container.*

I have previously specifically tied this lesson to my teaching of John Dewey's *The School and Society; The Child and the Curriculum*. But now, in the context of teaching *The Communist Manifesto*, the lesson serves to inspire inquiry about the lack of correlation between what is currently being produced (and how it is distributed), and what is currently needed relative to the non-sustainable culture in which we live. Students quickly observe that even the availability of the container, clearly a useful product, generates social contradictions that must be mitigated in order to promote relatively equal access to the goods and services we all need to thrive. Students quickly replicate the experience I have had in the past, where I have to initiate their consideration of the implications of our not wanting to voice a "negative" human social behavior like "hoarding food" even after they have already offered "war" as a possible consequence of having containers. They respond to me: "War is more amorphous, but hoarding food—somebody clearly *starts* that. We can acknowledge that we human beings in general cause wars, but nobody wants to be a hoarder of food" (Regenspan, 2002, p. 36).

This term, two students in my Core: Challenges of Modernity first-year seminar added another insight: they learned in their introductory international relations course the idea of zero-sum, or in their words, "the idea that every interaction has a winner and a loser; one person cannot gain while the other does not lose." I interpreted my work in response to support these students to understand the socially constructed nature of this "truth" of market relations. To disrupt the normalcy of these market relations is to reconnect them with the promise of re-situating their younger selves in Cowhey's classroom, where instead of losses entailed in zero-sum thinking, there are collective personal gains involved in learning not to step on ants, personal gains in extending wait-time to those children newly learning English, and now, perhaps, personal gains in advocating for the legislation my students recognize will become necessary to prevent the use of pots to hoard what all human beings need. The social imagination of my students can be ignited, but it requires me to project to them that they can remake the world.

Our discussion, then, was propelled by some of the following questions: what are the variables of high speed internet access in this context, and how useful are the cell phone apps that, along with social networking, absorb a higher and higher percentage of their/our "free" time? How might the pinch pot lesson help us think about private ownership of Internet access, and the imposition of fees for better access? I returned them to consideration of Badiou's proposition that our contemporary lives are circumscribed by a "suffocating reality principle whose distillate is the economy," a reality principle that emerges from competition for jobs in an environment of relative non-productivity and of income polarization not experienced since the days of the original robber barons.

How prescient of Dewey, theorizing in the era of the original robber barons, to have observed that even the capacity to breathe effectively is compromised in circumstances of artificial mind-body separation, now exacerbated by the current growth of the financial sector, as opposed to the productive sector. And might the convergence of descriptors related to unhealth of the body not offer us clues to the newer patterns of drinking on college campuses, where my students reported that they consume alcohol in order to become oblivious, as opposed to "high?" Here one of my students reinvoked Freud's conception of an "economics of libido" to propose that awareness of the incapacity to feel (and be) genuinely productive in the contemporary global economy might create the necessity for a redistribution of life force energy among the humans participating in such a dysfunctional system. We considered that future players in such a system might feel a need to literally waste their life energies (and I thought immediately of government farm subsidies that pay farmers not to grow crops in a world that continues to feature localized starvation). Some of my students were clearly enlivened by my interpretation that the prevalence of eating disorders among them certainly resonates with related conceptions of non-nourishing life choices for young people whose social imaginations are eroded by lack of use. And what exactly was the intention of that comment in the *Maroon-News*?

The lesson substitutes hauntagogy for ordinary pedagogy; its purpose complements the teaching of a particular text, in this case, *The Communist Manifesto*, by providing access to *thought*.

FURTHER IMPLICATIONS FOR MY COLLEGE TEACHING

Here we encounter the very paradox, whose lack of deconstruction in teacher education research often prevents more successful collaboration between critical foundational scholars in educational studies, and those primarily invested in the shaping of teachers for work in the public schools. This same paradox impedes the nurturing of healthy human development more generally, including in our humanities courses at universities: *thoughtful* people who interact with young people on a daily basis need to project genuine hopefulness about the potential of the students they teach to improve the political (including economic) realities that threaten social and environmental sustainability. Such genuine hopefulness actually contradicts the "soulful but futile idealism and spiritualism" derided by Dewey in 1932. In educational studies, we recognize and teach how conceptions of hopefulness can be co-opted by vapid and ultimately oppressive signifiers such as "excellence," especially for our students who are limited by their socialization under the circumstances of unearned affluence and privilege. Yet the more socially critical theory of our field can also serve to incinerate a genuine hopefulness that *is* the enlivened social imagination of which we see too little evidence among the students and fellow faculty we encounter daily. It is important that at any level of teaching we continue to reproduce the evidence of Deweyan social imagination in our students.

Further complicating the challenges of our work, Avery Gordon and Bill Readings together help us appreciate that typical uses of words like "poverty" in progressive social science research can represent part of the corporate university's project of "excellence," as opposed to *thought,* too. While Mary Cowhey's mother's use of the expression, "those less fortunate than ourselves at this time," to describe the reality of fellow humans living in poverty might seem quaint to us, the avoidance of the structuralist signifier "poverty" has a powerful influence on Cowhey. Like Dewey, she avoids most ideological constructions in her work with her students. She correctly understands the problems of such structuralist conceptions: they tend to deny agency; poverty becomes a fact of life, which the corporate university is happy to have students passively examine as part of their mission of excellence. Conversely, for Cowhey's students, poverty is a wrong and unfortunate reality that we, collective humanity, need to be in the process of addressing and alleviating. Its wrongness, the wrongness of poverty, increasingly linked to the wrongness of war, is implicated in our very humanity; we refuse to accept as a necessary reality what is inimical to the growth of a child (who could be in our classroom). For the students in Cowhey's classroom, social challenges become the reason to be alive and thinking. I see this same potential for the students in my classes, even though the idea of their own agency being applicable to the challenges we examine is novel thinking for the overwhelming majority. The question is the extent to which we college teachers have the power to further cultivate that novel thinking to make thought dominate their college education.

I do not want to oversimplify the differences between structuralist and post-structuralist conceptions of reality with regard to the focus on agency. Rather, I want to raise the possibility that the importance of agency is being marginalized in both: that structuralist perspectives defer the useful agency of working people until those people can function as a revolutionary proletariat for a specific process of social change in which we have lost confidence. At the same time, the post-structuralists can locate agency in, and therefore feel progressive about studying with their students, the practices of ordinary people that can function self-destructively with regard to individual and collective sustainability. I believe that both groups of theorists spend too little time investigating the educational practices that enliven or reawaken agency, and I worry that intellectuals and academics are often out of touch with the level to which discourses of "what it means to be a human being" are slipping from their moral moorings under the climate of neoliberalism that prizes what Readings calls subjective autonomy.

In this vein, my worry is that in giving up on the aim of the structuralist critique, which required collective organizing as its response, and moving to post-structuralist paradigms for our perspectives on the current historical moment, we may settle for understanding over action. Although we have good reason to privilege respect for differences over universalizing (humanistic) theory, our students need reminding about what all of us need: reliable sources of loving care, food, clothing, shelter, medical attention, belief in their usefulness and purpose, some sense of freedom (however debatable the conception), and educational opportunities outside of, as John Dewey reminds us, the local wisdom available in immediate geographic communities. It is important for us to remember that the limited nature of local wisdom includes, for our very privileged students, the market relations "wisdom" of Wall Street. If it is the case, as I believe it is, that access to fulfillment of these common needs is more ruled by the politics of social class than any other factors, then in giving up on the primacy of social class featured in classic (Marxist) structural analysis, we lose the clarity structural critique affords—that contesting the social class hierarchy might deliver us into a more humane world.

The continuing rapid concentration of wealth in the hands of fewer and fewer people clearly threatens the extent to which knowledge of our obligations to others will support healthy human development. How we act—literally how we collectively respond to all of the challenges that face us, including the destruction of the natural environment that sustains us most immediately—is increasingly determined by the extent to which our students will compete for a place in the One Percent (and increasingly choose inducements to quiet their frustrated agency, like alcohol and substance abuse), or the extent to which they learn from *thoughtful* teachers the gratification of living out our unknowable obligations to others. One might say, then, that the real job of a contemporary teacher and teacher educator is to not attempt to redirect students' attention *away* from the distractions (which, Avery Gordon reminds us, can emanate not just from the corporate media, but even from the theory we teach), but rather to examine their hauntedness, the hauntedness of the distractions, for clues to the something-to-be-done.

As an educational foundations professor, teacher educator, and mother, I trace the centrality of learner "agency" along with the contemporary marginalization of this agency I observe from my stance as mother and teacher. I tell stories from the unique positioning of my own complex personhood. I also correlate the emphasis on agency in a philosophy of mothering by Sara Ruddick, referring back to Madeleine Grumet's assertion that the first paradigm for teaching, whether men or women pursue that work, is mothering. This correlation supports my ability to appreciate the haunting available in the space between the story of teaching the *Communist Manifesto* during the economic collapse and the two childhood stories of Ben and Som Jet. It also provokes an interest in further developing the hauntagogy implied in my use of both the earlier and later stories in my teaching and writing.

CHAPTER 2

SOCIAL ACTION AS CURRICULUM

Unearthing a Something-to-be-done *in the Current Era*

> Since a democratic society repudiates the principle of external authority, it must find a substitute in voluntary disposition and interest; these can be created only by education. But there is a deeper explanation. A democracy is more than a form of government; it is primarily a mode of associated living, of conjoint communicated experience. The extension in space of the number of individuals who participate in an interest so that each has to refer his own action to that of others, and to consider the action of others to give point and direction to his own, is equivalent to the breaking down of those barriers of class, race, and national territory which keep men from perceiving the full import of their activity.
>
> —John Dewey, *Democracy and Education*

In my analysis of my son Ben's experience with the bat in our kitchen (see Chapter One), I suggested that although my family could support his agency to plug the hole in the ceiling and to make the sign *DO NOT PULL OUT THIS PLUG*, I could not offer him the "conjoint communicated experience" that Dewey prizes as the primary mode of living democracy. What is necessarily missing from family life is precisely this "conjoint communicated experience" that Mary Cowhey designed around the needs of Som Jet in her social reconstructionist classroom. In our kitchen, Ben was deprived of what public schools are uniquely situated to do by their very mandate: to put everybody and their differences together in the same space by making misunderstandings and different interpretations of reality their shared text. Nobody required that Ben "refer his own action to that of others." He encountered nobody with a different or better idea, and nobody suggested that non-English speakers would be unable to read the sign, therefore missing the direction to not pull out the plug. He lost out, too, on the experience of having to go down to the boiler room to ask the custodian if we might borrow a ladder.

The issue here is not to deny the enlivening experience of Ben, our family, and friends when that bat suddenly appeared and he was empowered to do something about it. It is rather to suggest that public conflicts have the potential to model "conjoint communicated experience" as private ones cannot. More specifically, public schools have the potential to be wonderful places because they can help children learn that being part of a public has very valuable rewards and challenges, connected with the capacity Dewey prized to "participate in an interest so that each has to refer his own action to that of others, and to consider the action of others to give point and direction to his own." Further, we know that this potential of public schools to be the place where the mode of democracy, "conjoint communicated experience," teaches young people how to enact active citizenship throughout their lives remains largely a potential (except in the rare example of a classroom like Cowhey's) (see Chapter 1).

PLANNING TO ENACT "CONJOINT COMMUNICATED EXPERIENCE"

In our passion to promote enlivening socially critical education for our elementary education students in the social justice-focused Master's program at Binghamton, the faculty recognized that not only had our students typically lacked the model of social reconstructionist education in their past schooling, but they had also typically lacked personal experience with active democratic citizenship. The possibility of "conjoint communicated experience" was therefore unfamiliar to most of them in both contexts when they entered our program. We reasoned that practice with the behaviors of active democratic citizenship was a necessary complement to our focus on the literacies and methods of socially critical education. As a faculty, we had already focused our curriculum-making work in the program on social reconstructionist philosophy and practices like those of Mary Cowhey, and now decided to experiment with the requirement of our students' engagement in a social action project. We conferred about this possibility with a number of cooperating teachers with whom our program had built significant positive relationships over time. The result was our eventual experimental conversion of the course that accompanied student teaching into Social Action as Curriculum. The conversion followed a pilot offering to the general student body of the University, intentionally planned so that we might forge connections between our students and students drawn to social action who were not necessarily going to pursue certification. We could not know how our hopes for this course would collide with global events, especially because its early enactment was so promising. The circumstances of that collision, including their context in my own life as a teacher, offer a powerful illustration of the process of haunting, as well as the usefulness of its unearthing for clues to something-to-be-done.

In this chapter I theorize, and then examine the enactment and demise of my Social Action as Curriculum course rationalized by our small elementary team's intention to provide our students with the opportunity to enact "conjoint communicated experience" as envisioned by Dewey. I taught the course in the few years both before and after the attacks on the World Trade Center of September 11, 2001. Response to those attacks changed the meaning of the social in our lives, hollowing out the very intentionality of Social Action as Curriculum. I now identify Social Action as Curriculum as a haunted site, mourning its loss as I consider how shifts in the dynamics of political power at multiple levels combined with aspects of my own complex personhood to make the course a ghost of its former self. (I remind my readers that both power, with its often uncanny manifestations, and complex personhood, with its acknowledgement that human beings are not altogether rational creatures, are, in combination, what makes life complicated, according to Gordon.)

The chapter eventually narrates a complicated and forced abandonment of Social Action as Curriculum and a gradual evolution into the less potent, but nonetheless hopeful curriculum of my recent Seminar in Democracy and Education at Colgate. Guided by the principles of autoethnography, I use a reflective critique of my own teaching life at the time, illuminated by the actual feeling of being haunted that I experienced to underscore the creepiness of the political era. An intention of this account is to interpret the differences in character between Social Action as Curriculum in its earlier robust form and its later more ghostly iterations. The wider purpose of such an interpretation is to establish resonances between those differences and the contrast between human life more generally, as lived before and after 9/11. The comparison frames the narration of my process as a teacher succumbing to and partially recovering from the clobbering effects of the political aftermath of 9/11, in the hopes that my uncovering of a something-to-be-done, however partial and complicated by my complex personhood, might serve as inspiration for my allies who hope to "pierce holes in knowledge" with others in the present.

In this context, I theorize the non-instrumental education that confirms "the personal as political," and its process as "conjoint communicated experience." Then I offer an assemblage of stories featuring the interactions between and among my students, myself, and residents of Binghamton's new immigrant communities in connection with two public mural projects, and a tutoring project. The relationships forged through these projects expanded, though, to involve more students, groups, and organizations in the years preceding 9/11. Narration of the process of that expansion provides illustration of "conjoint communicated experience" in Social Action as Curriculum. In the haunted ethos of the period of the build-up to the two wars the U.S. finally declared, it is precisely that quality of conjoint communicated experience in both my course, and in social life more generally, which was defanged. I define this defanging as a haunting because in addition to "[registering] the harm inflicted or a loss sustained by a social violence" which would qualify it as a trauma, it also engendered "disturbed feelings that could not be put away," "[exposure of] the cracks and rigging," and created the conditions where "something different than before, seems like it must be done," (p. 16) in Gordon's words.

Tracking this haunting, in a story from after my departure from Binghamton from my first teaching at Colgate University after I left Binghamton, a Politics in Education course, I explore and attempt to theorize my uncertainty about whether or not we were engaged in "conjoint communicated experience." Then, out of the long process of transition from my role as a teacher-activist at Binghamton to a more sedate, circumspect, and consciously qualified professorial identity at Colgate emerges a recent promising teaching experience in a seminar called Democracy and Education. I share a number of positive developments of this more gratifying experience of teaching Democracy and Education. Still, I end the chapter facing the depth of haunting that will need to be addressed in order to pursue global egalitarianism through education, with a meditation on how socially marginalized children are so readily being turned into ghosts.

CHAPTER 2

THE PERSONAL AS POLITICAL: RATIONALE FOR SOCIAL ACTION AS CURRICULUM

For myself and many of my peers in social justice-focused teacher education programs, a critique of instrumental knowledge, so prevalent in this era where market relations dominate everything, is accompanied by our already established Deweyan structuralist sense: non-instrumental knowledge is knowledge that can be usefully integrated with one's (Deweyan) project of seeking personal growth in the context of community. This personal growth project will require awareness of the structural realities of inequality and related non-sustainability that are imposed by capitalist market relations. Such awareness will support us to pursue our own individual growth in the context of social action to redress inequality and lack of sustainability. Instrumental knowledge, by contrast, is knowledge prized for its specific and limited exchange value within market relations—knowledge valued because it is likely to lead to good performance on a test, a good grade, or a higher salary. Clearly, there is significant overlap between these broadly generalized categories of knowledge. However, the term "instrumental knowledge" invokes subjective autonomy, the illusion of a self primarily in competition with others to get the goods—high test scores, grades, and salaries—the markers of success or failure in the contemporary non-sustainable global market-driven culture. Knowledge is construed as an instrument of this market-driven culture, which is, in turn, literally structured to enforce competition. In such an anti-Deweyan culture, all resources become instruments for potential personal advancement, and the resources so directed to private institutions, like liberal arts colleges, are associated, as Bill Readings confirms, with the signifier "excellence." By contrast, Dewey recognizes the problematic division of labor into thinking work and doing work, which is enforced by social class-determined education, as driving a non-sustainable culture and a less-than-enlivening motivation for schooling. Instrumental knowledge will tend to perpetuate non-sustainability, as opposed to the sustainable culture that situates the individual's mind-body integrated growth in the process of maintaining (and improving) the democratic functioning of the communities circumscribing the individual.

Though Dewey predated contemporary feminism, the feminist aphorism the "personal is political," with its implicit rejection of instrumental knowledge, taught many of us to understand the social construction of our personal experience as reflective of socio-political realities in the public world. We learned from this conception of our personal interdependence with political reality what we would need to do in order to shape gratifying personal lives. (Such lives are characterized by depth, including joy and sorrow, creativity, and rewarding commitments to others. We came to understand, too, that a certain level of anxiety was a normal companion to a life of depth.) We would need to use our agency to help shape a world that was less violent and related, more equitable in its distribution of resources. We would need to eliminate war and its supports in imperialism, colonialism, racism, sexism, and classism. We experimented with different rules for negotiating among our different perspectives. We grew in our skepticism about the utility of national boundaries, too, hoping to find ways of appreciating cultural differences without supporting nationalisms.

Significantly, we learned that those "isms" had shaped the people who shaped us. Many of us were educated towards a complicated self-reflectiveness (perhaps anticipating the work of Avery Gordon) by the gradual awareness that constraining or oppressive beliefs, lessons of the economic and political structures in which we lived (named by philosopher Ernest Becker "hero systems") were likely to have been internalized by the families and communities who raised us—and then by ourselves—as "psychology."

Becker specifically identified the "industrial-commercial" hero system as the reigning internalized ideology of the era when he wrote *The Birth and Death of Meaning* in 1974, a psychodynamically inspired broad social critique that effectively linked the individual's efforts to control anxiety with the accommodation to—even *heroic identification with* the reigning ideology of the day. He offered us a pre-feminist version of the personal as political, and an early corrective to Freud's overemphasis on the intra-psychic as cause of most personal pain (see Chapter 1). Then feminists helped us appreciate that the personal hurts we suffered, and the personal hurts we delivered to others, often represented political relations of power and domination internalized. We came to define what we had internalized in summary form as patriarchy. Nurtured by this understanding, political activism opposing war, imperialism, racism, and sexual abuse; advocacy for full productive employment, regulations to prevent obscene concentrations of global wealth for the very few, quality schooling for all children, equal rights for women, gays, lesbians, and transgendered people—such efforts were not only rewarding when they appeared to affect policy, but also because they affected our personal lives. They offered new emotional wisdom when we acted in concert with others against the patriarchal practices that had hurt us personally.

What attracts many of us to the field of social justice-focused teacher education is the opportunity to address such political, cultural, and personal challenges, and to do so in relation to our aim to reverse the global assault on socially critical education. In our field, so clearly belonging to the waste economy named by Bill Readings, we enjoy greater than average permission for interdisciplinarity, along with its potential to restore the affective bonds that make life experience differently educative from decontextualized knowledge. Avery Gordon cites Roland Barthes's rich understanding of interdisciplinarity, which has continually nurtured my own:

> Interdisciplinary work, so much discussed these days, is not about confronting already constituted disciplines (none of which, in fact, is willing to let itself go). To do something interdisciplinary, it's not enough to choose a "subject" (a theme) and gather around it two or three sciences. Interdisciplinarity consists in creating a new object that belongs to no one. (2008, p. 7)

To Barthes's affirmation, Gordon helpfully adds, "Not owned by anyone yet, this interdisciplinarity is in the public domain, which does not guarantee anything except that there is still some room to claim rather than discipline its meaning into existence ….” Moreover, Gordon defines her own interdisciplinary project as the search “for a language for identifying hauntings and for writing with the ghosts [that] any haunting inevitably throws up” (p. 7). In my own interdisciplinary project of Social Action as Curriculum, it is the language “conjoint communicated experience” that signifies precisely what was eventually made ghostly.

SOCIAL ACTION AS CURRICULUM PRE-HAUNTING

The course titled Social Action as Curriculum was an interdisciplinary project as Barthes intended, designed after one experimental iteration described below to coincide with student teaching as the capstone event of our social justice-focused elementary education Master’s program at Binghamton University. In its two earliest iterations my students and I, with the support of a talented consulting artist funded by our modest Council on the Arts grant, collectively produced two community murals. The first mural, in some ways the most ambitious, was actually the product of the pilot course that did not involve (then) current student teachers, and attracted a number of graduate students from the most socially critical programs at Binghamton including Sociology and Women’s Studies. We had engaged the support and active participation of a local African-American minister who not only led Sunday services for the local Haitian community, but also directed the Binghamton Housing Authority residence where a significant percentage of the refugee population of Binghamton lived. We painted the mural on the exposed wall of its Building #7. (On account of the presence of the massive and paternalistic Endicott-Johnson shoe business, Binghamton had been an officially designated refugee resettlement area for many years, but the decline and final closing of the factory complexes by the 1990s precipitated its loss of designation; since then new immigrants have continued to settle there in smaller numbers.)

This mural-painting project involved active participation of over one hundred new immigrant residents, including many school-age children who attended the same elementary school relatively close to the University where I supervised a number of student teachers on a regular basis. (The elementary school became the site of the mural project featured in the next iteration of the course one year later.) Perhaps the most exciting event associated with this first mural project was the pancake breakfast attended by a hundred residents representing seven different language groups, with four official translators present (also funded by the Arts Council grant), and much active informal translating occurring spontaneously over the course of our three-hour meeting. At that gathering in the Housing Authority’s social hall, my students and I facilitated heated discussion between two Somali families and the four young adult Kurdish women who became personal friends with two of my students, and continuous supporters of the project. These young women objected to the first near-consensus that had been informally negotiated by the many residents who were actively participating in this huge conversation to negotiate the content of the mural. (In order to speak you had to be holding the talking stick, an empty cardboard holiday wrapping paper roll elaborately decorated with wood glue and findings at an early meeting with children in the after school program sponsored by the Housing Authority's Boys and Girls club.) A diverse group had agreed that illustration of the charming Somali folktale narrated by a fifth-grade Somali student should become a central image in the mural. The Kurdish women argued that the mural should feature an image of the strafing of their families by the Republican guard as they sought escape from Iraq into Turkey during the brutal repression of uprisings against Saddam Hussein's regime in the spring of 1991. (All four of the young women had survived this experience as children.) "We thought this mural was going to be political; it should show the history of how our people were brutalized, not some fairy tale!" was their opening statement. Two of my students quickly developed remarkable skills at negotiating compromise in this very large and diverse group: it was eventually agreed that a snaking trail of barbed wire, symbolic of the refugee camp experiences of the many Iraqi families, would divide sections of the mural. These sections would feature the contributions of multiple constellations of residents, including the preschoolers speaking seven different first languages, who scoured our global bird, fish, and assorted animal and flower guidebooks and identified the flora and fauna from their countries of origin that would (all mixed-up, we agreed!) grace the borders of the mural. The eight-times-successively-translated joking comment of an older Caribbean man, "it takes the little ones to bring us together," engendered widespread laughter that especially delighted one of the young Kurdish women who was moved, as my students were, by both the laughter and the astute comment reflecting the balkanization of the mural. Ultimately, the twelve-week project that followed this meeting represented one of the greatest joys in my academic life, its complexity defying numerous efforts to systematically capture its lessons in my subsequent scholarship.

The second iteration of the course marked its transformation into both the seminar coinciding with student teaching, and capstone event for our elementary education Master's students. Its goals were now quite complicated, as the course was now being offered very specifically as a complement to student teaching. Our students and cooperating teachers were informed that this arrangement was intended to underscore the elementary team's perspective that we conceived of the work of teaching as political, in addition to intellectual and spiritual. We also offered the hope that social action might ultimately find a place in the actual curriculum of public school classrooms. These purposes had to co-exist with the necessary other varied aims of a seminar coinciding with student teaching, however. To this end, however, our elementary team had adopted the necessary practice of reserving a collection of challenging readings for the student teaching seminar intended to reawaken, for use in their placement classrooms, the students' knowledge gleaned from their previous three full-time terms of required coursework. The assigned readings reflected not only that vast array of knowledge, but also new attention to social action research. I also included the novel, *Animal Dreams* (featured in Chapter 4), for its examination of the process of a fallible young adult teacher slowly coming to live a life of intentional commitment to the global egalitarian project, and engaging her students in social action as part of the curriculum of their biology class. In seminar we also needed time to collectively process student teaching experiences, in support of my bi-monthly individual post-observation conferences. Yet, despite competing priorities, this class was able to complete another mural project at the elementary school mentioned earlier; the project was characterized by similar qualities of delight and social complexity as the earlier pilot one.

We were even able to respond to student critique of the first mural project regarding the balkanizing of its cultural content: the students and I had been disturbed by the lack of collaboration between and among the adult representatives of different ethnic/nationality groups to negotiate their group's contribution to the design and eventual painting, a limitation of the project so astutely noted by that Caribbean resident. We interpreted that the balkanization reflected what was actually happening in the world, precisely what Deweyan "conjoint communicated experience" is intended to contest. We decided to officially join an International Peace Mural association whose rules supported the anti-war and anti-oppression ideology of our program, in the hope that our membership would offer us leverage to critique those decisions of our community co-participants that we judged constraining in light of our highest goals for the project. Our choice to join the association proved prescient, as one of the association's rules caused an educative conflict for my students when the school's principal, after we had left the site one day, directed our consulting artist to paint a flag on the representation of the school in the mural. The association's rules banned representation of flags in the murals they sponsored, in consonance with their principle of discouraging expression of nationalisms. My students had to negotiate with both the principal and the PTA in order to have the flag painted over, and one PTA leader boycotted the mural opening in protest of our lack of sufficient patriotic spirit. We also had to console a tearful Puerto Rican third-grader who had planned to paint the flag of her homeland above her representation of her grandmother's village on the island. Yet, my two student teachers who provided the consolation voiced their pride in seminar that the child had gradually grown more wide-eyed and dry-eyed as they explained to her the intention of the rule. The policy of never patronizing children was a cornerstone of our program, but these two students provided the most potent reinforcement for that policy that I had ever experienced.

Both "Mural Openings," associated with these two first iterations of the course were gala events, to which we provided transportation for all families. Municipal and even state legislators attended, a practice that continued in all future mural openings. In the third and fourth iterations of Social Action as Curriculum, student teachers pursued indoor mural projects at another socially diverse elementary school and the middle school attended by most new immigrant and working class students in Binghamton. As a result of the expansion of this first project into a collaborative multi-grade social studies unit on immigration, and the second, on a study of the Harlem Renaissance, all of my students were drawn into these projects, and I was able to assign readings that supported their direct curriculum-making for their classrooms. My students were involved in providing after-school writing support for the children designing their contributions, as well as contributing to the significant clean-up operation required by the painting of a mural by young people in the front hallways of busy urban schools. The organic nature of my students' involvement eliminated the pressure of original project development.

LESSONS FROM OUR WORK WITH IRAQI FAMILIES

In another iteration of the course, we were able to focus directly on the anti-war commitment of our program. Two of my student teachers had befriended a group of local Iraqi men who were interested in improving their English speaking skills. These men, all fathers of young children, had the specific goal of more effective communication with the public about their own experience related to the negative effects on their families of the sanctions against Iraq in response to Iraq's invasion of Kuwait. The sanctions, imposed by the UN Security Council in 1990, represented a nearly total trade and financial embargo, and disproportionately affected the least wealthy Iraqi citizens. The wives of these men developed an interest in improved English skills too, as they hoped to volunteer in their children's public school classrooms. I shared a vision with my students: the eventual collaboration of these Iraqi mothers with teachers like Mary Cowhey. These women could potentially play the role of the guest visitor and local expert in the classroom of their children, providing a new voice about any subject matter of interest in the curriculum, as well as information about their relationship to Islam, or the experience of being an immigrant.

A total of five of my student teachers became involved in this project tutoring for English-speaking skills in these two different groups, the men and the women, during this iteration of the course. The students involved in this tutoring initiative characterized their experience as transformative, and specifically cited the opportunity to connect with the socially conservative Iraqi wives and mothers who initially avoided interacting with us, the welcoming spirit of the local mosque where they met for the tutoring sessions, and the opportunity to listen to the compelling life experiences of the Iraqi families. My students were particularly moved by the feeling of success they experienced when the men were able to share these stories in the public context of the downtown YM-YWCA's Anti-Racism day.

The writing of African American educator Lisa Delpit (1995) regarding empowerment of socially marginalized students, which we studied in our weekly seminar meeting, were richly complicated when we were able to consider the usefulness of improving their oral communicative skills in English in the two different contexts of the Iraqi men and the Iraqi women. Though Delpit does mention her own and some of her colleagues' activism in her now classic writing, we noted in our seminar that she tends to emphasize the importance of assimilation of the *codes of the culture of power* for socially marginalized students in order to make possible their successful competition with dominant culture students. She does not focus explicitly on their potential ability to build movements against oppression as they become better schooled in these codes. Yet for both groups of

Iraqi parents, English education held this potential. Any of us who respected only the popular post-colonial assertion that English is the language of oppression, revalued the work of Delpit not only in her own important context about the necessity of mastery of the codes for successful competition of socially marginalized young people in the market relations context, but also in this context of support for the ability to struggle for social change. Such consideration opened us to ponder the manipulative possibilities of all language use, as well. Janice Radway's understanding of the divides created by market relations could help explain how the discourse of justification for the Iraq War focused on "the failure of the sanctions," implying that the act of starving ordinary Iraqis of necessary medical and other supplies would somehow lead to their ability to topple the heavily militarized, totalitarian regime of Saddam Hussein. My students involved in both this, and a later tutoring project, involving only Iraqi women who wanted to prepare for a college education here, were allied with a community that opposed both, sanctions and war, considering both initiatives wrongly motivated. At the time, we had to consider these realities without the wisdom of Janice Radway—with only an intimation of the artificial divides imposed between and among people by the power of global market relations.

In another Social Action as Curriculum seminar our consideration of the personal as political led to a focus on the continual patience and care we observed as the Iraqi women attended to their children, whose typical quiet play in the background accompanied our informal meetings at the local mosque where my students tutored. We compared the quality of their maternal attention to their children to the education offered children from affluent professional families as characterized by Jean Anyon (1981)—in her classic article "Social Class and School Knowledge," which we were also studying in seminar at the time. Anyon's argument did not employ Readings's term "subjective autonomy" but she found in her research that the attention paid to young people in affluent professional schools (loosely correlated with "upper middle class" and matching the aspirations of most of my students) made them more self-centered. The paradox she uncovered is that affluent professional young people have developed a more nominally progressive critique of the society through a curriculum that is more socially critical than the curriculum available in public schools in working class and lower middle class neighborhoods. Yet, despite this curriculum, these affluent professional students are more focused on their own achievements as centrally important. Anyon labels the theme of their education "narcissistic."

The intimation in Anyon's article that made it relevant to our observations of the Iraqi mothers is that progressive social critique and socially revisioned curriculum, although they *can* lead to personal commitment to systemic social change, are readily defanged by pervasive belief in subjective autonomy. In our observation, the Iraqi women my students tutored were extremely attentive to each individual child, yet they tended to emphasize to their children the importance of their bonds with one another, as well as their responsibility to behave in a way that set a respectful tone. The respectful tone clearly conveyed their appreciation of the important work being pursued by their fathers in their attempts to receive the tutoring in English they needed in order to educate the broader community about misguided U.N. policy. Nevertheless, the children were allowed to be physically active, and even to occasionally interrupt their parents who were in dialogue with us. We ended our last seminar meeting of the term with a review of our readings from the perspective of how they had informed our projects and how our projects had offered new interpretations of our readings. Students articulated that Anyon's study, "Social Class and School Knowledge," although dated, helped us understand that progressive curriculum itself will not typically lead to action towards social change. Such an education must be accompanied by a focus on learner agency related to our obligations to one another. We reaffirmed that in their future teaching in their own classrooms, knowledge of our obligations to one another would need to produce the interdisciplinary glue for the curriculum.

EXPANDED ALLIANCES

A highlight of this period was a speaking engagement by the Iraqi men at our downtown YM-YWCA's Anti-Racism Day, where they spoke about their opposition to the sanctions. There we learned of Voices in the Wilderness, the U.S.-based anti-sanctions movement directed by long-time bold international peace activist Kathy Kelly, who also gave a talk on the Binghamton campus as part of her U.S. tour to garner support among students. It is significant that we had no connection with the invitation that brought Kathy Kelly to speak on campus. I include this discrete fact here because it confirms the reality that there were other colleagues in different departments who experienced her specific progressive activism as in alliance with the curriculum of their courses. This was particularly true of the Binghamton University sociology department, which specializes in world-systems analysis; I believe that it was a group of graduate students and faculty in the sociology department who invited Kelly to campus, and along with a number of local anti-war activists unaffiliated with the University, they were terrifically moved by her talk, as I was. In our seminar, we were reading Barbara Kingsolver's novel, *Animal Dreams* (see Chapter 4), and were able to identify Kelly's full-time political activism with that of the character, Hallie, who was strafed by the US military in a village in Nicaragua while sharing her expertise in plant biology. We noted that the level of activism of Hallie's sister, Codi, the biology teacher whose curriculum saved the local river from deadly pollution, modeled the level of social action consonant with being a teacher, even balancing a teaching career with a gratifying personal life. We noted that our demands on ourselves to be activists would always represent a tension in the practice of being a teacher.

I was fortunate to receive an affirmative action grant from Binghamton University that gave me the full-year sabbatical to complete my first academic book in 2000. During that time I did not do any teaching, but I did participate in the growing movement against high-stakes testing, collaborating with a number of students in our doctoral program, one of whom was a local principal, as well as a faculty member in our literacy program. Parent and community participation grew so dramatically during a period of about two years that on the evening of September 11th, a teacher educator friend and I were to be featured on the panel of a forum on high-stakes testing being sponsored by the alumni association of Binghamton University in one of the campus' largest auditoriums. This forum represented a culmination of work we had been doing towards the construction and distribution at meetings at the downtown public library of "testing boxes" to families who agreed to host anti-testing parties for neighbors in their own homes. The literature in the boxes became assigned reading in my introductory elementary methods seminar that term, the term of 9/11. Further, the most politically conscious of the families who opposed excessive testing were astute about both the connections between neoliberal wars and neoliberal evisceration of the curriculum in the service of standardization, as well as the steady defunding of public schools. A few of these parents were scheduled to speak that evening. The cancellation of this large university-sponsored community forum out of respect for the tragedy of 9/11 and the public's state of shock presaged what would become a permanent shift in the country's allocation of attention and resources. This was a haunting transformation both for those who acknowledged it as such and for those who knew "just enough to scare normalization into a state of nervous exhaustion" (Gordon, 2008, p. 64).

POST-9/11 HAUNTINGS: OUR WORK WITH TEACHERS FOR PEACE

Half of the students in Social Action as Curriculum that term regularly joined members of the Broome County Peace Alliance and me in weekly anti-war demonstrations outside the Hall of Justice against the brewing War in Afghanistan. Our participation coincided with our fifteen-minute break from Social Action as Curriculum, which met downtown a block away from the Hall of Justice. Here the university leased a building in order to encourage projects that represented community-university collaborations. Later, during the period leading up to the Iraq War, a small group of students in our Educational Theory and Practice doctoral program had founded an organization called Teachers for Peace. Teachers for Peace held periodic meetings attended by an average of ten local teachers and some of my elementary pre-service students. The largest meeting, facilitated by a recent graduate of our program, now teaching in her own classroom in a Binghamton public elementary school, attracted twenty participants, and featured discussion and sharing of children's anti-war literature. Once war against Iraq was declared, we sponsored a workshop on using media literacy to teach the complexities of the Iraq War at all levels of the curriculum. I also led one meeting where we considered the ways in which spiritually rooted anti-war discourses could support our work. During this brief time period, a productive synergy developed between the work of the two programs: our EdD Program in Educational Theory and Practice, and our social justice-focused Master's Program in Elementary Education. A few of the Master's students who were unsure about their position on the Iraq War nevertheless appeared to feel gratified to be included in the vibrant conversation that characterized these meetings.

The first Tuesday anti-war lunchtime vigil called for by Teachers for Peace on the main campus of the University was attended by a few faculty, a small number of graduate students (both white and students of color) and a group of Muslim teachers and their older students brought by the director-principal of the only Muslim school in the region, who was a student in our doctoral program. We circled the fountain in the center of campus for about a half hour, and a few students and faculty who were passing joined us. One faculty member in my own department participated. Soon after the first vigil, the Muslim school's director, on whose dissertation committee I served, told me only that there had been repercussions to her community after the demonstration that she would not discuss. I became frightened, and felt responsible for having incurred no consequences myself for an action that was damaging to a student of mine. Most of my Master's students were teaching full-time and unavailable, but as we moved towards the declaration were less ready to participate in anti-war activities. Two students in my seminar had family members in the military, which made discussion in class difficult. From this time forward, I tended to involve my students less in my anti-war activism, and turned to the few faculty members at Binghamton who developed an anti-war list-serve and sponsored a few teach-ins.

During the spring term that featured the bombing campaign sickeningly but accurately described as "shock and awe," which early elementary school teacher Mary Cowhey boldly deconstructed for her student teacher (see Chapter 1), one of my students had a boyfriend serving in Iraq and another had a father in the military who expected to be sent to Iraq. When I met informally with a group of my students in order to brainstorm possibilities for social action projects for the following year, none of them proposed projects related to either the Iraq War or the continuing war in Afghanistan, but they did feel enthusiastic about the program's brief history of collaboration with the large new-immigrant communities of Binghamton. Related to the keen interest in music of a number of these students, we devised an intriguing proposal to create a jazz symphony from fragments of music created in the various communities with which we now had warm relationships. In the next few weeks, we collectively drafted and submitted the Arts Council grant we needed to fund the local eclectic musician and composer whom we had already enticed to support us in this work. We were very surprised when notified that we were denied this grant. Significantly, the rejection letter, although regretful in tone, suggested that our program had already received "its share" of funding. This assertion contradicted the previous reception by the Arts Council of our proposals, which had conveyed the sense that our work elaborated their own highest vision of community arts activism and encouraged others to consider similarly ambitious projects. I do not believe that this denial had anything to do with politics, writ either small or large. I think it had to do with gradually shrinking governmental and private contributions to Arts Councils, which represented a pattern that contributed to my own graduate demoralization. Funding priorities were, in a global way, shifting public monies from the arts into the financing of wars.

Military recruitment in the public schools would begin shortly. Simultaneously, a discourse of "learning self-discipline" and being socially responsible would pervert Deweyan language so as to not only encourage high-school students increasingly stressed and bored by high-stakes testing to join the military, but also to excuse the appropriation of former federal contribution to public school budgets by the military-industrial complex. The patriotic upsurge quickly encouraged the demonizing of Muslims that had been foreshadowed by the experience of my doctoral student who was director of the only local Muslim school.

Kathy Kelly was arrested and declared a terrorist by the U.S. government after 9/11 when Voice in the Wilderness attempted—in violation of the sanctions—to bring essential medical supplies to Iraq. Voices in the Wilderness was declared a terrorist organization, and Kelly was arrested numerous times for similar offenses, including a visit to Iraq during "shock-and-awe" bombing with an international delegation from her organization. I remember writing a small personal check to her defense fund, while feeling increasingly impotent with regard to the fragmented nature of responses to the war at the university. During this period, a young white man whom a number of experienced activist graduate students at B.U. did not trust, who worked for information technology at the university, kept turning up at our small anti-war events, and then twice joined us on the busses to the larger demonstrations in New York and Washington, asking odd questions and jotting down notes. Was this man a government plant? Such trust issues were exacerbated when two of our doctoral students, carrying our Teachers for Peace banner, noticed men, literally in suits, seated in black limousines with frosted glass, rolling down the windows and taking our pictures at a demonstration in Washington, D.C. It should not surprise my readers that I found such realities disheartening—the probability of an informant on campus who spied on lawful demonstrations, the likelihood that government agents were taking pictures of our students and other demonstrators. As was the case during the Vietnam War, government surveillance of its citizens increased, while public monies were being wasted accreting files on non-violent activists. As I reread this passage in 2014, I note that the current normalization of the National Security Administration spying on the e-mail correspondence of ordinary U.S. citizens, made public by a young man who now holds legal terrorist status, makes the earlier disturbing surveillance seem almost quaint.

I will never forget being greeted by the principal of the local elementary school in which I was paying a planned observation visit to two of my student teachers on the very day the Iraq War was declared. As I entered the primary/early elementary wing, he turned from the wall he was facing to greet me while cutting a piece of masking tape between his front teeth. He was in the process of festooning with red, white, and blue crepe paper the corridor of the primary wing, where I observed that, after every twelve feet of crepe paper banner, a homemade sign directing the five, six, and seven year old children on this primary wing to "Love your country. Be patriotic."

To drop bombs on the cradle of civilization was not too political, but to build a movement supporting teachers to make visible in the curriculum of their classrooms the painful contradictions of this war *was* too political. Advocating for war is not too political, but advocating for peace is too political. These are the politics that immediately emerged in the early days of the Iraq War, at a time when I did not generally feel personally endangered—politics that began to haunt me, and continue to haunt me now. The most painful awareness that periodically overwhelmed me at that time was that I was not taking enough risks, that I was too inhibited, too easily intimidated. To borrow a phrase from Codi Noline's (pregnant) student Rita Cardenal in *Animal Dreams* (4), "it was a creeped scenario" (p. 141).

Gradually, shifts in the political climate circumscribing both of my programs contributed to my own further personal demoralization. When I was asked by a new department chair at Binghamton to remove the Teachers for Peace collection boxes and bumper stickers from our Education Department corridor in the building in which we taught and had our offices, I initially ignored her. I eventually learned that I could not, even though I enjoyed respect and support in my generally liberal department. I recognized once again that, in order to keep the local peace, liberalism can fold so neatly into a personal disposition to accommodate. As long as its "illiberal" contradictions can be exported far enough away or otherwise rendered invisible in the local context, liberalism can offer an illusion of having done one's job. It seemed that there was enough tacit agreement that Teachers for Peace was "too political" at this time, that there was no way to effectively oppose the directive to make Teachers for Peace invisible. At this time I was called into my department chair's office and told that the politicization of our elementary program was costing all of our graduates jobs. The reality was that nothing could have been further from the truth. Our students were more broadly educated and more passionate about their work than most teacher education candidates; at that time our program's focus on creativity, experiential curriculum, and the use of multiple genres of text with children, including an emphasis on children writing continual response texts, made our graduates attractive to administrators in the area. My students were also getting the most sophisticated education about teaching math from a colleague whose depth of understanding of Vygotskyan theory was equaled only by her knowledge of effective curriculum-making. The most intellectually curious teachers in the region were anxious to work with us. Yet the fears of my department chair about our viability in the context of the overpowering noise of the justifications for this illegal war were able to drown out reality, and to erode my own confidence in my ability to be effective.

Although you could occasionally see dying and mutilated (school) children, the "collateral damage" of this war, on YouTube and other Internet sites, they were ghosts even before the bombing began. Why, when we study child development in educational studies classes, do we not begin with these ghosts when we are "covering" the amazing amount of global expert agreement about what children need in order to have their free intelligence supported? Equally useful would be the power to set the terms of the national discourse on child development with the now-haunted famous slogan, "War is dangerous to children and other living things." What if we were to introduce our Child and Adolescent Development syllabi with such a statement? Isn't it haunting that it would be unthinkable for me, a Dewey scholar, to orient my Child and Adolescent Development course around my actual belief: that Dewey's lesser-known efforts to introduce anti-war legislation in Congress represented more important advocacy for the world's children than his occupations-based early-childhood curriculum? Similarly, I'd like to privilege ecological mapping of the concentric circles of damage done to children as a result of war over foundational knowledge about the work of, say, Piaget, as significant as I continue to judge his contributions to the field. Yet, to pursue the organization of a Child and Adolescent Development course that would continue to include Piaget around our collective need to make war illegal would position me as unscholarly—even an anti-intellectual hippie. In most university teaching contexts, by making this choice I would sacrifice the authority I need to teach. This awareness alerts us to the multiple challenges we face in constructing the truly interdisciplinary learning experiences advocated by John Barthes, projected as the goal of the curricular change initiatives proposed by Readings in *The University in Ruins*, which are consonant with Gordon's charge to reconstitute the methodology of sociological research.

Now, in 2014, I understand the act of unearthing (for the future work of my field of educational studies) the haunted nature of my course's demise to parallel precisely Janice Radway's description of Gordon's (2008) unearthing (for her field of sociology) in *Ghostly Matters*:

> … the intricate process by which the reductive and universalizing powers of the market are lived at the level of the conceptual and the intellectual and how the resulting divide between the general and the particular, between the social and the individual, constrains our ability to recognize and to redress the profound human costs of a system utterly dependent on the repression of a knowledge of social injustice. (p. ix)

Again, I seek to reclaim precisely "the ability to recognize and to redress the profound human costs of a system that is utterly dependent on the repression of a knowledge of social injustice." Although I have acknowledged above that my reclaiming of this ability is "for my field," readers must understand that "my field" corresponds to the Deweyan conception of education, which he identifies as human life.

Thus, I unearth the haunted nature of Social Action as Curriculum, while reclaiming the commitment to the pursuit of social justice it represented, the global egalitarian project. I defend this work as the direction of *thoughtful* liberal arts education in an era where such education no longer supports a national culture, but invites the possibility of *thinking* about the construction of a more socially equitable global culture (Readings, pp. 62-69). Our work, then, is to seek the increasing depth that Bill Readings defines as *thought*, a depth of inquiry directed at unearthing the possibilities for social and environmental sustainability, or the replication of human culture with improvement that Dewey defined as education. Yet this focus on social sustainability, resonating with Dewey's call for improvement in each generation's reproduction of human culture, will require a new willingness for those of us who teach at the current moment. For while Dewey fully intended to situate his educational project in the mainstream dominant culture, we can no longer harbor the illusion that our project is compatible with the market relations that define the contemporary dominant culture. Rather, we must enthusiastically situate our work in a waste economy, whether the waste economy of the university of excellence, or the waste economy of any institution or community in which we commit our efforts to the global egalitarian project. Readings's point is that dominant culture institutions need us and need our work in order to maintain their moral justification for being, even though our work is wasteful in the context of the economy of calculation whose goal is profit-making to benefit a limited class. If we pursue this work well, my hope is that the altered consciousness of our students will invest in this waste economy, even as these students necessarily strategize to survive in the economy of calculation, as we do. Such a redistribution of their life force energies would be motivated by their discovery of the joys of living outside of the constraints imposed by subjective autonomy. Then, the waste economy might, in turn, grow to represent a model of sane economy for more and more people, and gradually compete more successfully for resources with the economy of calculation.

Most of our contemporary students are unaware of the implications of "the personal is political," so we need to teach it to them without assuming that they have any personal experience with political activism to support its truth. At the same time, the rightward shift in national priorities and politics following 9/11 created barriers to the most potent projects like those we had pursued in earlier iterations of Social Action as Curriculum—those that illustrated the haunted manipulations of power in global context, and gave us access to haunted sites, including those described below.

I taught Social Action as Curriculum on three more occasions before I left Binghamton University, and I would characterize most of the social-action projects that followed 9/11 as valid and useful to my students. Yet, they tended to be negotiated by individual students, and required much less parent and community involvement. My students supported socially marginalized young people to create and exhibit photo essays that featured the strengths of their immigrant family culture. They helped build a nature preserve behind a school, and they collected and distributed donated books to children who claimed them out of genuine interest. They advertised the cruelty of local puppy mills, and they investigated the social injustices buried in the "three-strikes" policy of the legal system. They helped refund a school in El Salvador following a devastating earthquake by successfully marketing cards featuring original drawings by the children of the village. In one case, a student met weekly with a group of fourth graders during lunchtime to review newspaper accounts of a toxic spill caused by the local and very powerful IBM Corporation. They succeeded in having a letter to the editor published in the local newspaper about their questions about the handling of this abuse to the environment. With enough advance preparation, this investigation could have generated a great project for the whole class, but my guess is that it was only approved by the school on account of its limited nature and the principal's personal trust in the particular student, who had subbed in the building extensively. I valued all of the projects, but mourned the loss of the expansive modeling of Dewey's "conjoint communicated experience" that characterized the early mural projects and the tutoring work with the Iraqi families.

Although minuscule in comparison to the horrendous costs of the war to concentric circles of sufferers—beginning with Iraqi families and the families of United States soldiers, and moving out to losses in the globe's natural and cultural resources—the loss of the projects that represented global structural critique whose enactment was my highest goal for the Social Action as Curriculum experience was hugely symbolic. Avery Gordon helps me conceptualize that loss. A haunted site—actually, multiple haunted sites—were buried deeper, made less available for the efforts of education to do what Badiou calls "hole piercing." For Badiou the goal of all education is "to pierce a hole in [dominant culture] knowledge"—to expose the absences and distortions imposed by the effects of power on shaping what we think we know and learn.

MY OWN COMINGS AND GOINGS HAVE POLITICS

I left Binghamton University knowing that a number of my colleagues were disappointed with my decision to leave, and I felt little personal bitterness, recognizing, without having the words at the time, that we were living in a haunted era. Fortunately, a former doctoral student of mine who was a very respected elementary school teacher, Joan Koster, did (and currently continues to) keep the Teachers for Peace movement alive in the Binghamton area.

I accepted my present position at Colgate University without illusions, and knowing that Social Action as Curriculum would be difficult to revive at any college or university, as I had originally conceived it. Still, my move to primarily undergraduate education at Colgate was energizing. I was welcomed by my new group of colleagues with whom I continue to enjoy mutual respect and a collaborative spirit in our work together. Yet, regardless of where we teach, teacher educators continue to face multiple contradictions as we pursue this anti-oppression work: for example, the current curriculum at Colgate for prospective secondary English and social studies student teachers and for our more numerous social foundations of education/educational studies majors and minors has focused quite directly on dynamics of oppression and on the need for a multiple-perspective view of history, literature, and the sciences. This curriculum revalues the narratives and accomplishments of the marginalized and "speaks truth about (and to) power," although it does not typically focus on the question of concentration of wealth that continues to preoccupy me. Although race, gender, immigration, and LGBTQ issues are a strong focus in our courses, the rapid polarization of income garners less attention. Overt critique of capitalism is softened by our own uncertainties, or conflated in a critique of neoliberalism, consumerism, and sometimes, imperialism/colonialism. In universities like ours, with powerful departments of free market economics, and Boards of Trustees dominated by One Percenters, there are strategic impediments to harsh direct critiques of capitalism (although our mandated teaching of *The Communist Manifesto* provides one such opportunity; see Chapter 1). Movement building is analyzed historically, and comparative education courses offer a window for study of some contemporary movement building. However, I would argue that most national or local current events that directly implicate the rapidity with which the top ten percent of the One Percent are accreting an unconscionable share of the world's resources remain buried haunted sites. This is the case not only in my department but also in most schools—public, private, K-12, and higher education. James Loewen's *Lies My Teacher Told Me* still offers the most compelling explanation for this reality: Living history, that is, the history whose actors and observers are still alive, is the most controversial kind, as it directly invokes the politics of the present, and places front and center the political contradictions within which scholars and teachers live (1995). Certainly, a share of my salary is paid for by people whose investments and values helped (almost) bring down the global economy just a few years ago, some of whom represent the One Percent I'd like us to occupy. These realities are almost unspeakable at universities, despite the fact that the contradictions they engender must be navigated on a daily basis.

POLITICS AND EDUCATION AT COLGATE

My first term at Colgate, coinciding with the Hurricane Katrina disaster, provides an example of such contradictions. I was teaching our department's Politics in Education course at the time, and felt it necessary to displace my planned introduction of the course in order to focus attention on the experience of the public school children of New Orleans. This teaching experience supports my intimation that courses can rise and fall in response to our efforts to keep haunted sites on the radar, given the social contradictions in which we do our work.

During one of the first classes in this course, I showed news footage of a very old African-American woman dying on the baggage belt at the New Orleans airport. I used the word "genocide" to describe the response to the Katrina disaster, and correctly predicted that many displaced children (all of whom had lived in relative poverty before the disaster) would lose months of schooling. But I also lost the class, except for a few students who desperately tried to educate me about the social privilege of the majority of my students. I was even offered the advice of one marvelous student in particular (who has since gone on to win awards for her inspirational high school English teaching in South Central Los Angeles) that these students could be drawn into significant social critique, but slowly. I could not effectively hear my potential rescuers at the time, although the course was salvaged for many of my students by some unpredictable dynamics.

One particular saving grace was a young man in the class who was a leader in the umbrella fraternity organization on campus, and he had a certain amount of clout, including clout with the more conservative students. This young man was taken by the idea that the quest for greater social justice might direct our lives, which is an idea I introduce at the beginning of all of my courses. I believe that he had honestly never considered that a certain degree of other-centeredness could offer concrete, and, I argued, joyful, direction for one's future. I came to understand that he had felt genuinely gratified by a few of the more earnest "Greek life" charity initiatives on campus, and that for the first time, he was considering more sophisticated ways of facing social inequality that could help define his own potential usefulness as a human being. It also turned out that this same young man was dating a young woman in the class who wanted to be a teacher, and the two of them became my allies. She, too, appeared delighted to consider the possibility that a teacher could shape students' perspectives on their potential to impact significant social dynamics in their society. (She later did some wonderful work with me in an independent study on curriculum for developing consciousness around social justice.)

The dynamics of my Politics in Education class included an undercurrent of student feeling that I was requiring them to agree with my own beliefs. I conceived of myself, rather, as requiring thoughtful citation from course texts and improvement of the generally mediocre writing I experienced in their first set of short papers. Despite this feeling that I was politically biased, one struggling student became genuinely invested in my promise that I would offer one-on-one sessions to support any participants in our course to significantly advance their writing skills. This particular young man, M, was from a family who owned and operated a family farm, and the farm was suffering from competition with agribusiness. His parents were struggling and quite unhappy; he relied on his football scholarship to Colgate as his ticket to an elite education and a noble escape from the farm. When we read Julia Weber Gordon's *My Country School Diary* (1946), her pre-World War II chronicle of her Deweyan social reconstructionist teaching in a one-room schoolhouse in rural central New Jersey, M objected to my enthusiasm about the teacher's involvement of the students in a dialogue with a local Cooperative Extension administrator about how to address some of the irrationalities of local dairy farm produce marketing. For me, this use of a local community resource by a teacher reflected both her commitment to authentic investigation of social problems, and her commitment to the public good in a particular local context, textbook Deweyan teaching.

M worked diligently with me to craft quite a beautiful essay in which he attacked Weber Gordon for promoting a perspective that would keep her students "trapped on the farm" instead of supporting them to consider "overcoming their fears of the more affluent urban lives that might be available to them if they pursued an elite education" after graduating from Weber Gordon's one-room schoolhouse. Serendipitously, M was interviewed for the *Colgate Scene,* an upbeat campus publication connected with the development office that features often-compelling profiles of particular faculty research initiatives and interviews with students on a variety of topics that might engage families investigating Colgate as a possible college for their children. In M's response to the reporter's inquiry about Colgate faculty expectations of their students, he named me as the most demanding teacher he had ever had, and also suggested that he learned to write a college essay in my class. Subsequent dynamics in this class revealed that being viewed as "demanding" proved a partial antidote to being seen as dogmatically political.

I also asked M to share the thesis of his paper in class, and I connected his presentation to my own genuine apology to the class for having presented a laudatory perspective on Weber Gordon's teaching, making it less likely that students would feel encouraged to think for themselves as they considered their responses to the text. This incident also allowed me to introduce the idea of "tensions in practice," a theme that would not only gain traction throughout the course, but would offer me a discourse out of which I could sometimes publicly (in class) rethink my own political certainties.

Course evaluations confirmed my own sense of this class: its significant potential was compromised by both student perception of political bias on the part of the professor, and by periodic announcement of changes in expectations based on my own sense that "things were not working." But the course was disappointing to me not only because I had clearly not projected the respect I actually felt for my students, but for another reason as well: it featured only relatively insignificant interaction with any real community outside of the classroom in which students might test the theories to which they were exposed, even though some active connection with an organization "in the service of the public good" was required.

Maxine Greene's (1988) use of the conception of "the public good" automatically calls up associations with struggles for greater democracy and/or a notion of personal efficacy tied to both hard-earned growth and the qualitative good of some community. However, the "public good" can represent a vague concept for our students who are not steeped, as we are, in her tradition. Many of our students equate charitable fundraising with "serving the public good," despite increasing research that much charity giving is counterproductive. Such research contends that charitable organizations can erode public expectation that part of the mission of government is to provide a safety net to its citizens, especially during economically vulnerable times like the present (Poppendieck, 1998). For instance, one popular student in Politics in Education had a personal connection to an organization related to childhood survivors of heart disease, and she organized many students to support her to both raise money and involve local children in designing a new heart logo for the organization. I considered this project only very minimally educative for the students, and would certainly have disallowed it had I felt I could risk additional charges of dogmatism. At the time I was certain that this conflict served as an example of how we as teachers sometimes appear to, or do actually, confuse empowering opportunities for students to exercise independent initiative with poorly motivated, and therefore, meaningless offering of choice, as a result of the vulnerability of our own authority. Now I am less certain.

DEVELOPMENT OF MY DEMOCRACY AND EDUCATION SEMINAR

In the academic terms following this shaky first one, the goal that organized my teaching evolved into creation of well-rationalized opportunities for personal engagement with the ideas encountered in the excellent texts we offered in educational studies courses. I also gradually re-learned what I had known earlier through the enactment of Social Action as Curriculum. If we could couple text that offered structural critique and also tended to invite personal engagement with some well-rationalized and collective community project, we might be in a position to move beyond the usual limitations of community service projects that simply supported and replicated the nominal sense of our students as "givers" and "rescuers." Projects that did move beyond giving and rescuing also provided genuine stimulation for transformative thinking for many of my students, removing the temptation for me to fill in too much interpretation and thus to appear too politically dogmatic.

Having been at Colgate long enough to have made genuine alliances with a few schools and community groups, I was able to co-design one such well-rationalized community project with the principal who invited it during spring 2012.

I redesigned this Democracy and Education seminar in light of the success of the community participation components increasingly featured in my own and my colleagues' courses: This time I wanted to pursue one significant collective project in which there was a likelihood of focused structural critique emerging to address a problem identified by the community partner. A condition I hoped for, but did not articulate, would be the welcoming of a structural critique on our part by the community partner. Fortunately, I was approached by a principal of a rural elementary school; Deb Dushko asked us to evaluate her school's efforts to encourage parent involvement. Principal Dushko, a former doctoral student I knew in the doctoral program at Binghamton University, was deeply invested in the pursuit of social justice in her work. I also knew her to be a community partner who would be direct in her dealings with me and my students, as well as willing to deal with complex data with both integrity and sensitivity.

The excerpt below is the introduction to a letter, crafted collectively by my students and Principal Dushko following her visit to our class, which was sent out to the parents of the children in Morrisville-Eaton's Edward R. Andrews Elementary School. This letter was accompanied by the district goals pertinent to our project. Since Principal Dushko proposed the project six months before we publicized this seminar, I had been able to inform most of the students of my tentative commitment to it in advance of the seminar's beginning. A certain amount of excitement had been generated, I would argue, precisely because I had sought out their responses to my idea of significantly crafting the course around the project.

> *Dear Edward R. Andrews Families:*
>
> *Working with parents and families is possibly the most important part of what we do in our learning community. In light of this, I have asked Dr. Barbara Regenspan's Educational Foundations class from Colgate to help us determine how we can help every family feel that they are welcome and find ways to make sure everyone's voice is heard.*
>
> *Communication and involvement are important to us as a district. The Morrisville-Eaton Board of Education has maintained the following goals within our five District Goals in regard to creating and maintaining our school community:*

> · *Goal 2: To foster an educational climate where all staff, students and community members are treated equally with respect and dignity.*
> · *Goal 5: To cultivate a partnership with parents and community members that enables us to realize the district mission.*
>
> *The purpose of working with Colgate University on this project is to improve the children's educational experience by creating an atmosphere where parents can be involved in their child's education. I have asked students from Colgate to do research on this so we can get a different perspective on some possible solutions to improving our relationships with our families.*
>
> *The Colgate students will be talking with parents and families to help us better understand:*
> · *how parents are involved in their child's schooling*
> · *ways to increase parent-teacher communication and interaction*
> · *how to create a learning community where everyone feels they belong*

The letter went on to assure confidentiality and provide two means for parents to offer their contact information to us, should they volunteer to be interviewed by one of our student pairs.

I selected course readings with an emphasis on both democratic educational philosophies and specific ethnographic research featuring efforts of school districts to improve what they conceived of as parent involvement. Our readings reconceptualized parent involvement by considering the parent community as an active party in negotiating the school curriculum. One reading represented contemporary progressive research on emergent literacy, as it conceived of parents as primary determinants of a child's invitation into meaningful literacy. A key reading which we studied with great intensity of attention was Dewey's *Democracy and Education*, with the understanding that it would provide the philosophy to ground this specific project. Students also read the dystopian novel by Ursula LeGuin, *The Dispossessed,* as a complicated and troubling account of a planet organized around "conjoint communicated experience." (The use of imaginative literature in courses like this one is further explored in Chapters 4 and 6.)

Students retrieved parent invitations both from a website and the main office of the elementary school, and took responsibility for arranging interviews in pairs. By the third week of class every student had completed one long interview with a parent or family. We collectively recognized a need for more clarification from the principal of school policy related to parent involvement. Shortly after Principal Dushko's second visit to our class, we also recognized our need to speak with the teachers, and were able to coordinate student schedules with those of the faculty of Edward R. Andrews to make possible our participation in a regular faculty meeting, where we interviewed the teachers in small groups.

As a class, we were self-consciously congratulatory about how effectively we were able to use class sessions to study challenging texts and to organize the process of our work with the school, including agreements about interview content and goals regarding deepening faculty conceptions of what parent involvement could constitute, given our somewhat idealistic readings. Student responsiveness was impressive throughout the course. But most dramatic was the articulation by the students who had confirmed, initially in conversations outside of class, a reality which had not influenced course readings: rural poverty was emerging as a barrier to effective communication between parents and teachers at this school with a significant population of families living in poverty.

In my earlier overzealousness as a teacher projecting my own urgency for the pursuit of social justice through our work, I had overpacked my syllabi with readings, creating a sense of breathlessness in the very process of my courses. Fortunately, I had learned from this painful former experience to leave some space in the syllabus to add readings that would become necessary over the course of a term where our project might evolve in unpredictable ways, probably requiring new research literature grounding. At this point in my career, I had also learned the value of intentionally treating that space as an invitation for student engagement to express itself in student determination of a certain percentage of our readings. After much thoughtful discussion, it was agreed that we would take a week to individually research and agree on assignments of readings about rural poverty. Shortly after this conversation, we revisited our tentative findings and recognized that we needed support in research literature in another area as well: to help us interpret what was emerging as the complex personhood of our parent informants.

The complications encountered by the students in reporting the experience and meaning of this work in a final paper that they were invited to write in pairs (completed in three evaluated stages over the course of the term) led to continual negotiation in class and re-evaluation and feedback on my part. We found that my re-evaluations themselves actually became valued readings for this course; they were appreciated by the students as responses to their collective negotiations reflecting their immediate problems. (At three different times, the handouts that reflected my own rethinking based on our collective negotiations in class were accompanied by a new article that students agreed to consider.)

A couple of my own re-evaluations during this course led to suggestions about new ways of thinking about how to organize their final papers, reflected in their own work in stages. I created and distributed clarifying explanation in class following a session wherein students voiced their frustrations with the necessary ordering of their textual reflections on Dewey's *Democracy and Education* in relation to their multiple interview experiences. I excerpt it below as representing an innovation that led to further innovation (possibly eventually being included in the scholarship that reflects new methods of reporting research findings):

> *The Deweyan critique of school curriculum and practices with regard to relating to the multiple communities which circumscribe the school might need to open out to encompass many contradictions. Consider thinking about each section of your paper as a dialogue between two primary sources, text plus interview w/parents, teachers, Morrisville-Eaton's principal, Deb D., and with profs. John Palmer and Sheila Clonan, with Deweyan philosophy providing the glue. Then allow a source or both sources to angle out near*

> *the end of the section, so that you introduce the next section by identifying a common theme or a contradiction which connects the two sections. Keep doing this until you have exhausted your sources. Then create a "findings" section where you summarize the contradictions/tensions you can now articulate, then a section called: "suggestions for future practice," and then a section called "disconfirming evidence" in which you consider issues that could invalidate the possible reliability of our project/process.*
>
> *For instance, you might want to suggest in "disconfirming evidence" that there may be no point in pursuing such a project as this one without national agreement on whether we are going to prioritize "nurture of the soul of the learner" (directed by a Deweyan conception of every learner being the future citizen who contributes her "best stuff" to the society), or whether, instead, we will prioritize keeping a non-sustainable economy afloat by feeding students into the current class structure and preparing the upper middle class to be this economy's managers, while the most socially marginalized kids will be prepared to be the new "reserve army of labor," chronically underemployed or unemployed. So, until we get an agreement about what our priority is....and further....that we agree that it's "nurture of the soul of the learner," then our project stands on shaky grounds. This would be a dramatic perspective, but it could be quite valid, depending on how you angled your earlier interpretations. However, this dramatic critique is also premised on the belief in a time of fewer and/or less dramatic social contradictions, and that belief is probably an illusion. So, if we agree that all research is going to be conducted in the context of an incredible number of social contradictions....then this project represents "the best we could do" and that's all that is possible for any research! You might reflect this type of uncertainty of interpretation throughout the paper, and articulation of the layered uncertainties could become its own organizing strategy.*

Notice that in this handout, I am responding to the students' professed need for more procedural direction, but I use the opportunity to teach about the unavoidable contradictions in our work, here addressing the reality that there is no national consensus that education be directed to nurturing the souls of the learners. Kerr's article (considered at great length in Chapter 7), had already generated particularly lively discussion in this class, where students were in contact with specific children and their parents—able to appreciate some of the many impediments to nurture in families, poverty among them—who professed the best intentions for their children. But here I place that same priority on nurture, in a context that helps the students understand that ideas so enlivening and appropriate to us can be dismissed in other discourses. This is a reminder of pervasive hauntedness in the reality of human dependence on different and often competing discourses, the existence of which we can be only partially aware. Interestingly, it is only during the actual writing of this chapter that I recognize the conflation in my own philosophy of education between the "souls" of all learners and their social imaginations, a conflation I could not have articulated even two years ago when I taught this course. And because I believe that this useful conflation represents my having pierced a hole in what I thought I knew, I am inclined to interpret that I unearthed a haunting.

LAYERS OF FINDINGS, ENDING WITH HAUNTING

Related to Deb Dushko's integrity, we were invited by the school board of Morrisville-Eaton to present our findings at a Board meeting; we were invited by the teachers to present our findings at a teachers' meeting; and we were invited by the Parent Teacher Organization to present our findings at a PTO meeting. The students accepted all three invitations and we created three separate Google documents in order to work collectively on the individual political challenges of these presentations. All three meetings proved very gratifying for the students, who left with the impression that we had been effective. Despite the critical nature of much of our data, we received much positive feedback from our audiences.

Our findings included the discovery that unarticulated social class conflict led to the marginalization of a small, materially impoverished, extremely alienated group of families. There are haunted realities hiding in this finding, but we could not have been effective at these forums using such language. We also reported carefully on our discovery of what some families themselves identified as their increasing attention to their own immediate concerns only, and a lack of interest in the functioning of the collective school community. Some parents spoke openly of being concerned only with the progress of their own children. We learned that belief in subjective autonomy was not necessarily tied to social class, and also recognized the challenge it presented to the administration and the teachers who were genuinely invested in deepening the feelings of community in the school, including its parent community. This recognition that belief in subjective autonomy was a significant force in a generally working class, even high poverty rural school, surprised my students, and deepened the empathy they already held for Deb Dushko and her most committed teachers. My students and I had to face a disappointing aspect of all social action projects: the limitations of our ability to unearth hauntings for other people, especially those not in our immediate community and in relation to whom we have no leverage in the economy of calculation. Our presentations delicately drew attention to issues of unaware privilege on the part of some parents and teachers, and to a lack of trust on the part of the most socially marginalized families. We had to modify the material we presented to the different audiences, especially our finding that some teachers and middle-class parents did not understand the stresses of families living in poverty. We expressed the reality that these families generally felt a lack of appreciation from their children's teachers of the supports they *did* offer their children, including those that met their basic needs. We suggested some type of forum in which the interdependence of all members of the school community was presented as reality and supported by selected testimony.

It was inspiring to us that a number of teachers told us after our presentation to them that they wanted and needed more information. Especially appreciated, for instance, was a research finding that when families living on tight budgets heard from a teacher that a child of theirs was especially able in any academic area, that that family was likely to invest a greater percentage of their scarce resources in educational experiences for their child. Although we did detect a certain amount of teacher demoralization and cynicism in our early small group meetings, we also experienced exactly the opposite both in the attitudes of teachers who spoke to us and in the appreciation of particular teachers by a number of our parent informants.

In our discussion of the research findings, we tried to offer realistic assessments of how students in a future Colgate seminar could help to enact some of our suggestions for action, including supplying one-to-one assistance to specific children and their families so that they could participate in a reinstated science fair, whose recent sacrifice to budget cuts was regretted by many families with whom we spoke. At the present time, I am teaching a class in which the students will be able to commit to such limited kinds of strategic enactment for follow-up social action in Principal Dushko's school. Principal Dushko and I are also proposing a teacher study group of Mary Cowhey's *Black Ants and Buddhists*, which I hope to lead, possibly with the support of some of my current students.

Final papers in this course were generally remarkably strong, and because of their experimental quality, involved some exceptionally moving passages that read like creative writing. For instance, two young women in the course narrated their experience arriving at a trailer park in a snowstorm, being unable to locate the trailer of a single mother they had planned to interview, whose cell phone was not working. Eventually, finding themselves in a deep ditch, they were towed out by a number of both male and female trailer park residents, all anxious to help the students, no matter how long it took. These students used their lyrical writing to introduce a meditation on their own unearned privilege, and the foreign-ness to them of a neighborhood in which people would work so hard and take so much time to assist people they did not know personally. I appreciate a parallel here between Readings's contention that the work I pursue with my students represents a kind of "waste economy" of the corporate university, and the reality that the availability of residents of the trailer park to pull my students out of the ditch is, in part, related to the "service" of those residents to the contemporary relatively non-productive capitalist economy as the purposefully undervalued reserve army of labor. Their ghostly membership in the economy belies the presence of a social imagination unavailable to the "gainfully" employed: My students appreciated that when fellow human beings needed help, the residents of this trailer park did not question their obligation to offer it.

In retrospect, my own after-the-fact musing helps me deconstruct how certain kinds of haunting happen. The economic discourse, "stiff competition for jobs," validates the necessity of a reserve army of labor. It normalizes the creation of "the non-competitive," "the losers." One reason why that discourse can be so readily normalized is that there is no contesting discourse coming from the field of Child and Adolescent Growth. Such a contesting discourse would establish that nurturing the social imagination of learners *is the fuel* for "child and adolescent growth." We might say that this latter discourse of obligatory nurture is buried, and that its denial, despite the fact that it is true, is an aspect of our culture's hauntedness. As they come to understand that discourses direct social practices—that discourses are also, in fact, culled from social practices—students can increasingly appreciate that contemporary public policies are negotiated in the public absence of Readings's discourse of our unknowable obligations to others. With such a vital discourse absent, our culture literally makes ghosts of its children.

Although Social Action as Curriculum became a ghost when it was forced to sacrifice genuine "conjoint communicated experience," its hauntedness announced that kind of experience as the very essence of democracy. Interestingly, the process of the course's demise emphasized how precious that quality of my students' experience was to me as a teacher. Its absence left me wounded, a ghost of myself who needed a process of healing to restore my own confidence to teach out of my complex personhood. Now at least somewhat restored, I see that placing "conjoint communicated experience" at the center of my courses positions me as an empowered and empowering vampire-slayer.

CHAPTER 3

FAILED LESSON

The Unteachability of the Mayors' Anti-war Resolution

> If the instructor wants to spare his student surprises and difficulties he cannot help but falsify his material. If he wants to do justice to the facts, he runs the risk of demanding too much from his students and losing their interest and continuing attention.
>
> —Anna Freud, as quoted in Deborah Britzman's *Freud and Education*

In the *University in Ruins*, Bill Readings helpfully offers "that when faced with a disciplinary project, a crucial way of situating that project is by considering what it is *not*, what it excludes" (p. 176; emphasis in original). This chapter examines the very literal and traditional "disciplinary project" of lesson-planning from such a perspective—that is—I ask what considerations are excluded when our assessment of success is guided by conceptions like Vygotsky's "zone of proximal development," and/or the emphasis of the Common Core Standards, for instance, on "allowing the text to take center stage" (Shanahan, 2013). Avery Gordon tells us that power makes life complicated. How might the metaphor of haunting help us understand the complicatedness added to lesson planning by the reality of power relations making some texts invisible? Might hauntagogy reveal the reality of unteachable lessons?

In this chapter I trace my encounter with a development in national current events, the Mayors' Anti-war Resolution, that speaks to me of Deweyan democracy reawakened. Because this news is both marginalized by its positioning and stripped of its global egalitarian implications in its reporting in mainstream media, I anguish over how I can restore its appropriate power for consideration by my students. This is a crisis of haunting, so I invoke my colleague Mark Stern's hauntagogy—haunting + pedagogy = hauntagogy—in order to address it. Finally, I compare my frustration to that of the photographer of the Rwandan genocide, Alfredo Jaar, who buries his photographs rather than exhibiting them to a public whose misunderstandings about Africa have been internalized by parallel absences, erasures, and distortions as those that (mis)shape the consciousness of my students. Jaar interprets that his public is not appropriately haunted to experience their implicatedness in the history of racist imperialism by the West that is implicit in his photos: I interpret that my students are not adequately haunted by the mainstream normalizing of the evil of war to appreciate their implicatedness as potential teacher-activists in the profoundly hopeful current event I want to teach. Finally, I share my frustration with my students, entertaining some hope that my emotionality will have some power to stimulate hauntedness in them, or at least the creepiness one feels in the presence of a teacher who is not in control.

I AM INFORMED OF THE MAYORS' ANTI-WAR RESOLUTION

In June 2011, my husband forwarded me an article from deep within the pages of *The New York Times* about The U.S. Conference of Mayors, this one attended by the mayors of major cities, including Los Angeles, Philadelphia, Minneapolis, Oklahoma City, Santa Fe, Knoxville, Charlottesville, Eugene, and Ithaca (Cooper, 2011). At this conference, the mayors voted to pass an anti-war resolution that called for ending the wars in Iraq and Afghanistan, and investing the considerable *war dollars* [emphasis added] in the pressing needs of U.S. cities, including their/our beleaguered public schools.

At the time, I read the article with great interest and conversed with friends about it in the following days. On the radio I heard a brief National Public Radio report, too. I remember wanting to fruitfully use the mayors' public articulation of a connection between the wars and the consequent losses in quality of life at home. The mayors had framed a resolution using the power of representative democracy to make a demand in the interest of the public good. For me, the resolution represented a symbolic retreat from the increasingly technical discussions of both the wars and the budget cuts in the mainstream news. Both (wars and budget cuts) were typically portrayed as inevitable, playing to Badiou's "suffocating reality principle" which quashes awareness of the deadly consequences of wars and budget cuts to human beings and the planet. So I filed in my mind the thought that I might use this historic event in my teaching, even as I pictured John Dewey agreeing with me from his grave that the Mayors' Resolution should have been front-page news. I also wanted to retrace the slippery language curriculum of our public life that had brought us *war dollars*; I wanted to wonder aloud in class if I could buy lunch with such dollars, and whether they could be used to pay teachers.

NEL NODDINGS MAKES A SPACE IN MY CLASSROOM FOR THE MAYOR'S ANTI-WAR RESOLUTION

In a student teaching seminar the fall of 2011, I thought that I had found a useful way of positioning the article in my work with our students. We were studying the classic article by Nel Noddings, "Social Studies and Feminism" (1992). We had just considered Noddings's discussion of how "[in the early 1970s] … curriculum makers responded to the questions, 'Where are the women? Where are African-Americans?' by adding women and people of color to the standard story" (p. 59). Noddings explains that since that time, women's names and/or pictures were often sprinkled arbitrarily onto the pages of contemporary history textbooks, because beginning in the 1970s "it was required that important publications include women." But their names were typically detached from the revolutionary significance of their life's work.

Noddings's powerful example was Emily Greene Balch, who won the Nobel Peace Prize in 1946, and whose photograph was not included in major encyclopedias or textbooks until the 1970s. More troubling to Noddings, however, was the reality that even today, the significance of Balch's work is missing from textbooks. Noddings asks:

> How many students know that women from thirteen countries organized to stop World War I in 1915? That women started the Women's International League for Peace and Freedom (WILPF) in that year and that the organization is still active today? How many know that these women suggested a permanent arbitration body before the League of Nations was established? … Although Balch now receives an entry in encyclopedias and texts, high schoolers are left ignorant of the content of the WILPF's proposals and totally in the dark about how women organized and what procedures they used. (p. 60)

I noted a flurry of underlining on my students' printouts of the article. I appreciated that they could articulate Noddings's point: that high school social studies textbooks are saturated by "coverage" of wars, which are typically presented as inevitabilities, and almost completely lacking in information about the anti-war movements that contested the sense and/or legitimacy of those wars at the time. But I also experienced the relative flatness of my students' reception of the information.

I tend to read student engagement on a scale of "visceral responsiveness" to "cagey processing" and, at the lowest end, "thorough boredom," and find that such assessment sometimes offers me useful guidance for what to do next as a teacher. Though my students were not generally bored by our discussion of the article, I understood that only one was making a painful identification with the "in-the-dark" high schoolers cited by Noddings. That one student was aware of the ghost, although the majority of them had no way of appreciating an absence in their own consciousness. Taking into account the deficits in their knowledge of how people in the past had organized themselves to oppose wars, and without the benefit of a women's studies course, they were not likely to have considered why women especially might have been likely to initiate such organizing, given their traditional role as primary caregivers of the human beings in their lives.

For the purposes of developing a practice of hauntagogy, Avery Gordon helps us understand that an intimation of this absence would have created a feeling of "hauntedness" on their part. For my purposes as a teacher seeking student alliance with the global egalitarian project, the presence of such feelings would, as Gordon suggests, potentially make accessible a something-to-be-done hopefully on multiple levels: in my students' classrooms with their students in terms of appropriate curriculum and assignments, in the world by us teacher-activists, and (again) in the world by my students' future students, each developing personal agency under the guidance of one of the bright-eyed young people in front of me. I had a strong stake in providing some of the background my students lacked in order to help them appreciate Noddings's message for their future work with young people. It occurred to me that a contemporary account of ordinary people organizing against war seemed promising.

I left that particularly unlively class with the self-appointed project of researching archived online coverage of the Mayors' Resolution, thinking to position it as "intertext" in dialogue with the Noddings' article. Returning to my office, I Googled "2011 mayors anti-war resolution." The first eight sites that appeared were (in order): (1) Commondreams.org, (2) *Code Pink*, (3) uslaboragainstwar.org, (4) Truthout.org, (5) *Huffington Post*, (6) Institute for Policy Studies: Ideas into Action for Peace, Justice, and the Environment, (7) *Daily Kos*, and (8) *Berkeley Daily Planet*. In fourteen pages of listings, averaging eleven per page and with many repetitions, there was no listing of *The New York Times,* nor any listing from a mainstream national or local newspaper other than *The Baltimore Sun*, no less than the thirty-fifth entry down.

According to the eight websites named above, at the annual "U.S. Conference of Mayors," which met in Baltimore in 2011 from June 17-21, the mayors (of cities with populations above 30,000) passed two resolutions, one of which addressed nuclear disarmament. The other resolution bemoans the costs of the wars and "calls on the U.S. Congress to bring these war dollars home to meet vital human needs, promote job creation, rebuild our infrastructure, aid municipal and state governments, and develop a new economy based upon renewable, sustainable energy" (as cited on *The Huffington Post*, 2011, para. 15).

The political perspective of these first eight sites matched my own—that there is only one side to the story about contemporary wars: they are wrong and we can't afford them. They hurt the ordinary working people who become soldiers and fight in them, they divert attention from the compelling need for a more reasonable distribution of the world's resources, and perhaps most important, they destroy the capacity to nurture children. This latter reality will produce the totally predictable outcome that should especially haunt those teachers and prospective teachers among us: war will always cause an increase in damaged people whose intolerable pain will be projected outwards and generate more negative social realities—like future wars.

However, a willingness to entertain only one side of a story, especially in a teacher, is associated with dogmatism and totalitarianism. I would propose, in fact, that the truism, "there's two sides to every story," is typically considered a fundamental philosophical stance that is foundational to all good teaching. We know that "there are two sides to every story" is taught and reinforced in schools as regularly as the Pledge of Allegiance. Indeed, the weight of its assumed wisdom is so great that it obliterates the potential conflicts among the numerous perspectives on assessing validity that claim it: "multiple perspective," "liberalism," even traditional conservative "fairmindedness." Almost all of my students in teacher education have been captive to "There's two sides to every story," and I have only supervised a few student teachers in twenty-five years who have understood its actual hauntedness (see Chapter 5). Far more elegantly than I can, Anthony Wilden articulates why it is important to contest this orientation to "stories," with "stories" of course standing in for "knowledge," and/or "understanding." Educational philosopher Thomas Peterson (2010) cites Wilden's critique of the "illiberality" of this neo-liberal truism, asking what it might look like to teach instead out of an understanding:

> That certain questions and kinds of questions—such as racism and torture (and, I add, slavery and war)—have only one side; and that other problems can't be defined by the word "sides" at all, since they don't have any to start with. (pp. 162-163)

My students typically maintain a fairly simplistic "conservative" versus "liberal" naming of political realities, with "conservative" loosely correlating with the political perspectives represented by the Republican Party (when not dominated by the current extremist Tea Party-ers), and "liberal" corresponding to the current political perspectives of the Democratic Party. Most of my students who typically identify as "liberal" have not recognized that such a construction is typically "neoliberal" in the sense of its broader orientation, which refers back to the conception of government as positioned to "give," and therefore also able to "conserve" resources. This neoliberal conception does not include questioning what sorts of alliances with the profit motive of capitalism heavily influence governmental priorities. There is no interrogation of why the government has or does not have access to greater resources, (increasingly claimed by the One Percent on whom the government paradoxically depends for stability because government functions in the market economy where the One Percent has clout based on it huge resources).

What's become clear to me is that the conception "multiple perspective teaching," while it has the potential to interrupt this broader "liberal" (now neoliberal) discourse on social issues, usually does not do so. Instead it offers multiple voices that support the broader neoliberal conception of reality, which assumes capitalist economic relations—market relations—as the given *structure* in relation to which the reasonableness of our thinking and behaviour is determined. Anthony Wilden helps me conceive of a way to explain this problem to my students, and also to help them understand why the conception "structural" can be so useful to us teachers.

Imagine that the *structure* on which our conception of reasonable thinking and behavior rested was our knowledge that all human beings need decent food, clothing, shelter, education, an outlet for their ingenuity and love. In that case, we would know that any system that functioned to fabulously enrich some people and impoverish others was wrong. We could not entertain another side to this story. It is the case, however, that the current *structure* on which our conception of reasonable thinking and behavior rests is market relations, buying and selling for the purpose of generating profit. This structure not only tolerates, but encourages the fabulous enrichment of some and consequent impoverishment of others. A parallel argument: Although Anthony Giddens recognizes that torture is only wrong—that there is no other side to the story of torture's wrongness, and therefore it has no sides, under contemporary neoliberal thinking, our government's policy of torture could be debated, and has been, and continues to be.

French philosopher Alain Badiou's "suffocating reality principle whose distillate is the economy" plays out significantly here. First, there is an absence of certain perspectives in the "multiple perspectives" considered. Second, there is the tendency to weigh the multiple perspectives under consideration as though they were not influenced by dynamics of power and privilege—as though they correlated with equal power to determine reality. The absence of genuinely multiple perspectives, coupled with the tendency to ignore power dynamics, together affect the reality that the content is only minimally enhanced by the move from an unbroken narrative centered on a dominant culture perspective to a "multiple perspective" approach in interpretation of historical eras and events.

Like the view of many of the authors taught in our educational studies department, the news sites mentioned above espouse socially progressive ideals. They do not represent mainstream politics. I recognize the absurdity of this statement even as I want to ask, "Do you appreciate the haunting here?" To many, perhaps most, Colgate students (perhaps fewer who major or minor in educational studies), information that appeared only on these sites would seem suspect. Paradoxically, none of these websites carries the weight of mainstream validity warranted by such an event as the Mayors' Resolution, yet these sites offered the most thorough and relevant coverage.

Ironically, *The New York Times* is probably perceived by most students and faculty at Colgate as reliable, even though this assessment was exposed as false: Articles later proven to contain fabrications about the presence of weapons of mass destruction in Iraq were specifically and publicly used to bolster the Bush administration's case for waging war. In terms of the haunting metaphor, this reality is mind-boggling—that a well-regarded newspaper helped to lead this country into an ill-conceived war with its lies, yet paid no consequences. Beyond the outright lying was the very poor coverage of the significant global anti-war movement in which I participated along with many other anti-war teachers' groups that were made invisible to the public.

And now, how to calculate the double marginalization of the Mayors' Anti-War Resolution as covered by *The New York Times*, first buried on page ten of the New York edition, and then made a ghost, not even available to historians and student researchers checking generally for online information about the resolution, as I was? Again with regard to the Mayors' Resolution, what an insult to the bold elected officials modeling this quite dramatic exercise of their very purpose in a representative democracy, only to have their mainstream hometown newspapers avoid the most educative parts of the documentation from wire services, sources generally even more limited than those of the *Times*.

By prefacing my Google search keywords with "*New York Times,*" I was able to access the article that my husband had e-mailed me the previous June. Comparative examination of the progressive websites' articles with *The New York Times*'s coverage was upsetting enough. *The New York Times* gave only lip service to the critically important Mayors' 1971 Resolution, which represented a first foray into U.S. foreign policy, an area it normally refrains from commenting on in its resolutions. The significance of this earlier recognition is that it recalls the knowledge buried after World War II, the recognition that war, even war not fought on U.S. soil, impacts the resources available to U.S. cities, including the public schools in those cities. (A major theme in the history of American education is how preoccupation with war has distracted attention from the quest for appropriately challenging curriculum for all students.) The *Berkeley Daily Planet* offered analysis of the uncommon move at the 2011 conference, including commentary from the first resolution's sponsor, Mayor Kitty Piercy of Eugene, Oregon, who called for "a real investment in the future of America" (2011, para. 3). Yet *The New York Times* failed to take the necessary step of even naming the individuals who make up the Mayors' Conference, a key to understanding the implications of the resolution on a national level.

Other progressive websites also provided immediate access in their more easily accessible articles to the resolution and its signees, including copies of the earliest text of those articles. According to the website, "Environmentalists Against War," the mayor of Kabul, Muhammad Yunus Nawandish, gave a speech at a luncheon at the Mayors' Conference on June 18th. Their reporter at the conference, Jackie Cabasso, further reported that after she approached him, "He told me he'd heard about Mayors for Peace and immediately filled out the membership form! He told me that Kabul had been 90% destroyed, like Hiroshima and Nagasaki. Kabul has a population of over 5 million. I think this development nicely links the two pending resolutions" (2011, para. 7).

The other resolution, which also passed, was introduced by Oakland Mayor Jean Quan, and was sponsored by Mayors for Peace, an organization with 4,700 city mayor members in 150 countries—more than 170 in the United States, according to the *Berkeley Daily Planet* (Smith, 2011, para 9). That resolution, calling for complete nuclear disarmament by 2020, was not covered by *The New York Times* at all. Nor was the information about the long-term organizing that led to both resolutions being brought to the floor included in the *Times* coverage.

Like high school history textbooks, the knowledge of how citizens of the United States might enact our democratic rights, beyond voting, is not deemed useful or legitimate information. As Badiou reminds us, such denials are not motivated by cruelty or nastiness, but rather typically perpetuated, even announced, out of "extraordinary circumspection" (in Peterson, p. 162). In the terms popularized by the Occupy movement, the mostly circumspect ninety-nine percent is willing to continue to impose the sacrifices in quality of life, and related, sacrifice of real freedom and fraternity, required by the needs of the One Percent. The latter is that tiny group of people who profit from wars with money that could fund schools. Such money could even fund the education of prospective teachers whose curriculum features readings by Dewey, Greene, Paley, Kerr, Nussbaum, and Stern. Imagine the explosion of possibilities should a high percentage of schoolchildren consider "normal" a more equitable distribution of the capacity to generate wealth and resources. The status quo alternative, as Avery Gordon indicates, represents denial on a scale that exacts a terrible toll in hauntedness:

> To look for lessons about haunting when … entire societies become haunted by terrible deeds that are systematically occurring and are simultaneously denied by every public organ of governance and communication; when the whole purpose of the verbal denial is to ensure that everyone knows just enough to scare normalization into a state of nervous exhaustion… To broach, much less settle on, a firm understanding of this social reality can make you feel like you are carrying the weight of the world on your shoulders. It simply cannot be carried with any delicacy, a strict requirement in these circumstances. (Gordon, 2008, p. 64)

It is important for me to keep repeating Badiou's conception of the "suffocating reality principle" identified with and causing "extraordinary circumspection." I forgive my students for the reality that their consciousness is gripped by both, and I must continually forgive them in order to teach them. Our students (and I am referring to not just my students in social justice-focused educational studies and teacher education, but to most students, including those in the K-12 continuum) are a product of artificially induced "nervous exhaustion." They believe that they and "the country" have made significant and continuous "sacrifices" in efforts to level the playing field. They have further absorbed the mainstream media's perspective that these social problems are intractable. Even if they do not identify with this exhaustion, they identify with "compassion fatigue." This is the price they pay to fit into the categories of normalcy, which become associated with an increasingly suffocating reality principle. That price is reflected in the slide in mental health of college students: the precipitous rise in incidents of serious depression, eating disorders, and out-of-control drinking. Our own campus counseling centers publicize the data regarding numbers of all of these psychological and behavioural symptoms, though they tend to be very weak on interpretation, denying that the "personal is political." How else to explain the continuing attraction to fraternity and sorority life, so banal in its perpetuation of the habits of "normalcy" as to be embarrassing, even to many of the students who remain in it? Finally, what is particularly helpful about Gordon's conception of the denials "scar[ing] normalization into a state of nervous exhaustion" (1997, p. 64) is that it also explains why our students don't know what's going in the world, except what they catch by watching Jon Stewart and similar television satirists. (The last thing I want to do here is minimize what Jon Stewart accomplishes; indeed, there are lessons for hauntagogy in his work!)

Not being Jon Stewart for better and worse, I found it confusing to determine what to do in my class, where "piercing a hole in knowledge" (as per Alain Badiou's definition of education) is a dicey undertaking, as Avery Gordon confirms. It would be difficult to move these students, students who have not been actively critiquing the presentation of their world in traditional news sources, to a place of profound appreciation of what is absent from *The New York Times*. In my muddle about what to do in class the next day, I again reread the various online sources. I thought I might project (from the websites of both *The New York Times* and *Berkeley Daily Planet)* a statement from the mayor of Los Angeles that I remembered having heard on the radio that June during the time of the Mayors'

Conference: "That we would build bridges in Baghdad and Kandahar and not in Baltimore and Kansas City, absolutely boggles the mind" (Smith, 2011, epigraph). But I immediately became distracted by a question: why hadn't Mayor Antonio Villaraigosa of Los Angeles asserted, "That we would *bomb* bridges in Baghdad and Kandahar, and not build them in Baltimore and Kansas City, absolutely boggles the mind?" It suddenly seemed to me that the actual statement of the Mayor of Los Angeles muddied the waters, and did not serve as an appropriate intertext to examine in dialogue with the Noddings article during class.

At the last minute, I experienced a crisis in confidence. There was a risk of marginalizing what was probably the most important point. The more progressive websites featured organizers in action, offered information on how ordinary people met with the mayors in order to help shape resolutions and then reshape them to get them to pass. Readers could hear the delight of the organizers in their albeit gradual and necessarily compromised gains. This content would represent real education for my students, but would mean projecting only the *Berkeley Daily Planet* or similar overtly progressive sources.

I recognized that the example I wanted to use was too flawed for me to make a clear point. I imagined that most of my students would find too many processes of unraveling in the way of the interpretation I had hoped to make about Mayor Villaraigosa's statement: how it had erased the reality that we had bombed those bridges now requiring rebuilding, as surely as those history textbooks had erased the possibility of citizens organizing themselves into a movement powerful enough to refuse a war. For myself and for the few of my students who already had feelings about being left in the dark, our readings about wars in high school history textbooks are haunted by the absence of visible enough organizing efforts of women (and men) who try to stop wars. The goal, then, is to figure out how to make readings haunted for the others. How do we tie Noddings's research on the absence of Emily Balch's anti-war advocacy (beginning with the earlier absence of her picture) from the American history textbooks that have mis-educated my students, to the marginalization of the Mayors' Resolution without presenting ourselves as conspiracy theorists? What are the implications for our ability to tell and elicit useful stories with our students and our readers, if our goal is to win commitment to a not precisely defined global egalitarian project? Perhaps Noddings offers a clue in the resonant metaphor of being left in the dark. Might consciousness of being left in the dark precede and prepare for that state of hauntedness?

AVERY GORDON SPEAKS TO PHOTOGRAPHIC ABSENCES

Both Gordon and Noddings are preoccupied with our being left in the dark. Avery Gordon deepens Noddings's use of absence of women in the photographic historical record as entry point for questions about the nature of the historical record itself—both Gordon and Noddings write about women who are never brought to the photographic light. These two scholars are also interested in the implications of leaving domesticity and love, traditionally women's interests, in the dark as well. Gordon, although clearly critical of Freudian psychoanalysis on many counts, intentionally brings us its essential wisdom, applying its directive to look inside with passionate curiosity to potential revelation of a something-to-be-done. In the specific case examined by Gordon, it is a something-to-be-done about a specific brilliant woman being multiply marginalized—with the implication that the direction for action is to make the historical record more "imaginative."

In *Ghostly Matters*, Gordon expresses her own befuddlement as an academic sociologist. She is facing one specific representation of an issue, described by Maxine Greene, which has significantly shaped our contemporary field of educational studies. I understand the issue to be as follows: Because we know that we, all human beings, all potential knowers, are always individually and specifically positioned in the world, our knowledge is necessarily partial. As well, our positioning means that what we know and the identities we claim are, at least in part, constructed by the concentric circles of people and media that circumscribe our lives, and these, too, represent different types and amounts of power which have shaped that knowledge, those identities.

Gordon arrives at an academic conference in her field of sociology with "an abstract and a promise" (p. 32). Her abstract makes no claims about her methodology, but affirms the reality that social construction issues already make all knowledge questionable. Citing Cary Nelson, Gordon describes this issue as, "aggravated by the often deluded sense of the state of theory produced by the narrow framing of the social terrain in which we do our intellectual work …" which Nelson also characterizes as "traditionally male academic practices" (p. 37). Gordon's promise is that she will unearth a new research methodology that embraces radical uncertainty: it "must question the boundaries separating the truth from delusion, the fact from the artifact, the visible from the invisible, science from literature, the ghost from the empirical, and the mode of producing knowledge from the product that mode creates" (p. 37). But Gordon was invited to raise questions about how the postmodern recognition of the social construction of knowledge and identity complicates ethnography, which is the premier methodology of contemporary progressive sociology (and socially critical education studies). Her colleagues pose to her the obvious question, "What method have you [emphasis added] adopted for your research?" (p. 38)

Gordon collects her thoughtful responsive narrative under the heading "Distractions": She begins with the "distraction" of becoming preoccupied with the absence of the brilliant Sabina Spielrein from the photograph of the Weimar Conference, the 1911 Psychoanalytic Conference, where Spielrein should have been, given the then recent acceptance of her doctoral dissertation. Presenting in collage-like manner entries from Spielrein's diary, letters between Freud and Jung, her own brilliant interpretations of selected bits of psychoanalytic theory and finally, an apology to Spielrein for her (Gordon's) use/abuse of her (Spielrein's) life for her own academic purposes, Gordon leads us to an acknowledgement of profound and incalculable losses. Yet the complex and gorgeously lyrical story Gordon reveals offers multiple layers of information about haunted teacher-student relationships as well as the recovery of wisdom for the school curriculum.

Gordon examines her interdisciplinary array of evidence to show that Freud suppressed, or at least avoided, examination of his awareness of the dominance of the social, as opposed to intrapsychic origins of the uncanny, those periodic experiences of us ordinary human beings that have about them a quality of "hauntedness." The evidence in "Distractions" of Freud's intellectual suppression parallels a different sort of evidence of a possibly more conscious form of suppression in the affect-laden fragments of the life story of Sabina Spielrein derived by Gordon from Spielrein's scholarly writing, letters, and Gordon's imaginative speculation. Among other things, we find that Spielrein, a brilliant student of psychoanalysis at the time, wrote about the death instinct in her dissertation published in 1911, ten years before Freud proposed its essence in *Beyond the Pleasure Principle*. Further, during the period of time in which Spielrein experienced a complex relationship with Jung as both patient and lover, the relationship that paradoxically may well have cured her, Freud read her manuscript.

Yet in the story as told by Gordon, Spielrein appears to be helped to separate from this relationship with her married advisor and therapist by a haunting of her own—the uncanny appearance of a wolf reflected back at her as she looks in the mirror. The wolf's reply to Spielrein's effort at good-natured engagement, "The great chill is coming" (p. 49), apparently eased her ability to separate from Jung, even to make peace with her chillier reception from some in the psychoanalytic movement. She is educated by this ghostly apparition and, in turn, educates us about the reality that we have tended to psychologize what are, in fact, political realities. Here Spielrein has been healed enough by psychoanalysis to both appreciate the wolf in herself—that ideological certainty of the men—and to see that these men would now reject her romantically perhaps in order to deny her intellectual originality and their indebtedness to her. What an important lesson for our students—that our psyches have been socially constructed by the very oppressive relations of daily life that are imposed by the capitalist economy that finds support in patriarchy!

Thus we are offered Gordon's own scholarly discovery beholden to and reflective of Spielrein's ghost: that Freud seriously and—perhaps intentionally, perhaps unconsciously—underestimated what he knew about the haunting of the human psyche by the actual historic (oppressive) behavior of ourselves and our fellow human beings. For my purposes, this point could not be more important: Because of the contemporary culture's obsession with empirical evidence, those of us who embrace the reality and importance of the unconscious are often on the defensive. In our defensiveness, we can underestimate the extent to which Freud's legacy has colluded with individualism by emphasizing the intra-psychic over the relational.

At the end of "Distractions," Gordon confesses to Spielrein her "uneasiness for using [her] story, or the story of the places [she was] between, as a pretext for speaking about methodology and other matters, about needing or seeming to need a dead woman to enliven matters, to make them have some material force" (p. 59). Gordon's apology for having examined only very selective fragments of

Spielrein's productive, generous, but ultimately tragic life is incredibly poignant for us teachers, especially because perhaps the greatest of Spielrein's gifts to the psychoanalytic movement was a model school for children (based on nurture!) that she opened when she returned to the Soviet Union. In Gordon's same letter of apology, we learn of the subsequent banning of psychoanalysis by the Soviet government and the closing of Spielrein's school on false charges, which proved devastating to her reputation. Through the apology, Gordon continues to narrate Spielrein's disappearance from the psychoanalytic movement, followed by overwhelming tragedy between 1935 and 1941: the murder of her husband and three scientist-professor brothers by Stalin, then the murder of Spielrein herself and her daughters by the Gestapo when Rostov was occupied by the Germans and all the town's Jews were taken to the synagogue and shot. Gordon closes the apology to Spielrein:

> I admit that I may have gotten only so far as to insist on our need to reckon with hauntings and to ponder the paradox of providing a hospitable memory for ghosts *out of a concern for justice.* (p. 60; Gordon emphasizes that phrase previously used by Derrida)

Avery Gordon is facing the possible triviality of the project of searching for ghosts in order to create better scholarship, and for us teachers, better curriculum, *out of a concern for justice*. For in the end, even a satisfactory revelation by each ghost of a specific something-to-be-done is up against the weight of global, historical hauntedness. The evidence unearthed at the collective sites of hauntedness, is, of course, evidence of the ongoing horrors inflicted by war, racism and colonization, murder of our fellow human beings and their cultures, and rape of our planet. Gordon briefly considers here if, in her attention to the precise strategy for hearing from each single ghost, she is insulting the memory of Spielrein and her family, whose probable torture and documented murder by the Stalinists and the Nazis hardly even figure into her "scholarly" use/abuse of Spielrein's life in "Distractions." Is this scholarship a distraction? Will the "*somethings*" be done, even when the ghosts succeed in revealing them? Am I correct that education ought to be the process of unearthing haunting in order to seek the something-to-be-done?

Isn't this the question that contemporary teacher educators and teachers ask ourselves every other moment in the current ghostly era? Do we trivialize what the human race is up against when we rail against high-stakes standardized testing because that testing takes the place of a teacher listening to the story of a child, the very essence of the curriculum of Spielrein's Soviet-era school? Can anybody hear the point over all the ghostly howling? Using data from Spielrein's life in this constructivist manner, Gordon not only suggests more about what kinds of welcome and unwelcome lessons hauntagogy is uniquely suited to reveal to us teachers in this world. She also revives the Deweyan conception of imagination along with the use of autobiographical inquiry to guide research. She proves that such revival can represent more than a distraction.

Yet for those of us hoping for a bigger "payoff" from Gordon's "distraction," which is invited in the recognition of hauntagogy, there is disappointment at the end of the chapter. The wolf's prediction, which clearly helped Spielrein navigate her personal problems of lack of recognition both as lover and theorist, did not articulate a way for her to achieve protection and participation in two necessary anti-totalitarian movements, first to defeat fascism and then to defeat Stalinism. As we know from our students (who are mostly educated by confused and confusing teachers like us, by history textbooks, and by "reality principles" that do not often serve their needs or best interests), students are not usually situated to receive the lessons that might be most helpful. And even if they receive them, they might not be able to hear or use them anyway, at least at that specific time in their lives. In Spielrein's case, extreme political repression creating a series of absences, of hauntings upon hauntings, made such reception and resistant action impossible.

In the article, "Presence, Absence, and the Presently-Absent: Ethics and the Pedagogical Possibilities of Photographs" (2012), my colleague Mark Stern originally developed the formula "haunting + pedagogy = *hauntagogy*" in response to a lesson that could not be taught. Inspired by both Derrida and Gordon's concerns for finding "a hospitable memory [for a ghost] ... out of a concern for justice" (Derrida as cited in Gordon, 2008, p. 58), Stern examines the ultimate haunted phenomenon of an artist's attempt to make an invisible genocide visible. In Stern's words:

> In August of 1994, a few weeks after the 100-day genocide in Rwanda, Chilean-born conceptual artist Alfredo Jaar and his friend Carlos Vasquez arrived to the area with cameras and other recording equipment. With help from the United Nations, they were able to travel through Rwanda and the refugee camps in surrounding countries talking with people about what they had seen and experienced and taking photographs of what they witnessed. Responding to the silence of the international community during the Rwandan genocide, Jaar attempted to use the photographs he took to interrupt viewing habits that objectified violence and seemed to make the horror of violence, especially violence in Africa, generically comprehensible. Pictures in European and American press of Rwanda fell into a longstanding genre of Africa and African suffering that seemed not to outrage viewers but led them to what Barthes has called "intellectual acquiescence." Attempting to make viewers uncomfortable about this acquiescence, Jaar chose in his exhibits not to expose the photographs of the horror and the people he encountered. Instead, Jaar hid and buried his photographs, sometimes completely and sometimes partially out of sight, to keep the dead and the horror from Rwanda visually obscured from viewers. Burying the photographs this way signified a silence that represented the "barbaric indifference" of the international community (and implied viewer). By obscuring a viewer's line of sight, Jaar offered a theoretical critique of the idea that photographs can present all that there is to see about any situation, specifically a horrific one. (p. 1)

* * *

In the historical context of this case, the wisdom of hauntagogy points to the unwillingness of the imperializing West to recognize the normalization of Belgium's murderous practices of racist colonization, practices including the identity cards that officially "entitled" the Tutsis to Catholicism, education, and non-agricultural jobs. The Hutus, meanwhile, were forced to remain peasant farmers. Belgian policies thus deliberately created the classist, racist, inter-group hatred that played out in the contemporary genocide. And these practices of Belgium followed an earlier imperialism: Rwanda was "given" to the Belgians to punish the Germans through the terms of the Treaty of Versailles in 1919. Germany's earlier colonization of Belgium and the First World War itself were part of the same pattern of the more developed West using colonies as looting bases, and periodically warring to contest one another's rights to certain spoils. This specific historical evidence clearly implicates all of the West and its global accumulation practices in the "erasure" of the humanity of those exploited that *are* imperialism and colonization.

A question for teachers is how to best connect the global accumulation practices that have been normalized for our students with the damage those practices have done. Such an accomplishment would, in Badiou's terms, "pierce a hole in knowledge." Jaar sought to bring attention to the silence of the international community in the face of the murderous conflict—itself the direct result of former imperialist conflicts—that could have been stopped by a serious global commitment to peacekeeping forces. But he saw that the members of the public who would view the photos could not receive them usefully because they did not have the capacity to be haunted by them. Africans killing Africans has been normalized in a consciousness shaped by ghostly absences of knowledge. In his contemporary time frame, Jaar correctly saw that his photographs would reinforce the pattern of us knowledgeable students in the West blaming the ghosts for their own genocide. So Jaar buried the photos in a pile of sand at his openings, offering a graphic lesson in a specific something-to-be-done guided by hauntagogy. In effect, he was offering a new curriculum of marking unteachable absences. Hopefully these burials would fulfill their educational promise to us students alerted to the need to have our knowledge pierced by successfully delivered ghost stories like the one told by Jaar. At some point, will our students or their students exhume Jaar's photographs and use their power to build the movement to outlaw war, once and for all?

This bitter lesson of history shows that hauntagogy makes it necessary to face "erasures" in the curriculum that amount to tombstones for these actual erasures; paradoxically the erasures of the erasures are part of the stories told as knowledge. When Badiou asserts that education is the act of piercing a hole in knowledge, he is referring to the act of deflating the power of knowledge distortions, including its erasures of erasures, which continue to misguide human affairs and enforce an increasingly "suffocating reality principle." While Western colonization has rarely been presented in our public schools as "murderous," despite the obvious truth of that characterization, the murder of Africans by Africans is normalized in the public mind as *what those people do to one another on the Dark Continent.* The unwillingness of the international community to respond to the Rwandan genocide as a global tragedy in which the racist (and even murderous) policies of Western imperialism and colonization left the country with deadly patterns of hatred among the various identity groups is, in the end, a product of the same ghosts that haunt the curriculum. Hauntagogy helps us face the ghostly, haunting powers of the erasures.

So, emulating Jaar, I did the only thing that I had the confidence to do with the Mayors' Anti-War Resolution at the time: I buried it. Rather than teach the lesson, I came into the next class with a parallel distraction to Avery Gordon's, when her feelings connected to the photographic absence of Spielrein in that photo of the 1918 psychoanalytic conference distracted her from her planned presentation at the sociology conference. I made my feelings the focus of my lesson, and left my students, as I now leave my readers with the question of whether they were a worthy distraction or not. I shared with them the feelings of isolation I entertained as I processed my own difficulty conveying the Deweyan quality of inspiration I found in the Mayors' Anti-War Resolution, which I doubted they had the background to appreciate. I feared I could not haunt them with the facts. Could I haunt them with my feelings?

Maybe my feelings were simply a distraction from the point: The idea of people coming together to face obstacles, as the mayors had, so directly modeled the dialectic of freedom, identified by my early mentor, Maxine Greene. As early as 1982, she offered in her Presidential Address at the AERA (American Educational Research Association) conference: "Almost never is there an expressed concern about the public realm: there is silence about renewing the common world and about what that common world should be. What is it that lies in between, that holds us together, that we can cherish and try to keep alive? Where, when we ponder it, *are* we to turn?" (p. 4)

Avery Gordon, like us teacher-educators invested in the global egalitarian project, holds onto haunted stories as sites to which we might turn. Gordon ends her chapter of Spielrein valorizing the search for the best possible story, the most potentially educative story, as all there is. I feel that she is defending my decision to bury the lesson in my own anguish, as she defends her faith in "distractions":

> … because it would not have been quite the story I wanted to tell if I had just told you that sociology [read educational studies] needs a way of grappling with what it represses, haunting, and psychoanalysis needs a way of grappling with what it represses, society. No, that wouldn't have been the story at all. And so we are left to insist on our need to reckon with haunting as a prerequisite for sensuous knowledge and to ponder the paradox of providing a hospitable memory for ghosts. (p. 60)

CHAPTER 4

WHY IS DAVE BRUBECK CRYING?

> The ghost makes itself known to us through haunting and pulls us affectively into the structure of a feeling of a reality we come to experience as a recognition. Haunting recognition is a special way of knowing what has happened or is happening.
>
> —Avery Gordon, *Ghostly Matters*

The promise of attention to feelings in the classroom as a hauntagogical strategy is intimated in Gordon's appreciation of the potential leadership of the ghost. The last chapter ended with a nod to the hopeful possibility of attending to feelings as intimated by Nel Noddings in her article "Social Studies and Feminism." In this chapter I explore haunting recognition in film and imaginative literature that have proven compelling to my students. Such film and literature prompts emotional responses in the classroom and can be used to point students towards the adult responsibilities of coming to know their complex personhood*s* and their relationships to power; together, these two responsibilities constitute personal growth. Might these recognized emotions propel students forward into a haunted site and teach them to appreciate how the global egalitarian project supports their personal growth projects?

I offer three stories in this chapter—one exploring curriculum centered on use of a film clip from Ken Burns's documentary miniseries, *Jazz* (2000), the second on the teaching of critical theorist Michael Apple's famous article, "Cheap French Fries," and the third on my study with my students of Barbara Kingsolver's *Animal Dreams* (1990)—with the understanding that all three stories illustrate how affect is implicated in the translation from the personal to the political in the classroom. Summarizing the common lessons of the three stories, I propose the process of examining the emotional pulls that characterize (psychoanalytic) transference relationships. Sometimes, that examination uncovers a haunting, and sometimes, if we are lucky, the uncovery leads us to formulate a something-to-be-done. I end the chapter with the announcement that my philosophical allies and I find in social reconstructionist education our something-to-be-done, having been led to its practices by our attachments to freedom, equality, and fraternity.

ON TEACHING JAZZ

The first story examines use of a film clip that features beloved and recently deceased jazz pianist Dave Brubeck from the 2000 PBS (Public Broadcasting Service) production of the documentary mini-series, *Jazz*. The series was both widely appreciated and, in my opinion, accurately criticized for its attempts to tailor content for a middle-class demographic. While it is clear that this criticism has merit, I hope readers who were troubled by the way the series marginalized some of the complexity and richness of the contemporary jazz scene and/or failed to tap a more harshly realistic critique of race and class politics in the United States will still be able to hear my story.

I chose as curriculum a five-minute sequence from Episode Seven of *Jazz*, "Dedicated to Chaos"; its beginning images are set during World War II. Dave Brubeck begins by talking about freedom in relation to jazz against the backdrop of the war; he identifies freedom with the United States in one very specific metaphor. Describing what jazz players experienced that spoke of freedom, Brubeck says: "They were…away from the constriction of the written music…but improvising on top of it. This is the thing I love about jazz. It's about the United States—the way it expresses freedom." Brubeck is concerned with freedom, but his metaphor falters when it becomes clear that his conception of freedom includes freedom from racism. The interview with Brubeck leads into the disruption of his "jazz-freedom-United States" chain of associations through his recognition that white supremacist race relations had not changed in the United States during his absence from the country. When his integrated band returns from World War II, its African American members are barred from entering the front door of a Texas restaurant.

Tracking the clip sequentially, after Brubeck's positive introduction of his "jazz-freedom-United States" chain of associations, the series narrator, Keith David, tells us that Brubeck's dad wanted him to become a cattle handler and stay home and work the ranch in California: "But Brubeck loved jazz." After graduation from college, Brubeck enlisted, married on a brief leave, and was shipped out to Europe in the summer of 1944, fully expecting to go into combat. When he and his fellow enlistees landed, they were immediately transported to Verdun and assured they'd be sent to the front immediately. But when a piano player was requested to enhance the live entertainment organized for the newly arrived enlistees, Brubeck volunteered. A colonel who heard him play said he should not go to the front, but instead, stay behind and form a band.

The Wolfpack Band that Brubeck organized played for the soldiers through the rest of the war. Although the army was segregated, the band was not. The integrated group lived in close quarters, sharing their life stories and every minute of their waking and jazz-making lives. Their work included its share of soldiers' risks: because they played so close to the front they were once strafed by German planes, and at the Battle of the Bulge, the band was lost behind German lines for hours. The Wolfpack Band remained integrated and together right through the end of the war.

"When Dave Brubeck and the Wolfpack Band got home, nothing in America had changed," the film's narrator then tells us. Brubeck himself continues: "We landed in Texas and we went to the dining room to eat, and they wouldn't serve the black guys." One of them said he wouldn't eat their food, and crying, turned to Brubeck: "I wonder why I went through all this?"

Now we see Brubeck alone on the screen, without the war footage, without the scenes of the Wolfpack Band, without the delighted American crowds cheering the end of the war, without the black soldiers segregated in their regiment, away from the dining room in Texas. He narrates: "The first black man I ever saw, my dad took me to see on the Sacramento River. 'Open your shirt for Dave,' my dad said to his friend." The camera pans to this young black man with ropey markings on his chest; it's hard for us, the viewers, to look. "There was a brand on his chest," says Brubeck, the words catching in his throat, his eyes rimmed with tears. "My Dad said, 'These things can't happen in America.'" Dave Brubeck closes: "That's why I fought for what I fought for."

Brubeck's chain of associations, "jazz-freedom-United States," slams into the contradiction that the politics of equality (which characterized the life of the Wolfpack Band) were not the politics at home, where support for the war against racism/fascism had been generated. In this haunted history lesson, one African-American man and one white man cry about a similar contradiction, that U.S. citizens rallied behind a war in Europe against racism/fascism, while allowing the same force to remain uninterrupted at home. Racism's invisibility in the U.S. context of the time is a haunting. Further, in terms of the construction of this history lesson, both the white man and the black man were nurtured by their art (jazz) to understand the creative force that was possible for all human beings, "away from the constriction of the written music… but improvising on top of it."

Echoing many progressive American historians who associate post-Civil War Reconstruction with loss of democratic direction, Alain Badiou asserts that America sacrificed the values of the French Revolution: freedom, equality, and fraternity (see Chapter 7 for further elaboration of Badiou's assertion). Brubeck speaks from that loss, providing an opportunity for students' feeling to lead to understanding. It's easy to engage students in conversation about very different meanings of "freedom"; Brubeck is not talking about freedom from the intrusion of other people's desires and needs, and the related individualist freedom to buy whatever brand of cell phone appeals. He is speaking rather of freedom for African Americans to live with their humanity fully recognized and respected, freedom for whites and blacks to live as brothers, freedom to defeat the Ku Klux Klan and its sadistic "branding" of human beings—its torture and/or murder of them. Brubeck's model for fraternity consists of blacks and whites sharing living space and jointly contributing to the public good with their work, which the production and performance of the great jazz of the Wolfpack Band represents.

It also helps our students to appreciate that there are plenty of older white Americans whose understanding of the words "freedom" and "fraternity" are attached to an image of structural change that can happen only through awakening the political and (related) spiritual consciousness of the majority. For most of our privileged students, such a vision of awakening has been invisible. And in terms of Avery Gordon's highest hopes for how haunting can reveal a very specific something-to-be-done, perhaps we can help these students to understand that the branding by the Klan of the friend of Brubeck's dad haunts the brandings that are more familiar to them, the brandings of Nike and Apple, so thoughtfully examined in Naomi Klein's book *No Logo: No Space, No Choice, No Jobs* (2000). More accessible to my students in my experience, however, has been the lesson that tears can be markers of a haunted site, and that haunted sites are haunted by the presence of social contradiction.

What was contradicted in the case of Dave Brubeck's witnessing of his African-American jazz musician brother being barred from front-door entry to a restaurant? What was contradicted in the case of his being witness to the branding on the chest of his dad's friend? What hauntings are kept invisible when we perpetuate Freud's probably mistaken assertion that the pain we suffer is caused by mostly intra-psychic phenomena? Gordon's chapter "Distractions" is largely dedicated to showing us that Freud knew otherwise and was, for example, blind to the pain that he and Jung inflicted on Sabina Spielrein through sexism and poisonous academic competition. The hauntings that Gordon seeks to expose can convince us that most of our pain is the pain we internalize when we or others are treated cruelly, abused, even murdered by fellow humans. In turn, we externalize the suffering by visiting similar pain on others.

A visceral quality of engagement occurs with my students when we examine these questions and propositions about haunting, especially when they have had experience with Visual Thinking Strategies and/or critical media literacy. I ask them to consider the idea of the two experiences of moral/social contradiction narrated by Brubeck (discrimination and branding). They typically recognize that the moral weight of Brubeck's conception of freedom and fraternity is made even weightier when great jazz (art) is conceived of as a symbol and product of both. I ask my students to think about that weight as slamming against the first contradiction in this film clip, which everyone recognizes as the barring from the front door of the restaurant of the African-American musicians who lived as brothers with white musicians during the war in Europe against racism/fascism. Incidentally, this is a great time to play some jazz in the classroom, especially Dave Brubeck and Paul Desmond's famous "Take Five."

The hopefulness of the felt reality of freedom and fraternity is thus presented as having bodily weight when it "slams against" the ugly reality of racist exclusion, of the erasure of a Wolfpack Band brother experienced by Brubeck. Then Brubeck is brought (and brings us, the viewers) to the second, sickening contradiction. At this point in the Brubeck narrative, the weight of freedom and fraternity has already been contextualized by the sacrifices endured during the war to defeat fascism, plus the power of art that is "freedom from constriction of the music." Thus, already haunted by the erasure that Brubeck has experienced, we face the reality of an earlier brother, this time a friend of Brubeck's dad, having been marked as domestic livestock. To what extent are we, the viewers, "pull[ed] affectively into the structure of feeling of a reality we come to experience as a recognition," as Gordon describes? Are we identified with the powerful affective response of Dave Brubeck, and to what extent does the "recognition" allow us to identify with his feeling? My students give a range of responses, including crying. I myself am always choked up at this point.

What has been particularly promising to me about this lesson has been the way it gives students meta-knowledge about media literacy. Many find themselves personally pained by Brubeck's disrupted chain of associations. Since the process of questioning educates (to varying extents and differently) these students, it is easy for them to move to an alliance with the goals of the filmmakers. When this happens we can talk about what made the film effective, and what might increase its effectiveness. Positioning in the syllabus a digital storytelling assignment due around this time can be particularly useful (see Chapter 7).

The disruption of Brubeck's associations, "jazz-freedom-United States," can invite college students to explore their own chains of disrupted associations. They can consider the evidence that we are all, on some level, hoping for a life that offers a belief in the oneness of humanity. From a Deweyan education perspective, this would mean alliance with the view that we are here to contribute to the collective pot of emotional, spiritual, and material resources of all, ourselves included. I have taken the risk of suggesting to my students that if we have not been socialized against crying, our tears often announce when we have slammed into a painful contradiction. The tears express a hope that might not even be consciously available to us, such as a hope that we truly can be one with all humanity. This hope is closely related to the belief that we are all worthy of nurture, regardless of how we have been treated.

Sometimes the contradictions identified by students are readily interpreted as personal. Sometimes a social element is accessible. Sometimes the contradiction first appears to be personal, but, with further inquiry, a significant share of the socio-political internalized as personal-psychological is traceable. When that happens, a good question for students who have read at least excerpts of Freud's *Civilization and Its Discontents* is: what if that feeling of "oceanic oneness" that Freud dismissed as infantile regression is actually an often-repressed desire to connect at the deepest level with the global egalitarian project? What if Vivian Paley's (1992) "you can't say you can't play" rule to social relationships in the classroom (see Chapter 7) re-stimulates a desire shaped in a shared social unconscious—one more aligned with the global egalitarian project than the hierarchical capitalist modes of relating? What if we can assemble our own array of new desires by pursuing this line of inquiry with students?

Here we also have an opening to discuss the difference between narcissism and radical self-acceptance, a tenet of American Buddhism (Brach, 2003). Radical self-acceptance, closely related to what social theorist Robert Lifton (1993) calls respect for the "protean self" is paradoxical in that it presupposes that only a self-accepting person can dissolve her socially constructed attachments and wants. By dissolving these attachments, a person leaves operative the very aspect of being that is, in Dewey's terms, life, and, in Badiou's, life lived in alliance with the global egalitarian project.

Although I have never observed this in a high-school history classroom, I can imagine showing the Dave Brubeck clip to students in order to inaugurate consideration of World War II opened by study of the French resistance and of the Lincoln Brigade of the Spanish Civil War. Such an approach would align well with the use of *Facing History and Ourselves: Holocaust and Human Behavior* (1994), an excellent anthology that is required reading for both our secondary English and social studies certification programs at Colgate. Most of our college students, including students of color, do not link the rise of fascism with racism, nor do they link both fascism and racism with colonization as related manifestations of the international trade in human beings.

Historian Bill Lowen (1995) asserts that it is not possible to teach too much about historic alliances of whites and blacks who made and continue to make connections between racism, fascism, war, and colonialism. Such alliances are typically degraded in high-school history textbooks where John Brown, for instance, is reduced to an aberrant individual, a violent, crazy person. Most of my students take Dave Brubeck's crying seriously. They have been able to appreciate, when they begin to consider how freedom was defined by those allied with liberation struggles, why Badiou writes about a "suffocating reality principle whose distillate is the economy." The conception of freedom as the freedom to make as much money as one wishes, regardless of the systemic violence to others with which it colludes, troubles many of them if and when that reality is brought to the table.

TEACHING "CHEAP FRENCH FRIES"

There are endless possibilities for readings and writing assignments to support this phase of what Gordon calls "recognition" on the part of the students. I have had some promising experiences when I pair the Brubeck film clip with the study of Michael Apple's (1996) article "Education, Identity, and Cheap French Fries." In this article he explores the connection between the cheap French fries we buy and eat at burger joints, and the lack of schooling afforded the Indonesian children whose families' land is robbed to grow the fry potatoes. The connecting theme between these two is our emotional ignorance about the world. Now I recognize that what I have named "emotional ignorance" is the lack of what Gordon, citing Marx, more appropriately calls "sensuous knowledge" and I call visceral knowledge (Gordon, 2008, p. 23). When recognition of this "sensuous knowledge" peaks in the classroom, and depending on the extent to which a mutually respectful classroom community has been built, student testimony can be amazingly educative. In my Curriculum Theory class, for instance, a Mexican-American student, Wendy, captivated us with her narration of her support for her Mexican grandmother's resistance to the use of a healthier cooking stove, arrogantly installed in only her home as part of an apparently underfunded U.S. venture to improve the health of the residents of her village. Especially effective was the informal pairing of Wendy's presentation with that of Katya, an economically privileged student who spoke movingly of how the psychological dynamics of her family impaired her ability to trust others. In a particularly engaging class session we were able to bridge considerations of emotional intelligence that we conventionally conceived of as psychology, with emotional intelligence that was clearly the product of political awareness. When the classroom community has appeared the most viscerally connected, I have briefly introduced yoga and/or meditation at this point, supported by excerpts from John Dewey's defense of the Alexander Technique (as described in Chapter 1). We consider socialized capitalism, the "suffocating reality principle whose distillate is the economy," to be powerful enough to literally corrupt our breathing.

Another visceral subject for students is their impending future in a shrinking job market. Indeed, many come to Colgate seeking a competitive edge that will assure them employment. Apple's essay can be studied with students by tracing the connections that he makes between those lucrative investment-banking jobs, the availability of cheap French fries at our burger joints, and the lack of schooling for Indonesian peasant children. Apple demonstrates that when peasant families have been dispossessed of their land by "legal" contracts between the multinational, corporate burger joints and the government bureaucrats who lease the land to the grower/owners of (eventual) cheap French fries, there are fewer residents for whom the government is obligated to provide schooling. Indeed, the government stops allocating money for public education for these children who have, in effect, disappeared. A useful rhetorical question, then, is: Whom do our students think negotiates such contracts for these international clients? What other kinds of contracts might cross the desk of a Colgate graduate working for a big commercial bank or investment house? How is such an employee positioned to deal with a contract dependent on land being expropriated from a peasant family who has no legal papers?

Twice in teaching this Apple article my students have reported feeling like they had been reduced to a package of appearances during summer internships at investment houses. At interviews, they were not asked what they were learning in college—indeed, the only focus was on the students' social connections. They were never told about the social worth of the banks' operations; they never had the sense that they were being asked to apply their intelligence. Largely as a result of these experiences, both of the students were re-evaluating their intended commitment to an economics major.

Such student testimony typically "pulls affect" as in the quotation by Gordon in this chapter's epigraph, and sometimes induces what I call a visceral level of engagement in class. Without such engagement, study of an article such as Apple's can do what Gordon fears: "[settle] the ground for a future cleansed of its spirit" as cruelty is reduced to academic fact (Gordon, 2008, p. 63). The ghostly and cruel dispossession of home and the loss of education experienced by these nameless Indonesian peasants is unavailable to my students. When the ground is settled, nothing is, in Badiou's term, "pierced," so the "suffocating reality principle" remains in place, and the Apple article is reduced to so much data. Such data is seen as significant only in its exchange value, a ticket to a college diploma that qualifies the student to work for an investment bank, approving contracts dependent on land stolen from peasants in a developing country.

Careers pursued without the determination to disrupt the unconscionable concentration of wealth in the hands of the few inflict damage whose energy will return to pain my students and me, not to mention people such as the dispossessed

Indonesian peasants. The disappeared Indonesian children, as well as former students approving impoverishing contracts, have hurting spirits, haunted spirits. Influenced by Freud (1961/1930), I remind my students and capture in my own poetry the idea that "everything is built on the rubble of ancient cities." This reality is one of the reasons why the dismissal of dialogue between Marxism and psychoanalysis, for all of the complicatedness of such dialogue, is so tragic. Only a limited group of academics and public intellectuals keep alive this conversation. Gordon's "settled ground" translates into one more levelling denial, one more layer of lies. A haunting remains in place of denied stories, and the ghosts will appear in the form of another global economic collapse or even genocide, as the photographer Alfredo Jaar understands (see Chapter 3).

The challenge for us, once again, is how to call up the requisite hauntedness in our students? How might we help them experience, as a haunting, the disappearance of those Indonesian children from the category of humanity entitled to education? Might we encourage students to consider the possibility that the feelings not available to them now are simply repressed, only to manifest personally as eating disorders, depression, and/or other forms of internalization of a "suffocating reality principle"? Apple offers compelling evidence to our students that the personal is political.

RATIONALIZING A CURRICULUM AROUND *ANIMAL DREAMS*

I return now to Gordon's piece of wisdom about what imaginative literature can do that theory cannot. We find that we can transfer energy required in the search for the perfect theory to the examination of the range of imaginative literature available to us. I experience as poetry a statement of Regine Robin, cited by Gordon, that "something crosses over the disciplinary boundaries which only fiction can apprehend, like a trace of unassumed contradictions, as the only way to designate the locus of its own production" (cited by Gordon, 2008, p. 36). I am only now able to understand what Robin is articulating, though intimations of her statement's truth have influenced my own practice as a teacher and teacher educator for many years. Robin is explaining that, in some cases, only imaginative literature can replace the interdisciplinarity of knowledge that compartmentalization has artificially ripped from its context in real life. Robin challenges us to use imaginative literature to return the life story to history, to return emotions to theory about privilege or the dynamics of oppression. She suggests to me that imaginative literature can structure narratives where complex personhood interacts with the multiple ways that power asserts itself; then the reader can identify with critical social theory as alive in the life of characters whose experience actually generates the theory in the first place.

I have found that Robin's wisdom also suggests the usefulness of pairing the reading of imaginative literature with autobiographical writing assignments. It is helpful for the students to experience a piece of their own lives reflected in a story whose characters offer a key to their own potential development outside of the "suffocating reality principle whose distillate is the economy." In my classes, I have paired an accessible "multicultural" novel that features a teacher with a writing assignment requiring autobiographical grappling related to personal memory, or fear of one's own power. This has proven promising in my experience in meeting the challenge offered by Robin.

Although I have told a story about teaching Barbara Kingsolver's 1990 novel *Animal Dreams* in earlier scholarship, I return to consider it here as an example of imaginative literature that provokes emotional responses from my students and leads them to uncover haunted sites. I teach this text in Curriculum Theory, as the strategic life choices presented to Kingsolver's characters, especially the protagonist who becomes a teacher, parallel the choices that my students typically face in their young adulthoods. From a Deweyan perspective, the curriculum of schooling ought to reflect the curriculum of life and vice versa.

In *Animal Dreams*, the main character and sometimes narrator, Cossima, or Codi, has a complex background and story from which she can call up a wide range of student life experiences and identities. When Codi was a child, her mother died, leaving Codi as surrogate mother to her younger sister, Hallie, with whom she remains very close. College-educated Codi, trained as a medical doctor, is resentful of the father, who raised her on his own following her mother's death. She has recently left a too-safe relationship with a fellow medical student who, like her, is ambivalent about love and commitment. She now struggles with her ambivalence in a bi-racial relationship with a (perhaps stereotypically) attractive Native-American man.

Codi has returned to Grace, the place of her birth, a town with a Latino, white working-class, and Native-American population. In Grace, Codi is not typical, as she is assumed to be white and is further positioned as privileged by her status as daughter of the emotionally unavailable town doctor. With characteristic ambivalence, she has accepted a position as the public high school's biology teacher. What makes *Animal Dreams* so especially appropriate for a Curriculum Theory course is that Codi succeeds in this role by helping her students to conceive a Deweyan curriculum that spirals out of their experience. Their initial discovery of the death of Grace's river due to the operations of an unscrupulous mining corporation launches a social reconstructionist curriculum that is more compelling than those offered by the rare progressive science teaching textbooks available in the field of science teacher education.

The motivation for Codi's return is complicated. While intending to maintain emotional distance, she wants to care for her somewhat estranged father. Her father, Homer, a doctor, is suffering from self-diagnosed Alzheimer's disease. This reality, as well as the early death of her mother, wins her the compassion of my students, who are otherwise irritated by what they perceive as her inability to enjoy her freedom. It is uncanny how many students use the words "spoiled" and "lost" to describe her. Most students also initially reject her father as a negative character. The aphorism "it takes a village to raise a child" has become comically ubiquitous with co-optation and overuse, but here the reader discovers that Codi has, in fact, been co-parented by the village. The village, in turn, has accreted a great deal of wisdom about her and her family, which she eventually learns to access. Another educative convergence here is that the wisdom of the village is indigenous wisdom; our students have the opportunity to consider the life-loving messages that may have been unavailable to them in their white and privileged upbringings.

TO BE INFORMED BY THE VERY THINGS THEMSELVES

For an introductory-level college course taught from the perspective of the promise of recovering memory and awakening life-loving pursuit of the global egalitarian project, this novel also contributes specifically inspiring metaphors. Codi's literal burial (when still a teenager) of her miscarried baby near the arroyo on the land where she grew up—the same land on which her father still lives—emerges as a decisive haunting in the story of her life. That burial also introduces the likelihood that other ghosts will be unearthed in the text. More ghosts are buried under Grace's soil. The water is being poisoned where the fruit trees have their roots, and Codi's lover Loyd's twin brother is entombed there. Loyd's dead twin is a casualty of the erasure of his people. The men in the town are partly erased spirits; former miners who once made a decent living in the copper mines but now serve as a reserve army of labor.

In Grace, the evil social realities of the purely profit-driven operations of the mining company largely have been buried (like the Mayors' Anti-War Resolution of Chapter 3) by these now ex-mine workers, who have given up their active struggle. One of their rightfully indignant Latino wives describes the situation: "Excuse me, but your husbands won't put Chinese arithmetic past no bulldozers" (p. 162). (Another great feminist question emerges in our discussion: what keeps alive the spirit of the women when the men have retreated into passivity and a limited kind of engagement with one another, often influenced by over-drinking?) The mining company is leaching copper sulphate into the ground as part of their effort to recover the last metal tailings. The copper sulphate is killing the fruit trees, thereby threatening the only possible livelihood of its working-class citizens who have been laid off by the same mining company when their labor is no longer profitable.

Pragmatically for teaching purposes, Codi's emerging self-reflective capacities are connected to her increasing awareness of the politics of class and race oppression and related U.S. imperialism, specifically as enacted in Nicaragua. Over the course of the novel, her beloved activist sister, Hallie, uses her expertise in plant biology to ally with Nicaraguan peasants in the struggle against the U.S.-backed war in which they are either directly targeted or at least positioned as collateral damage. Hallie's murder paradoxically points to a something-to-be-done by Codi and the town that raised both sisters—parallel organizing at home to that pursued by Hallie in Nicaragua. Codi is educated by the denials of responsibility from the U.S. government, which she knows to be false. Thus, she supports the local Stitch and Bitch Club's organizing to defeat the power of the parallel denials on the part of the mining company. As Hallie works with the peasants in Nicaragua to reclaim their land, Codi supports their efforts to reclaim the health of the river and the fruit trees in Grace, the land of her birth. She helps create the movement that defeats the power behind a greed that knows no limits, which parallels the greed of those financing the U.S. military in alliance with the fascists in Nicaragua.

Especially useful for our reading of this text in educational studies courses (or any course in which students are being positioned as future teachers) is the fact that the protagonist becomes a social reconstructionist biology teacher. Codi's role as a teacher reflects her recovery of memory, leading to respect for the people in the place that has always made a home for her. She becomes a key player in the something-to-be-done, the struggle against the mining corporation after her new community of allies in her personal struggles demands that she take political leadership.

Because of Codi's increasing recognition of her complex personhood, *Animal Dreams* is a useful text for courses other than Curriculum Theory, including Challenges of Modernity, Educational Philosophies, or Politics of Education. Perhaps most significantly, readers begin to understand the actual complexity of personhood. They come to associate the expression of the counterproductive behavior patterns that Codi must unlearn over the course of the novel with her experience growing up as a privileged human being in terms of race and social class. In other words, the two categories that determine life's complicatedness according to Gordon—complex personhood and power relations—are not so readily disentangled.

Codi learns how to be an ally to others, a lesson that becomes the most important gift she gives her students. But her college education, too, has left her with critical literacy and the expertise about the organisms that should have been present in the poisoned river, positioning her as a useful disseminator of ideas that, in this case, "pierce a hole in knowledge." Our students in educational studies have been schooled in Lisa Delpit's (1995/2006) emphasis on an education rich in what she calls the "codes of the culture of power," especially for the working-class and people of color. They are relieved by the reality that Codi offers so much expert information to her own working-class students, as opposed to keeping them comfortable with relatively low expectations of her science curriculum.

Animal Dreams, with its broad selection of hauntings, for all of its ultimate feel-good predictability, "pulls us affectively into the structure of a feeling of a reality we come to experience as a recognition" in unpredictable ways. One of the most fruitful processes I have experienced in class, in terms of this "affective pull," is the invitation for students to voice opposition to an aspect of my own presentation of the novel. In my experience teaching this novel, a number of students have contested my suggestion that Homer Noline, Codi's father, had his affect liberated by Alzheimer's. I typically ask if any of them have had the experience of loving someone who has developed Alzheimer's Disease. Students have typically responded by narrating their annoyance with Kingsolver and/or with me for perpetuating a romanticization of a reality that has brought so much pain to a loved one, themselves, and their family. Having lived with a grandparent who is now lost to them, they feel that Kingsolver romanticizes a disease that is only cruel. Yet each experience of such student reporting can support a classroom climate that begins to reverse the usual situation in which only students of color, working-class students, or students raised in poverty feel they have the right to speak about personal suffering. Inviting into the classroom storytelling about the suffering of people close to them can encourage relatively privileged students to recognize the ways they are affected by the pain of others. It can serve as an opening for realizations related to the ways all of us are haunted by poorly mourned or altogether denied losses and oppressions.

It is helpful at this time to read aloud in class Chapter 10 of *Animal Dreams*, "The Mask." Only one-and-a-half pages long, this chapter describes Doc Homer lying on his own examining table in his medical office, "drift[ing] between wakefulness and sleep, thinking of Codi" (p. 93). In this half-dream state, Codi is the pregnant teenager whom Homer cannot bring himself to address, as the darkened skin under her eyes reminds him of his beloved wife, who died giving birth to Hallie:

> The ghost of their happiest time returned to inhabit the miserable body of their child. He can't help feeling he has damaged them all, just by linking them together. His family is a web of women dead and alive, with himself at the center like a spider, driven by different instincts. He lies mute, hearing only the tactile way that a spider hears, touching the threads of the web with long extended fingertips and listening. Listening for trapped life. (p. 93)

Homer's confused daydreaming here is poetically self-reflective and evocative of our own empathy. Yet confusion begins to manifest itself when he is caring for patients, and especially for a young Latina woman with whom he shares an identity he has learned to abhor. "It's a creeped scenario" (p. 141), says Rita Cardenal, Codi's pregnant student, describing Homer's haunting behavior towards her as her doctor, confusing her with his own now-grown daughter whom he watched bury her miscarried baby as a teenager. Yet "creeped scenario" also comes to describe what we learn Homer experienced as a child in school, where, as the young Latino, Homer Nolinas, living in extreme poverty, he was targeted with racist and classist ridicule, even by his teachers. Referring to Regine Robin's claim about the deep philosophical mining whose impetus is study of imaginative literature, Gordon asserts that "[her] purpose is to encourage us to think that the very way in which we discover things, learn about others, or grapple with history is intimately tied to the very things themselves, to their variable modes of operation, and thus to how we would change them" (Gordon, 2008, p. 65). Rita and Homer offer us insight about how racism, with its variable modes of toxic operation, and the thickness of its historical blight, will propagate a type of confused story that makes it intolerable in all circumstances. There are no two sides to the racism story: it must be obliterated.

A fruitful question for students at this point in the study of the novel is: what are possible interpretations of "trapped life"? They understand that Homer is haunted by the Latino self he has denied, by the loss of his wife and the formerly redeemed, lively husband and father that he used to be. Having denied his identity, he has little access to the self that might fruitfully mourn his wife. So Homer listens for the trapped life, which resonates with the haunting by these now increasingly accessible memories, returning us to the recurring Freud-inspired metaphor of lives built on the rubble of ancient cities.

In *Animal Dreams*, Codi's students learn about the death of the river by examining samples and realizing the precise damage caused by the greed of the mining company. Thus the "creeped scenario" also foreshadows what we learn about the relationship between the mining company and the town. This biology lesson and its aftermath pose the possibility of education opposite to the reductive, sterile dogfish lesson used by Kerr (see Chapter 7). Codi's biology lesson mocks the contemporary technocratic and soulless curriculum supported by standardization and testing. And, as Gordon predicts, the something-to-be-done that emerges from the way students learn in Codi's biology classroom is informed by the "very things themselves, to their variable modes of operation, and thus to how we would change them" (p. 65).

Just as Codi's students collaborate to uncover the damage to the river, the Stitch and Bitch Club collaborates to create and sell the peacock piñatas (part of their historic craft culture) that fund their lawsuit against the mining company. Codi's biology students create an artful terrarium in the classroom to preserve the spirit of their scientific inquiry of the river; likewise the women of the Club incorporate an art project into their challenge. Then, paralleling the use of her biology lessons to educate the students about the very real problems facing their community, Codi transcribes her accreted knowledge about the mining company's damage to the river onto handmade scrolls inserted under each peacock's wing.

Modelled here is a marriage between art and science, the very necessary alliance most threatened by the contemporary technocratic curriculum, and the equally critical alliance between learning and activism, threatened by the "suffocating reality principle whose distillate is the economy." There is knowledge about how to organize here—the very knowledge suppressed by the mainstream media's accounts of the activism that led to both of the mayors' anti-war resolutions (featured in Chapter 3). Just as Avery Gordon has promised, there is a correlation between how the learning happens and how people in the town respond to crisis. One could even argue that the Stitch and Bitch Club collectively tells what Sara Ruddick (1995) names "maternal stories." Codi as a child of the town of Grace, allied with her students, learns that they all "have lives very much their own, and inextricably connected to others" (p. 98).

AFFECT, TRANSFERENCE, AND SOMETHING TO BE DONE

Unfortunately, we don't see movement in the husbands of the Stitch and Bitch Club members during the action of *Animal Dreams*, but Dave Brubeck's tears, especially combined with his cogent political analysis in the Ken Burns *Jazz* clip, does contest the gendered "reason/emotion split" explored by my fellow educational philosopher and mentor Wendy Kohli (1995) in her classic article, "Educating for Emancipatory Rationality." Kohli cites Alison Jagger's work in which Jagger "suggests that 'emotions may be helpful and even necessary rather than inimical to the construction of knowledge … [Jagger] argues that 'human emotions are neither instinctive nor biologically determined. Instead, they are socially constructed on several levels'" (p. 105). Kohli interprets Jagger's conclusions from anthropological research to suggest that "people can be taught different ways to understand and experience emotions" (p. 106). I have observed this reality in the unhaunting of beloved students of color as certain manifestations of internalized oppression dissolve, when they discover that they have a few genuine allies. Such undoing can even begin with exposure to educative text. Indeed, my MAT social studies student Moana Fogg (2012) (featured in Chapter 5), writes in her master's project:

> My relationship to knowledge was typically regurgitation of mainstream information presented by my teachers. Due to this deficit in my schooling, I struggled coming to terms with my black identity, and often tried to submerge it by assimilating in the mainstream culture. It wasn't until I started taking history courses at Colgate focusing on the black freedom struggle when I discovered the importance of self-actualization. Through internalizing these marginalized perspectives of history, I not only recognized how my schooling experience was limited, but also uncovered how my previous self-deprecation surrounding my racial identity inhibited my personal development. Instead of trying to avoid estrangement through assimilation, I learned to identify with the "desperate need to rekindle and sustain the flame of black liberation struggle" (hooks, 1994, p. 67). For the first time in my schooling, I was empowered by the classroom content; my experience as a woman of color was finally being recognized as central and significant. (pp. 2-3)

Kohli's work on affect resonates with Moana's focus on self-actualization and also reminds me of the many emotional conversations I have shared with Moana and other students with non-dominant culture identities. These students must listen to the often painfully oppressive comments of their white and/or unaware fellow students, and make decisions about the extent to which they want to educate their peers while navigating their own often-powerful feelings. Kohli writes:

> It is not just about including more voices or perspectives in the conversation. These newly included voices may be amplified by anger, even rage. They may be diminished by fear, embarrassment, or inadequacy .... What happens to these feelings when they enter the conversation? How are they incorporated? If expressed, can the communication remain 'reasonable'? ... Any theory of communicative reason that is reaching for more radical democratic participation must incorporate a strategy for dealing with the emotions that are intricately related to historically marginalized, disenfranchised groups. (pp. 110-111)

Kohli proposes possibilities with which I regularly experiment, including allowing students "to take turns listening to one another as they vent feelings associated with the forms of oppression they suffer due to their particular location in society" (p. 111). My classrooms often feature no-backtalk speak outs as well, where all students are required to listen without commenting as a fellow student makes requirements of potential allies.

I appreciate that the contemporary field of affect studies or affect theory draws scholars from multiple fields including sociology, anthropology, cultural studies, geography, philosophy, psychology, queer theory, and my own field of educational studies. Yet, as opposed to Kohli's work, which emerged from the desire to use understandings about affect to move forward the global egalitarian project, most contemporary affect theory tends to be very cautious about implications for classroom or community practice. I have concerns about the potential over-theorizing of the behavior of people who suffer from oppression, or related, from a "suffocating reality principle whose distillate is the economy." My hope is that more of our collective energy as teachers will be focused on political solutions to personal suffering, including the recovery of personal agency to build, and in the building of, political alliances. I wonder if the study of affect can represent a retreat from the collective action that might helpfully respond to affect as marking a site of haunting.

Related, another approach that I have found promising in the classroom involves interrogating potential psychological manipulation related to the presentation of affect. When students in a recent Curriculum Theory course studying *Animal Dreams* considered the usefulness of Loyd's revisiting the circumstances of his brother's death, a fascinating debate ensued about whether Kingsolver was more invested in her character's growth or her own stake in some peculiarly determinist growth of her readers. Related to the Ken Burns/Dave Brubeck clip, they can debate whether or not Ken Burns knew that Dave Brubeck would cry, for instance. Some students will want to consider whether the tears are sincere or not; in my experience in college classrooms students did not raise these questions, but a colleague of mine did. To make legitimate the consideration of the capacity of art to be emotionally manipulative as opposed to usefully evocative is another empowering aspect of media literacy lessons with older adolescents; the making of films, the construction of our lessons—these, too, are acts of power. The point is that the dialogue around legitimacy maintains a focus on affect and its uses and abuses. In many experiences with these types of conversations, I have found that there is always a compelling chorus in the classroom who voice my own perspective on the value of attention to feelings as worthy, whatever the context.

Perhaps most useful, in terms of the potential education of all of us when we choose to focus attention on the affective in texts, is the recognition of the terminology that can offer our students access to further inquiry in texts and within themselves. I recommend pairing Avery Gordon's magnificent page-long description of complex personhood (2008, p. 4-5) with the passage in *Animal Dreams* where Codi's student Rita Cardenal helps us appreciate the reality that in navigating any troubling social realities we often find that "it's a creeped scenario." Rita unwittingly offers us a marvellous colloquialism to which I return repeatedly in my work with students who have studied this book. We face that Homer's confusion of memories, which causes him to displace onto Rita his longing to have been a better man for his wife and daughters, is not all that different from the process of the ordinary transference relationships that shape us all for better and worse. Deborah Britzman teaches us that in transference relationships "new relationships conjure old ones." The variable effects of these relationships alert us to the importance of examining their power; they can pull us to behaviour better avoided, in both the personal and political realms. Yet they can also be the source of a something-to-be-done. We recognize that Brubeck and Badiou are captive to the emotional weight that makes transference relationships so powerful, as are John Dewey and Mary Cowhey, and even me. Having encountered much reinforcement in hope-inspiring relationships in the past for our attachments to freedom, equality and fraternity, we project these attachment relationships onto the new ones we encounter in our attempts to pierce holes in knowledge with our students.

CHAPTER 5

WHY IS SARAH CRYING?

"The illiberality of liberalism," a notion that continually frustrates my attempts to convey it to my students, relates to another significant autobiographical story, one that includes my daughter's introduction to literacy. Always aware of Madeleine Grumet's (1988) assertion that the paradigm for teaching is mothering, I present this story for the lessons it holds for the work of moving students to engage with the global egalitarian project. The story is also useful because it invites theorizing about critical literacy, notably through what it would mean to figure in Deborah Britzman's (2011) conception of psychoanalytic transference to the typically political account. Britzman's contribution to our understanding is her sense of the creative potential for the curriculum in our becoming aware of the unpredictable transference relations in the classroom, some of which we innocently precipitate by virtue of being authority figures. These relations can nurture what she terms wild education—and what Julia Kristeva terms "narrative revolts" (p. 96)—responsive to the multiple kinds of transference that group psychology assures us will always be operative in schooling.

A SCHOLAR ALLY INTRODUCES MY AUTOBIOGRAPHY

I had been planning to write another book about the spiraling of curriculum for educational studies courses out of my own autobiography. That book was to be modeled on Marianna De Marco Torgovnick's (1994) *Crossing Ocean Parkway*, which alternates autobiographical narrative about personal border crossings with complicated responses to troubling social conflagrations associated with cultural differences and inequality. Important for Torgovnick, who grew up in an Italian working-class family in the Bensonhurst section of Brooklyn, Ocean Parkway was the class divide separating her from the Jewish and (she perceived) more intellectual neighborhood, the street whose crossing represented upward mobility, a future college education, and a remove from the working-class Italian family in which she is clearly well loved but held too tightly. As sometimes happens in life, Torgovnick's dream materializes when she literally crosses Ocean Parkway, marrying a Jewish intellectual husband, getting an elite college education and, at least for a time, actually living in the Park Slope neighborhood of Brooklyn. She becomes a contemporary social philosopher and critic and takes on the very issues of cultural border crossings that are a focus of our work in critical educational studies. In the alternating chapters of *Crossing Ocean Parkway*, Torgovnick deconstructs a particular powerful social icon or culturally complex "current event" from multiple perspectives, always complicating her examination of race and racism with insight from the multiple cultural and social class positions with which she identifies, or grapples.

My crossing was somewhat parallel to Torgovnick's in that what I fantasized was a life more boundaried and less visceral. I grew up in a lower–middle-class neighborhood in Philadelphia whose demographics changed from white and multi-European–ethnic to majority African American while I still lived in it. My father was a sometimes miserable, tyrannical, and abusive Jewish Romanian immigrant, periodically capable of tremendous charm and genuine appreciation of his family and others, who came to the United States with "nothing but a shirt on his back." He was also the first intellectual I ever knew, and certainly the most powerful one. He provided economic security to our family by working in an electronics store that specialized in the export of televisions to Central America. My mother was a "housewife" (she would have found the term "homemaker" pretentious) until she became secretary to the head of curriculum at the Philadelphia Board of Education when I was in high school.

I remember being attracted to my own early notion of "the intellectual" because it seemed both safe and powerful, and I knew that my father was a "working-class intellectual," though I do not know how old I was when I could have thought in this language. There was always a mind-body split in my choice to privilege thinking over sports and body-centered activity, although swimming was the one physical activity actively pursued with pleasure by my entire family. I was the worst student in the ballet class that met at the public playground on Upsal Street; I had to go to special after-school sessions in order not to fail gym class in high school. I remember the wishes that propelled my early adolescence: privacy in the bathroom, and removal of the guilt I experienced around wanting beautiful store-bought clothes.

Beginning in junior high school, my intellectual ideas appeared to develop around the feeding of these particular wishes, and congealed into attraction to both Marxian and Freudian thinking. The first, Marxism—a bit oddly, perhaps—supported my right to fashionable, store-bought clothes, because I rejected the individualist hippie revolution in which only personal simplicity of wants mattered—what really mattered was the struggle for the International Workers' Party, not what I wore. The second, Freudianism, was attractive because, perhaps paradoxically, psychoanalytic thinking felt private and I needed space from intrusion. One could modestly embrace the consumer culture and still fight the revolution; one could consider Freud's assumption about our drivenness to connect to others in the context of wondering about the boundaries of one's own body, and still hold a conception of a common good.

Meanwhile, there was one constant throughout my young adulthood. From the time I could conceive of being anything, I knew that I wanted to be a teacher. I saw myself as the bright and energetic—and most importantly, the redemptive—daughter who would bring literacy and the promise of greater social justice to children of all ages, races, and ethnicities in schools. I would remake the world into one that would have been more hospitable for my angry, abusive, often charming, and intellectually gifted father. (I thought similarly about redeeming Edna, the

African-American woman who ironed clothes and cleaned our house on Wednesdays, a typical arrangement in the neighbourhood in which I grew up.) At no point can I remember thinking about remaking the world for my mother, raised working class in West Philadelphia, although it is true that she spoke often of having always wanted to be a teacher. I knew that a college education, especially for a female, was unthinkable in her family; I knew that her internalized oppression as a non-middle-class woman and Jew of that era prevented her from shining in school. By her own report, she was unaware of having ever experienced self-confidence before she married my father.

Although self-reflection, even psychoanalytically inflected therapy, was certainly not new to me by the time I had taught in many different contexts, my first reading of Deborah Britzman's (1998) exploration in *Lost Subjects, Contested Objects* of Anna Freud's concept of education as "interference" created a kind of shocked resonance for me. Britzman confirmed that the autobiographical narrative in which I had positioned myself "teacher as political organizer" had more depth than I had explored. It was, as I had suspected, given its quality of narrative certainty and political determinism, haunted. I recognized that it begged for what Kristeva, after Freud, calls "narrative revolt."

Britzman's book led me to begin writing poetry, but also to reframe the earlier narrative about my own innocence and goodness. I can now substitute for previous formulations about my childhood my perception that the predominant feeling I then experienced was one of being profoundly interfered with (it is purposeful that I end this sentence with a preposition, leaving me to wonder why I enforce the rule against doing so with my students). I now believe that my reaching out to determinist ideologies—Freudianism and Marxism—relatively early in life was connected with both the weight and the unconsciously perceived harshness of the interference, whose reality could not be explored. The confusing intimations of something wrong at home needed harsh ideology to both bury them and, paradoxically, to balance their weight with the protective certainty of other intellectual fathers. At the same time, I was left with ambivalence about asserting my own power. Again, conscious of Grumet's recognition that the paradigm for teaching is mothering, I see that I was the best at mothering when I was teaching: I could put text between myself and my daughter, Sarah, and empower her through helping her access literacy, even emotional literacy. Her quest for literacy kept us in communication with one another, but also moderated the direct intimacy, the stuff that potentially constructed her as a mirror of my own shame. Literacy protected her from the excessive criticalness I often felt towards her for being a girl with some similar energies to my own.

LITERACY HELPS A HAUNTED MOTHER EDUCATE A DAUGHTER

When Sarah was very young, she covered papers with long lines of scribbles and then recited quite elaborate stories that she imagined were encoded in her marks. Jerome Harste (1984) described this process, which exactly matches Sarah's, in his classic whole language text, *Language Stories and Literacy Lessons*. When she was four, her scribbles advanced to Xs, Os, Cs, and Ss, but the rest of the process remained the same. That is, she "read" elaborate stories that she imagined were encoded in her Xs, Os, Cs and Ss. But one day she handed me one of these papers and she asked me to read it, and I began to tell a funny story about a girl named Sarah and her mother getting lost on a walk. Sarah stopped me and said, "No … really read it. Read the letters!" and so I phonetically decoded the letters in front of me to the best of my ability and it came out something like "conoxocos." Sarah started to cry and wailed, "I knew I couldn't really read!"

I remember her crying as a moment when I appreciated at a deeper level what I had repeatedly seen confirmed as a primary/early elementary-level teacher: that the achievement of sign-symbol correspondence was hugely significant for a child. It marked another phase of entry into the symbolic world, the world whose codes give us access to conventional, dominant-culture power. In my identification with the politicized "reading the world" conception of the new literacies, I had minimized the weightedness of the accomplishment of sign-symbol correspondence from the perspective of the uninitiated. This experience with Sarah prepared me to understand the scholarship of African-American educator and social theorist Lisa Delpit (1995), who asserts that white teachers who fail to teach sign-symbol correspondence and conventional writing skills to young African-American children, in favor of validating the children's fluency, are depriving those children of the codes of the culture of power (p. 25). Such deprivation represents another manifestation of the racism regularly enacted, often without awareness, in schools. Delpit's thinking also complicated my understanding of Patrick Finn's (1999) distinction between empowering and disempowering literacies, in his *Literacy With an Attitude*, a book that continues, along with Delpit's work, to inform my teaching.

Delpit's theory could explain the reality that Sarah would gradually assimilate sign-symbol correspondence growing up in a household where the printed word, including books, lists, and letters, was a major force in the environment, but children growing up in more oral cultures were not likely to assimilate the "codes" as readily and/or without instruction. I understood that Sarah's tears were her way of processing her exclusion from the codes of the culture of power, which created a contradiction for her. The part of her belief in her ability to read, which was an illusion, slammed up against her understanding of just how powerful a force literacy can be. She feared that she was on the outside of the community that makes and controls the rules that shape our lives and provide a certain amount of order and meaning. She felt ready for that power but could not access it because she had not mastered the codes.

Still, Sarah's tears confirmed her recognition of literacy's highest potential. I took this opportunity to remind her: she understood that letters make words that carry meaning, and that you can put the meanings of your life and what you think and what you do and what you imagine down on paper. Meaning is held there so you can share it with others even when they are not in the same place as you. That is the important part—that we can understand the joys and needs and challenges in the experience of one another's lives through words that we write down and teach one another to read.

The challenge of figuring out how the individual letters sound, how they are put together to make the words in which what we mean is encoded—that is actually a more mechanical process than making meaning and recognizing meaning, and that mechanical process simply requires a certain amount of development and instruction to master. The complicating factor here is that any requirement of "mastery" holds the possibility of assimilation of the masters' reality principle, or the rules of its distillate, the economy. Remember that Alain Badiou reminds us of the especially suffocating quality of both the principle and those rules in the contemporary era. In other words, the student who masters the codes risks being absorbed by the dominant power-wielders' construction of reality.

This tension between our needs as learners to assimilate the codes of the dominant culture and yet find protection from assimilation into the masters' reality principle, which is especially toxic in the contemporary era, is not obvious to our students, and it needs to be identified for them. Unfortunately, the theoretical texts that do this work are often very difficult for college students, and certainly not readily accessible to high schoolers. I tried twice, for example, to teach Ernest Becker's (1971) *The Birth and Death of Meaning* in Curriculum Theory with only very limited success. Becker captures the gradual accretion of normalizing reality principles into "hero systems" that have profound impact on typical (mis)education in any historical era. Such "hero systems" tell us what knowledge and people we will value and who and what we will devalue and attempt to exclude. Becker is particularly helpful in that he does not minimize the understanding coming from psychoanalysis about the universal human need to keep in check potentially overwhelming anxiety. His thesis, however, is politically progressive: he emphasizes that our work as human beings is to defeat the normalizing, constraining effects on our development of the contemporary hero system. Though this lesson is precisely what my students need to hear, they can't hear Becker's paternal wisdom. Perhaps my maternal approach will prove more effective.

THEORIZING DOUBTS AND CONTRADICTIONS: RECOGNIZING HAUNTED SPACES

Interestingly, the period in Sarah's and my life featured in this chapter coincided with my introduction to post-structuralism, with its concept of the social construction of reality and knowledge. It theorized my dissertation research; I was studying the literacy curriculum of a gifted maternal thinker, the second-grade teacher who had been my cooperating teacher when I had student-taught in her classroom in rural and high-poverty Sodus, New York, twenty years earlier. Throughout this work, I began to understand that only a marriage of structuralist class analysis and post-structuralist discourses could address the important questions in both the academic study of curriculum theorizing and the parallel work of making and enacting curriculum in schools.

So my narrative with Sarah, in part propelled by my own personal hauntedness, was developing simultaneously with the narrative that shaped my dissertation, my teaching, and even my first book: this is how we stay together enough in this fantastically multicultural, though not always safe world, conceiving of ourselves as coalitions interconnected with coalitions—all of us, regardless of our differences, regardless of our individual hurts, motivated by the global egalitarian project. We must continually note what kinds of sustainable material, spiritual, and emotional security are necessary for all human beings. We must find the something(s)-to-be done in every circumstance where these securities have not been and/or are not currently available to everybody. And we must attend to our own hauntings, in order to minimize the creeped scenarios with which we can collude in the process of these pursuits.

I literally began to picture—and urged my students to consider—the population of the world as representable in the linked Venn diagrams I mused about with Sarah, common identity markers providing the material that bridged people who were in other ways different from one another. I shared with Sarah this conception of the interdependence of all people in the world, at the same time that this vision of all people as ultimately connected profoundly influenced my ideas about literacy and the teaching of literacy. Related, I began facing my discomfort about the way revolutionary theory continued to figure prominently in the progressive theories of my colleague scholars in educational foundations and myself, recognizing that most of us doing the teaching were no longer revolutionaries. My own tenure in the Trotskyist International Workers Party as an organizer in the Bronx for the New York City-based movement Workers and Parents United for Daycare had been short-lived, ending a full ten years before I became Sarah's mother. Although I continued to see Marxian social class analysis as foundational to my thinking, I began seeking ways of bringing into conversation class analysis and post-structuralist thinking.

Despite contradictions between the two, I found it useful to think of the space between the most positive conception of post-structuralism—a world in which the connected interests of all could gradually become more visible in interlinked Venn diagrams—and the revolutionary imperative in Marxism—as a space of haunting. The advantage of such a conception of a space, an openness, is the hopefulness that a continual array of revelations in the form of something(s)-to-be-done could replace the singular idea of a violent overthrow of one class by another, when uncovering sites of hauntedness in knowledge is taken seriously as a goal of education.

The conception of this contradiction and the space it makes explains my attraction to the work of Alain Badiou, because I see him as fruitfully navigating this space even as he remains a more certain structuralist than I am. Clearly convinced that both capitalism and the social class structure generate all other oppressions, he understands how post-structuralist shifts in interpretation can collude with the downside of identity politics:

> The name 'culture' comes to obliterate that of 'art.' The word 'technology' obliterates the word 'science.' The word 'management' obliterates the word

> 'politics.' The word 'sexuality' obliterates love. The 'culture-technology-management-sexuality' system, which has the immense merit of being homogeneous to the market, and all of whose terms designate a category of commercial presentation, constitutes the modern nominal occlusion of the 'art-science-politics-love' system, which identifies truth procedures typologically. (cited in Peterson, 2010, p. 167)

I do not share Badiou's certainty about "truth procedures," and, indeed, his identification of only very specific "lovers" as embodying love or his clarity about which poets represent "art" feel both arrogant and old-fashioned to me. I think he is naïve as well about the assumed purity of the "art-science-politics-love" system, which he sees as having been replaced by the market-driven "culture-technology-management-sexuality" system. He probably underestimates a certain degree of non-cynical thinking that led to the slippage involved in the "truth procedures" of science as well. Science has been profoundly implicated in the wants of the capitalist class for profit-making, following its earlier service to religionists for exploration of the harmonies of the universe in praise of the one and only God. Thus the truth procedures Badiou identifies with art, science, politics, and love were never certain, and there are good arguments to be made for the lack of truth in a discourse of science that constructed the natural world as an enemy requiring control. I find in Badiou's work a desire for certainly, for safety in "truth procedures" in which I cannot believe.

Yet, I do understand what he means about the "culture-technology-management-sexuality" system occluding the "art-science-politics-love" system. The former categories represent the most marketable aspects of the latter categories. And the former categories are tending to obliterate the latter categories in school curriculum; the discourse of neoliberal public school management very much offers to serve up our children to the capitalist economy. In my most cynical moments I complete the preceding sentence: "where a higher and higher percentage of them will function as a reserve army of labor and a smaller and smaller percentage will compete to market technology as they medicate themselves on intoxicants, including ADHD drugs and instrumental sexual relationships."

Interestingly, when I consider what I have perceived as my weaknesses as a mother, I confront the ways in which I could not present the world as wholly safe to my children. I think Sarah was exposed to a kind of hauntedness not only because I was continually fearful of personal boundary violations, but also because I had given up on my Marxian dream of an eventual safe world in which the "correct" and universal class was in charge. I was conscious of my preoccupation with the problem of how to struggle for social justice as both a haunted mother and a teacher when I no longer believed in overthrow of one class by another, but appreciated the limits of liberalism, especially in its new iteration as neoliberalism.

WHAT LITERACY MEANS (OR DOESN'T)

Even facing a world directed increasingly by instrumentalist agendas, rather than my hopes of expanding love and democracy as education, I had always felt confirmed in my understanding that most children can and do "get" the higher potentials of the written word. They do so before being schooled by school, and even earlier through the media, parents, and socialized others who convey messages both consciously and unconsciously. During the summer of Sarah's discovery that she could not really read, our son Ben, who was seven, taught her to decode the letters with the same Miami Linguistic Readers that had been used in his progressive and heavily arts-oriented kindergarten. One of the funny stories I used to tell my elementary teacher education students at Binghamton in the era of our fullest passion for invented spelling was that when Ben sat down to rationalize for Sarah what he intended to do, he pointed out to her that she might as well learn to spell words correctly, too, as "they would make [her] learn how to do this in second grade anyway."

I understand that there are cultural issues and class issues at play here, that my children are relatively privileged and that they have been immersed in conventional, traditional (even a bit scholarly) English since they were born. But I also know this truth about teaching reading from a great deal of experience with children not privileged like my children and young people from very different cultural and social-class backgrounds. Reading and writing is about the capacity to tell your own stories and to hear the stories of other people, but further, to actually educate others with your stories and to get educated from the stories of others. If literacy learners have confirmed for them their early awareness about what reading and writing could be good for—if they are confirmed in the reality that they are authors when they write something of interest to any audience—then the process of learning to decode is relatively mechanical, even when, in most cases, it has to be explicitly taught.

So the question becomes, why are schools stuck on the mechanical part of the process? Why are schools, especially those with a high percentage of working-class or immigrant children, not adequately supporting the eagerness of the children to tell stories and listen to the stories of people not in the same room? Why do young people almost never hear the truth that I told Sarah at age four about her having already mastered the most important aspect of literacy when she was momentarily devastated by the understanding that she could not yet accurately decode words? And later on—when the young people who do get through the mystification and succeed in learning to decode and encode are really reading relevant and inspiring content—why, at that time, is this not presented as the hope-inspiring miracle it is? This is the miracle: that we can connect with others in different places and circumstances, share our stories with them, help them solve problems, and get their help in solving ours by communicating across the world.

Jean Anyon's (1981) now classic "Social Class and School Knowledge," despite its Marxian determinism, has been a very useful reading for my students. The article presents mostly compelling data (except its income correlations which are too dated to be useful) to support Anyon's structuralist argument that the economic system and a family's social class in relation to that system will largely determine the extent to which their children will acquire the socially critical literacy to which I was introducing Sarah. In other words, Sarah was prepared to read that some groups of people were being wrongly targeted with social problems for which we are all implicated. Yet for many years, my students overwhelmingly confirmed that their experiences had been somewhat similar to Sarah's. Those who were brought up in families Anyon characterized as "affluent professional" and "executive elite," did, in fact, learn in school about social inequality and to some much-lesser extent, racism and sexism as organized systems of oppression.

With John Dewey's non-revolutionary support, I, along with many researchers in critical literacy, were often successful at teaching our students about the global economy's division of the world's work into thinking/managing/controlling work versus doing work. It was not a great leap for our students to understand that the world's people are artificially divided into thinking/managing/controlling people versus doing people, and related, that the thinking people were always a minority and the doers the overwhelming majority. This meant that the highest potential of literacy did not correspond with the needs of the global economy that has had a stake in a very small group of people controlling the doing work of a very large group of people.

The story continued: public schools, particularly the public schools serving the world's potential workers and/or reserve army of labor, prepare students for the very lowest level of literacy possible. It is not an active conspiracy, but rather, a confluence of negative social forces: low expectations towards often-resistant students are held by white and middle-class teachers who are often unaware of the classism and racism they have absorbed in the combination of both the personal transference relationships and the societal hero systems that have shaped them. Perhaps more significantly, they are typically unable to appreciate the power underneath student resistance. Not appreciating that power, teachers are unable to access it on behalf of their students and themselves, as cultural workers constrained by the increasingly neoliberal bureaucracy of schooling. Without a structural critique of inequality, these teachers and their students are doomed, though Anyon doesn't say that. The testing and standards regime, even in its earlier and less-brutal iterations, further supported the forcible inculcation of children into an instrumental level of literacy against the wishes of those who had managed to enter school with their hopes for literacy's high potential intact. We also have compelling evidence from activist educational researcher Michelle Fine (1991) that the adolescents who drop out of the most underfunded urban schools are less depressed than those who continue to attend. Though she does not romanticize their futures, Fine convinces us that they literally leave the norms of low-level school literacy in order not to sacrifice their mental health, their preservation of some sense of agency to do, to work, to have families, and to some extent, to speak to others across differences of experience and expertise.

This is the story, variations of which I have breathlessly rushed along constructing for my students (making the assumption that they had received the message Sarah received), similar to the message received by other children whose parents were affluent professionals. But what I have come to appreciate is that I can no longer assume that even my majority affluent professional students were inculcated into empowering literacy. Coming to us in the contemporary era, they are much more likely to have absorbed a more affluent version of the largely instrumentalist education typically offered to working-class children. And when they have seen themselves as being capable of generating knowledge, it is a much more limited conception of the capacity to generate knowledge than that implied by Anyon. I now believe that for the past fifteen years, outside of the experience in the rare classroom taught by a Vivian Paley or a Mary Cowhey, literacy has not been generally presented to even affluent professional children as the empowerment to share stories and to share knowledge with people outside of talking distance whose lives we might impact, and vice versa. It is a much more commoditized skill most of my students received, a skill intended to give them purchase in a corporate society, not to mention purchasing power, in an era where an expectation of economic security has been slipping away from the middle and upper-middle classes.

Now when I reconstruct this account of my mothering of Sarah, I am aware that the terms of my gift of a literacy in consonance with the global egalitarian project was, at least in part, a result of my own shame and lack of confidence. Out of my fear for my daughter of too close an identification with me, I gave her a feeling of empowerment through connection with all of the others in the world; I led her out but, literally, perhaps too far away from maternal protection. I sacrificed the provision of a kind of safety I believe now that she needed. For all of her current hard-won self-confidence and the beauty and general fulfilment she experiences in her life, I believe that I left her with too much responsibility for others, and not enough protective self-regard. That leading out, the very Latin derivation of the word education, is precisely what I believe most of my privileged students did not experience, although many of them got too much, or the wrong kind of self-regard that so readily colludes with subjective autonomy. Except for very few of them, I note an absence of what we call "voice" in their early college writing; from their upbringing they acquired a comforting identification that did not allow them to develop confidence in "a life very much their own," nor the voice that comes from the wide assimilation of stories of others to whom they recognized their "inextricable connectedness."

We might say that their parents are the contemporary manifestations of those Dewey accused of "educat[ing] their children so that they may get on" (1916, p. 95). But I know from conversations with some of them that these parents are at least subconsciously anxious about the non-sustainability of the current system, a reality that was not as obvious in Dewey's era, and they have some sense that this new iteration of robber barons is more dangerous, even when these contemporary parents collude with them. Many retain a socially liberal edge, especially about gender issues, and most of them teach their children that racism, at least the unsubtle kind, is wrong. Yet, I rarely see the signs in my students of what Jean Anyon interpreted as the socially critical consciousness of the affluent professionals of the later sixties and seventies. I do, however, continue to observe evidence of the theme Anyon correlated with affluent professional education, which is narcissism.

I hope it follows from the preceding that my interest is to make use of what I believe is a new source of social contradictions in our work with our students who are prospective teachers, and to consider the possibility that the metaphor of haunting could be particularly helpful in usefully navigating these contradictions. It is also clear that we need to remain open to different ways of thinking and talking about the possibility of a something-to-be-done if, in fact, our students have recently been positioned to find the global egalitarian project more foreign, with not even a resonance from their earliest schooled consciousness. I entertain the possibility that the discourse of hauntedness may support a way of conceiving of the contradictions between a necessary socially "liberal" approach to our work, and an equally necessary "structural" approach to our work. We must respect both the parents of our students who are in the military and those who are anti-war activists. Yet, we can no longer support our students to conceive of war as a viable option. We must treat with respect the young people in our classrooms who are prone to narcissism, and the young people who are prone to too much self-doubt. Yet we must teach our obligations to one another, while we convey the importance of appropriate self-regard. Teacher education is literally haunted by these contradictions. Perhaps haunting recognition can help us navigate the tensions in our practices, practices ultimately *for* piercing holes in knowledge—for pursuing the global egalitarian project in the context of these inevitable contradictions, including those generated by our own complex personhoods.

"THERE'S TWO SIDES TO EVERY STORY" REVISITED

In Chapter 3 I used educational philosopher Thomas Peterson's citation of Anthony Wilden's critique of the "illiberality" of the neo-liberal truism "There's two sides to the story" to examine the problem of its implications for my students' reception of current events and their sources. Here I examine the problem of the tendency of student teachers (again, as stand-ins for all those committed to educating themselves and others in the interests of the global egalitarian project) to replicate the above problematic truism in their teaching of humanities and social sciences. Relative to the "two sides of the story" view of multiple perspective teaching, Wilden asks, "What does it look like to teach instead out of an understanding that sometimes "the story (as in racism, torture) has only one valid side, other times it has many sides, and often, 'sides' is the wrong formulation altogether?" (Peterson, 2010, pp. 162-163). I hope to show the relative intransigence of the "two sides of every story" paradigm, and then offer some possible approaches to the problem, figuring in, too, Britzman's support for our understanding of how group psychology affects and generates transference relationships.

There are further complications of these dynamics in the current era. As both major political parties fail to challenge the unconscionable accumulation of wealth in the hands of a tiny percentage of people, we need to especially avoid oversimplifying the critique of liberalism; unfortunately, to avoid dangerous oversimplification requires historical background that most of our students are lacking. Teaching to that background knowledge always competes with other goals of teacher education, like inspiring a capacity to connect with young people and to relate to them in ways that contradict their cynicism about the study of the past and/or the study of texts, as well as any doubts they have about their own capacities and worth. The goal of supporting our students to learn to listen well to their own students in order to show them (their students) how their thinking can be further complicated in a more general sense is a demanding goal in itself.

So there are multiple considerations that affect the curriculum. Our student teachers at Colgate typically come with significant enthusiasm for "bringing history (and canonical and non-canonical texts in English classrooms) alive" for their students. Even when the content area information they attempt to convey remains confined by the "there are two sides of every story" paradigm, student teachers who are intellectually curious and conventionally knowledgeable can be effective at engaging their own students who might ask more complex questions later in their lives. This is especially the case if our student teachers are determined to engage students who are marginalized by virtue of social class, race, religion, gender identity, sexual preference, any personal eccentricities, or learning challenges associated with disabilities. In other words, I often appreciate that my student teachers are going beyond liberal formulations in their successes at making empowering connections with their students, even though they perpetuate the paradigm "there are two sides to every story." As a compromise, I express the expectation that my students seek what I loosely name "depth" in their work with their students, especially when more emphasis at contesting "the illiberality of liberalism" will be received as too dogmatic and/or as political indoctrination.

Additionally, in a small town like Hamilton, resources to operate the town's vital functions are increasingly limited on account of the same neoliberal policies that threaten public education. In this context, a global egalitarian perspective can appear to have very little connection to the needs for competent maintenance of crucial public services, jobs to which many of the town's active citizens devote themselves. We do want local city council members to support, for instance, the sustainability-oriented rejection of fracking and community forums around the increasingly complicated politics of wind power. Yet it is sometimes the case that years and years of experience doing the relatively thankless work of overseeing maintenance of local roads with limited budgets ought to be simply appreciated! Colgate students who are community-minded enough to consider becoming public school teachers are likely to have pleasant contact with the well-intentioned citizens who are focused on these immediate local issues, and can readily appreciate these citizens as community activists. When town councils with limited funds need to focus all of their attention on the immediate issues related to preservation of the most necessary services, the political choices that have determined the minimal and continually cut budgets within which they operate become invisible. Possibilities for improvement of the quality of life that require social imagination can appear impractical, even foolhardy. Respect for the appearance of apoliticalness continues to complicate the work of supervising student teachers in their local classroom placements in English and social studies.

Commitment to the community's needs often involves deepening a totally appropriate commitment to general public service that does not necessarily educate about issues of oppression or even greater social justice. Is it useful to think of these discourse issues as haunted by unstated structural political realities, typically masked by "cultural" concerns? I think it is. To complicate matters further, the competition for state resources between Upstate New York towns and New York City is a minefield, exacerbated by neoliberal policies, in that Upstate resentment is sometimes expressed in racist and classist terms. New York City has been viewed as the African American and Jewish city, draining all of the resources from the legitimate "business" of the rest of the state, where people see themselves as struggling (somehow more honestly) to make a living. The efforts of a few Colgate faculty members and Hamilton residents to organize a local Occupy movement failed; however, the politics of resentment of New York City are also linked to its association with the unconscionable accretion of resources by the top tenth of the One Percent. Supporting appropriate political opposition to what I increasingly conceive of as theft of public resources by this tiny fraction of the population without condoning destructive resentments towards identity groups, is certainly confusing and challenging work.

Relative to the challenge of inspiring a structural critique to guide my students' work is another reality: the likelihood that, as student teachers generally supported by their experienced cooperating teachers, they will speak of "U.S. interests" in the liberal/neoliberal sense that conflates democracy and capitalism. In this interpretation, which actually organizes the typical social studies curriculum, it was "in the interests of the US to enter World War I," because Germany had resumed submarine attacks on British passenger and commercial ships. From a structuralist perspective, the US ruling class observed that its European class allies were busy carving up the world's markets, and they could lose out on the spoils. To examine the issue of liberal versus structural standpoint more generally it would be useful to consider the longer passage from the Peterson (2010) article capturing Wilden's perspective:

> The basic structure of the liberal ideology rests on the illiberal belief that there are "two sides to every question"—and no real hierarchies of power, where the questioner has the power and the authority to harm the person or family or other treasured relations of the one under interrogation. By its very structure capitalist liberal theory (born in the English Revolution of 1642–88) ignores the fact that many questions have many "sides" (religion is the best example); that certain questions and kinds of questions—such as racism and torture—have only one side; and that other problems can't be defined by the word "sides" at all, since they don't have any to start with. (p. 162)

Multiple student teaching observation reports show how consistently the "two sides of every story" paradigm plays out in the work of white and middle-class student teachers in powerful resonance with Wilden's critique. This is the case, for example, when my social studies student teachers are teaching the Federalist/Anti-Federalist Debates, where none of them investigate with depth the growing power of the Boston bankers until and unless I specifically require research on this. Related, they fail to access the newest scholarship that confirms Shays' Rebellion as a quite reasonable response to the growing power of those Boston bankers. Even in their teaching about slavery, examination of the Three-Fifths Compromise is often presented without moral outrage. Likewise, many will proudly teach "the stock market game" without any accompanying social class critique or critique of capitalist ownership.

During a more ordinary kind of lesson on the history of American cotton production taught by a few of my elementary teacher education students, the children in their classrooms were certainly delighted to examine both sheared wool and cotton bolls and to work with an actual cotton gin. They were to determine which was a more likely source of the hand-woven clothing of American colonists. Indeed, a very similar lesson is well rationalized by Dewey (1915/2001) himself, in *The School and Society; The Child and the Curriculum*. Having examined the practical considerations related to the process of cleaning, carding, and weaving wool, versus removing the seeds from cotton bolls, the lessons went no further. Interestingly, at the time of his writing of that text, Dewey's consciousness did not include enough awareness to expand his consideration of colonial ingenuity to the specific way ingenuity was later coupled with the ultimate exploitation/degradation of slavery to produce the capitalist accumulation on which future economic growth was built.

Increasingly, I note that my English education students teaching Larry Watson's *Montana, 1948*; Elie Wiesel's *Night*, or Harper Lee's *To Kill a Mockingbird* will typically do a better job of confronting the historically accreted weight of the social construction of the characters' racism, classism, and sexism, sometimes even overtly contesting the tendency of their students to reduce analysis to individual (liberal) morality and/or psychology plays. Again, I believe this reality speaks to the importance of coupling historical survey knowledge with documentation of the lives of specific non-dominant culture "players" of the era under examination, either in the historical record, or in historical fiction. The students in English education who work to examine the lives of individual social actors with their students appear to be more able to make visible the structural realities that contest "the two sides of every story" paradigm.

SUCCESS STORIES

In my last fifteen years of supervising student teachers in social studies, first in elementary and then in secondary schools, I have experienced only three exceptions to that powerful resonance with Wilden's critique in the work of my student teachers—all of these young women marginalized by virtue of non-dominant culture identities. The most recent exception was a study of the Peasants' Revolts of 1381 taught by Starr, a part-Native American student in Colgate's MAT program. Among other work with her students intended to question the historic inevitability of both local and imperialist exploitation as growth strategies, Starr used both the poem "Piers Plowman" by William Langlund and a graphic representation of Wat Tyler's confrontation with a landlord (who was in the process of claiming ownership over a male peasant's wife) to stage a media literacy lesson whose outcome was insight about the interrelatedness of all oppressions.

Teaching against the typical liberal cotton production lesson featured earlier, Jill—a white working-class "non-traditional" (older than typical) student teacher in the elementary master's program at Binghamton University—helped fifth graders reason through the connection between profit-making and slavery (with the advent of the cotton gin) by emphasizing profit. That the labor required for the planting and harvesting of those cotton bolls with their nasty seeds could, with the cotton gin, engender quite a bit of profit for the owner of those fields if he did not have to pay for that labor emerged in conversation during a lesson Jill introduced as "about the relationship between slavery and capitalism." This was the first lesson so named that I have ever personally experienced in an elementary school. The conversation between Jill and her students went so far as to produce the awareness that the possibility of such profit invited slavery "if you had a greedy mind." I remember the particular child who shouted out that phrase following a classmate's effort to convey the haunted (and correct) premise that the idea of slavery was something thinkable in the social imagination at that time and place. I also remember two tow-headed boys comically rubbing their hands together and making Scrooge-like smiles. It was an all-white classroom with a white student teacher, and I remember that the conversation did not illuminate the other obvious haunting of racism.

Moana—a bi-racial student in Colgate's MAT program in social studies—(an excerpt from whose Master's project was featured in Chapter 4)—confronted the same material with her seventh-grade students when student-teaching "slavery" as a social studies unit. To begin with, she used the term "slave labor," which brought front and center the theme of ultimate exploitation of other human beings for their labor power. She used concrete data from the daily life of slaves such as the fact that one third of children in slave families did not know their biological parents, and that punishment by beating feet was administered to make escape more difficult. These seventh graders were impressed by this specialized and visceral knowledge to which they were given access. Moreover, through positioning this lesson as one of a series on "various avenues of slave resistance," Moana put the curricular emphasis exactly where it needs to be: on the struggle of groups for the rights that are not automatically guaranteed by government. Such a theme contradicts the naïve view of most young people (which is typically reinforced by their textbooks) that governments give rights and make things better for people as a function of being government.

The conception of most young people about government is peculiarly abstract and remains that way for most of our college students. My former colleague Kay Johnston is a theorist who studies moral reasoning. She asks her students to consider to whom they believe themselves morally responsible and finds that most of them initially identify only those closest to them, the people to whom they could offer personal care. She notes that they do not appear to recognize that government could organize their link to the others in relation to whom they cannot directly "take care." So although they may have an abstract notion of government doing good, they do not generally have a sense of their ability to participate in such goodness coming about politically, even as they do, in her compelling classes, grapple with the limitations of their own personal capacities to offer care in the name of their moral responsibility to others. Especially for those who anticipate teaching children, their processing of the contradictions they perceive between moral responsibility and their capacities to make a difference in the lives of others can be quite emotional. I would add here the connection I perceive between this reality and the difficulty of the students committing to the global egalitarian project. Not understanding the potential for expansion of the kind of organizing pursued by the mayors (in Chapter 3), and living inside of the "suffocating reality principle whose distillate is the economy," students often consider commitment to the protection and love of those nearest and dearest to them as the best they can do. Then the discourse of the importance of taking care of oneself, in which I, too, am invested, colludes with the necessarily limited purview of those who have no conception of either unknowable obligations to others or struggle for political change in governmental priorities. It is also the case that my students are often lacking the sense of what's in it for them. As has been previously stated, they have generally not experienced the expansiveness of self and personal happiness that accrues to those who defeat aspects of their own internalized oppression (and oppressive patterns) through activism.

My observations of hundreds of history lessons have repeatedly confirmed that the students need continual reinforcement to learn and retain their understanding of the reality that whatever has been granted in the way of rights has been fought for by groups. Particularly helpful was Moana's emphasis on supporting students to understand the nature of violent resistance, without glorifying violence. Evidence to rationalize the perspective "it makes sense why the slaves would want to revolt" was built up throughout her lessons. Furthermore, she interrupted the typical sentimental view that would affirm the good/bad individualist discourse around slavery for both masters and slaves—that "good" masters were personally nice to their slaves and that "good" slaves did not violently rebel. This is the vapid discourse that often organizes slavery units at this level. As well, Moana included visceral considerations of other forms of resistance—breaking of tools for example, or feigning and exaggerating illness, continually reinforcing the "slaves' use of their intelligence in order to lessen the profitability to their masters of their unpaid labor."

Perhaps the most evocative response to Moana's teaching was offered not by her students, but by her cooperating teacher. Moana's ultimate message to her students was that oppressive policies must be met by opposing action. Her cooperating teacher, a lifelong resident of this small rural district, had a marvellous directness herself, and admired "that Moana's passion was rooted in her own life experience." The period during which she mentored Moana coincided with the announcement of a new round of devastating budget cuts to this rural district ten miles from Hamilton. In our three-way conference following one of my observation visits to her classroom, the cooperating teacher shared with us a protest letter she had written to the governor. She had asserted in this letter that these cuts evidenced both poor priorities and short-sighted thinking by withdrawing investment in the high potential of her current students. I cannot remember which of the three of us first proposed that this letter resonated wonderfully with the slavery unit (and its theme of the need for resistance in the face of social injustice being propagated and/or tolerated by government) and should be shared with the students, but the fact is that Moana's cooperating teacher projected it for the whole class to read. I am of the strong opinion that it was Moana's influence that freed this seasoned teacher to take a public stand against oppressive government policies and to share that stand with her class. Now imagine Moana in her own classroom, having been in a school long enough to have made trusting relationships with colleagues and parents, and being able to regularly connect active resistance to current policies related to local school funding explicitly in her unit planning. (Here is a high level something-to-be-done in response to one of the very specific historical hauntings investigated by Avery Gordon in her magnificent deconstruction of Toni Morrison's *Beloved*, which I recommend to my readers.)

In Moana's culminating master's project cited earlier, there is significant evidence that her provision of a structural critique to her classroom of white early adolescents from mostly financially struggling rural families was deeply connected with her personal struggle for the necessary self-esteem that empowers what she and bell hooks (1994) identify as "self-actualization." Further, she came to understand her own process of growth as fuelling her ability to give appropriate weight to "marginalized historical subjects" in her curriculum:

> I began to see how using my vulnerability as a woman of color could be an asset in navigating complex issues related to privilege and power in the classroom. I understood how using the knowledge I have acquired through navigating the tensions of my biracial identity brought weight to the marginalized historical subjects from class. Through this recognition of the layers of my vulnerability, I understood the complexity of Silin's demand that "teachers do not simply implement curriculum, but actively bring their own knowledge to bear on its instruction." (Silin, 1992, p. 260)

Moana "brought to bear" on her curriculum the very structural critique of power relations in our society she needed in order to grow as a healthy human being in this society's racist culture. Indeed, the most moving content of her master's project was a transcribed conversation with one of her students in which the student raised the possibility of "good" slave owners. In response to this question, Moana literally and successfully deconstructed with seventh graders the potential "illiberality of liberalism" by unearthing the structural nature of a system or institution (in which one human being owns another).

To Badiou and all other progressives who, without any caveats, deride identity politics, I want to say, "Not so fast!" In the current era in which a "suffocating reality principle whose distillate is the economy" grips our students, it appears that those who have internalized the power of structural, as opposed to liberal, critique are most likely to be those who have had to do so in order to construct their identities as full human beings, a status automatically granted to our typical dominant culture students. Ironically, most of our educational studies majors and applicants to our teacher education programs are women, yet being female has not typically supported young affluent professional women to identify with oppressed groups in this era. For Moana, by contrast, confrontation with the structural impediment that is racism shaped the nature of her own critical study of history in college as empowering. This critical education, the very education that "pierces a hole in knowledge," offered Moana a window into the inscription of racism in the history that shaped both our country's sense of itself as white supremacist, and her own reception of herself according to the norms of white supremacy. In teaching, especially teaching predominantly white working-class rural students, Moana was able to offer/assert the very education that had restored to her a sense of legitimacy and power as the work of being a classroom teacher. The students were moved by her implicatedness in this work, and wanted to identify with the critical scholar as teacher whom she represented. Moana embodies "the personal as political" model for teaching when she refers to having to deal with her "vulnerability" as a bi-racial teacher who offers her students a structural critique of the institution of slavery.

I want to offer a plea for us to make generous scholarship assistance, especially for socially marginalized students, a necessary part of our MAT programs and undergraduate teacher education programs. I include in the category of marginalized identities: African American, Muslim, American Indian, working class, developing country-origin, women who present as seeing the connection between the historical oppression of women and all other oppressions, and any LGBTQ locations. I know that it is not the case that these students will necessarily perceive structural realities as determining their linked oppression with other oppressed groups, only that there is a greater likelihood that they will do so. I can imagine as well that such students could especially relate to a conception of their own marginalized identity markers as haunted, because of the ways they have had to position their identities for different audiences. I already know that learning to code-switch more effectively has offered some of my students increasing insight into other kinds of social contradictions that had been buried/invisible in contexts other than their own. Naming such once-buried knowledge "haunted" might open to their curriculum planning the fruitful trajectory proposed by Avery Gordon that has as its goal the realization of a something-to-be-done.

MEDITATION ON WHOLENESS, BOUNDARY INVASIONS, AUTO-EHNOGRAPHY AND UNANSWERED/UNANSWERABLE? QUESTIONS

There is personal resonance for me in the challenges of Starr, Jill, and Moana navigating non-dominant culture identities as women who are teachers. They are more successful than the average teacher in unearthing hauntings with their students because their healthy human development—their achievement of a sense of wholeness, has required that they unearth repressed knowledge of the social oppressions that have targeted them. They correctly understand that the problems with personal confidence that they have faced (and mostly overcome) are, in fact, reflective of structural inequalities, which are political problems. They have each had some experience with socially critical education that has educated their autobiographies by piercing holes in (faulty and/or absent) social knowledge. They understand the personal to be political.

As I have already intimated, one of my intentions in writing this book is to uncover the meaning of the "personal as political" for my own teaching. The inclusion of a story about my own mothering, connected with interpretation about its lessons for my teaching, was a way of implicating my complex personhood in the narrative, without turning this book into a memoir, which I did not want to do. Yet I held a vision of what autoethnography might have the power to *do* when I conceived of the book that has proven not completely realistic either. I thought that I might be uniquely positioned to write an autoethnography of a social reconstructionist teacher as a woman who has reasonably healed the most painful hurts that have, in part, constructed her complex personhood. I recognize that my privileges have made this healing possible by giving me access to an expansive and socially critical education, psychodynamic therapies, yoga, meditation, and participation in pro-democratic political activism (with the best of what the Left and feminisms have had to offer); all in combination with the joys of a gratifying personal, marital and family life, including participation in Jewish and Buddhist spiritual practices. I thought that I could make the case that having healed from the damage of what I conceived of as "boundary invasions" that could not be acknowledged in public, and, related, which were powerfully associated with the workings of patriarchy, that I had special insight about the unearthing of a haunted site in order to uncover the what-is-to-be-done. My own feelings of reasonable safety and confidence were compromised by my father's inappropriate attention to my body, taking the form of continual invasions of my privacy, (which fortunately never developed into what is commonly regarded as incest). I never wanted to make this intimately personal revelation a focus of this book, yet it's clear to me that there is something significant about an experience of personal haunting that *does* offer special insight about education, and particularly teacher education in this neoliberal era. As a public, we are experiencing continual boundary invasions that do not educate us as the right kinds of interference might. These boundary invasions include increased surveillance and a demand for accounting of every aspect of our personal lives, yet they also represent the opposite of what John Dewey conceived of as "conjoint communication experience." There is nothing democratic about their imposition, and nothing educative about the new standards of behaviour (and curriculum) that they impose on us. We are losing control of our capacity to shape our future because public material resources are becoming privatized in the hands of fewer and fewer people, literally the ten percent of the One Percent, while private spiritual resources are increasingly constrained by the "suffocating reality principle whose distillate is the economy." As we comply with each new demand for accreditation, validation, and verification, we forfeit more of our capacity to shape our collective socio-political future.

Returning to my own private focus, I must make peace with the reality that my need/wish to "lead Sarah out," which offered her the critical literacy that shaped her awareness of all others as having no lesser claims on the world's resources than her own, cost her in the form of periodic self-doubt, perhaps more of such self-doubt than optimal. By contrast, I see my dominant culture and privileged students as, with few exceptions, comfortably identified with their own parents to such an extent that they appear to lack confidence about their "inextricable connections with others" and the obligations those entail. It is difficult for many of them to process the fallacies of subjective autonomy. The comparison or analogy I create here raises some as yet unanswerable questions for me about the complexity of my motives as a teacher-activist-philosopher.

I want to close with a reflection on fathers. Like Codi's father, Homer Noline, (see Chapter 4), my father had his own story of survival of multiple oppressions, leaving him with doubts about his own wholeness which were re-stimulated by a daughter with a mind (and body) of her own. I find resonance between this reality and the reflection above about the comparison involving Sarah and my privileged students. Out of this resonance a question emerges about the nature of the relationship between the two categories Avery Gordon establishes to define the reality that life is complex: complex personhood and the unpredictable and varied nature of the forms that power can take. Perhaps these categories need to be considered an interdisciplinarity of human development as we, Gordon's allies, move to shape forms of social scientific and/or educational inquiry that better resist the patriarchal market relations that will distort our ability to appropriately evaluate each and both.

I find some solace in my full identification with Gordon's professed plight:

> The persistent and troubling ghosts in the house [highlight] the limitations of many of our prevalent modes of inquiry and the assumptions they make about the social world, the people who inhabit these worlds, and what is required to study them. The available critical vocabularies [are] failing (me) to communicate the depth, density, and intricacies of the dialectic of subjection and subjectivity (or what in my business we call structure and agency), of domination and freedom, of critique and utopian longing. (p. 8)

As Gordon writes of the awareness that motivated her book, so I feel troubled by the challenge of legitimizing the global egalitarian project as the focus of my teaching. I watch as a particularly toxic form of capitalism reshapes what it means to be a human being in this era where the world's resources continue to rapidly concentrate in the hands of the very few. At the same time, the depth of work we do as educators focused on the global egalitarian project is made even more politically vulnerable under the contemporary draconian neoliberal reforms. Anna Freud is correct when she claims that all teaching involves interference. My maternal tendency is to interfere mightily, raising the inconvenient question: in the context of so much hauntedness, how do we know that we are justly interfering with the consciousness of others?

CHAPTER 6

WILD EDUCATION

Teaching This Side of Brightness

> The test of misunderstanding … shakes our confidence in the capacity of things and persons to make themselves recognized. An acceptance of a kind of companionship with misunderstanding, which goes with the ambiguities of an incomplete, open-ended life world, has to replace the fear of error.
>
> —Paul Ricoeur, as quoted in Deborah Britzman's *Freud and Education*

> Everything rests on not being afraid of what is happening to you.
>
> —Avery Gordon, *Ghostly Matters*

This chapter presents my rationale for teaching in a Philosophies of Education course the gorgeous contemporary work of historical fiction by Colum McCann, *This Side of Brightness*; I contextualize this rationale in educational philosopher Deborah Britzman's *wild* education. My purpose is to suggest how formal education's preoccupation with the easy binary of rightness-wrongness, the illusion of the one right answer, keeps us focused on all but the really important questions about what it means to be a human being and how we will or won't collectively thrive. I propose as my model for paying such necessary attention to these really important questions examination of a specific practice of hauntagogy: focusing classroom inquiry on readers as witnesses of the hauntedness of the lives of characters in thoughtfully selected imaginative literature. The curriculum is then one of noticing our shifts in consciousness related to the complex personhood of characters who necessarily bear an array of different relationships to power. These are the kinds of questions that emerge from my understanding of Britzman's conception of wild education: How are the lives of the characters haunted by denials of their value? How do these characters stand in for human beings, and can we practice loving our fellow humans as we practice loving the characters, enough to imagine a future for them and for us?

At a time when the current cynical high-stakes testing environment in public schools places a special emphasis on rightness-wrongness, it is helpful to note that Ricoeur requires us teachers to challenge our human tendency to operate based on a fear of error. Avery Gordon would agree, I believe, that historically, many fellow human beings have been erased in the wake of collective enactments of "fear of error," ideologically manipulated to rationalize the erasures. For example, as I write the above, I experience a re-appreciation of specific erased connections; I consider the meaning of the politically bi-partisan agreement that the contemporary high-stakes testing environment in public schools and its "rigorous reforms" will ensure that our students are "competitive" future players in a globalized world, even as we fire teachers and close schools due to budget cuts, and even as an increasingly rapacious One Percent of our population accretes much of what was once public wealth (while sending most of their children to private schools). Meanwhile, many of those other children made "non-competitive" when we erase their teachers and their neighborhood public schools can claim recent ancestors literally erased by slavery, political disappearance, and hyper-exploitation; yet our privileged students are encouraged by the mainstream culture to objectify these young people, especially once they are no longer children, as "losers." This characterization suggests the limited or absent capacity of relatively privileged people like many of my students to both calculate what those "other" children have lost, as well as to recognize our own implicatedness in those losses. Further, something else has been sacrificed: the recognition of the loss to us of these erasures. (Perhaps no writer has described such loss to the white and middle-class mainstream as well as W.E.B. DuBois.) These multiple recognitions of loss would require "being haunted."

Teacher educator Deborah Britzman (2011) makes haunting central to her deconstruction of education's preoccupation with rightness-wrongness over the course of at least three ingenious and lyrical books of educational philosophy tied to curriculum theory. I did not know Britzman's psychoanalytically inspired wild education when I first brought insights from early childhood education into my work teaching college students. Yet her clarity about confusions of love and education suddenly seemed so obvious: "In Freud's view, the mix-up of love and education begins life, and its form will be wild education" (p. 59). Here, Britzman means that the infant's education begins at a time of her total dependence for loving care on her educators—parents, siblings, and close others, even before her conscious awareness. Learning what pleases and does not please these first educators, and therefore what is right in *the only context that matters in that vulnerable time* (my emphasis) is the first education.

Second, Britzman notes that Freud correctly placed education in the mind; we know the mind to be both an unstable place and a place that holds onto everything, never letting go of an experience or an idea, however many times the conception or memory of the experience or idea is revised, however much we *forget*. It is all there, still ready to be restimulated, called into consciousness by an often-unanticipated trigger. This is probably the most significant gift that our students can receive from reading *Civilization and Its Discontents*: the understanding Freud takes great pains to explain by using the analogy of the mind as Rome in its many historical iterations. This understanding inspired in me the poetic first line that I find myself continually re-using in my work with students and in my own writing (including this book): "Everything cobbles itself on the rubble of ancient cities." We know of our own irrationalities, the peculiar workings of our unconscious when wishes and desires bubble up, affecting our behavior in ways sometimes surprising to us, if only in the hold of a particular irrational idea we thought we had outgrown. We can articulate some of our own struggles and have intimations of the struggles of the people closest to us, "the reality and pleasure principles that make up our divided minds," and we can often examine how they and we are continually seduced by durable confusions about upbringing and "fantasies of the family romance" (Britzman, 2011, p. 58). Referring directly to Freud, Britzman adds, "His research representing the bodily mind and his discovery of psychoanalysis as a method of treatment, as theory of conflicted humanity, and as a means for analyzing social life lends a weird abundance to the work of trying to understand humanly created events such as war, art, group psychology, religion, and education" (p. 59).

EDUCATING AUTOBIOGRAPHICAL KNOWLEDGE

My experience working with mostly college undergraduates, following ten years with only graduate students, is that although psychoanalysis as a subject may be very difficult to teach, the abundance of which Britzman speaks is readily available to our students, once prompted by concepts like her (borrowed from Anna Freud) *wild* education. Working with abundant material is, I have found, the most useful antidote to the preoccupation with rightness-wrongness that impedes work of depth with our students. And to the obvious charge that autobiographical information is not the knowledge our students need, I am at this point confident enough to respond that educating autobiographical knowledge *is our job*. In other words, all of us need to have what we think we know about ourselves further educated. This means having the opportunity to filter our own autobiographies through multiple lenses—historic, philosophical, economic, literary. But it also means being supported to examine that aspect of our personal process of getting educated that I would describe as "what new experiences and ideas are coming up against"—and that would be, after Avery Gordon, our own complex personhoods. I believe that Ricoeur (above) is asking each of us to consider: to what extent can my complex personhood tolerate the "companionship with misunderstanding" that would allow me to accept "the ambiguities of our incomplete and open-ended life worlds," so that my life/learning/teaching will not be suffocated by fear of error?

Fortunately, there is a pedagogy implicit in educating autobiographical knowledge, for we are reminded that in "the mix-up of love and education [that] begins life" (Britzman, 2011, p. 59), the reality of transference comes into being and contradictorily both plagues education and makes it possible. In our own experiences, there are misunderstandings early on of which we might have no conscious awareness, yet, "one's past unresolved conflicts with others and within the self are projected onto the meanings of new interactions. Unexpectedly, new experiences conjure old ones" (Britzman & Pitt, 1996, p. 117). As well, the teacher is always the receiver of projections from each of her multiple students, and she, herself, generates her own, which bell hooks famously reminds us (1994). Assignments inside and outside of the classroom can become the sites where new knowledge is *placed* within the context of former experience, where both teachers and students can analyze their own reception of specific knowledge, processed wildly: teachers and students can become more self-aware of their own wild expectations and desires. Yet the effects of transference on education are not problems to be solved, for love—transference—is what makes attachment to the teacher and to knowledge possible. It becomes clear why one of Britzman's books is named *The Very Thought of Education: Psychoanalysis and the Impossible Professions* (2009).

The human pattern identified by Ricoeur, this fact of the human condition engendered by early total dependence on fallible others with ideas of their own—fear of error—registers early and holds on tight. Britzman assures us that such primal fear—fear of alienating those on whom one is dependent for everything and the remnants of this fear when one is no longer totally dependent—can only be deconstructed, and therefore mitigated, but not solved. The best of early childhood educators, including Vivian Paley and Mary Cowhey, devote some of their most moving work in the classroom to diffusing the energies around rightness-wrongness, including deconstructing with children the ways that inequitable distributions of power influence what passes for right and wrong; they build their literacy curricula around the play with such ideas. (It must be stressed that these are exceptional teachers, even among early childhood and early elementary educators.) Paley's (1992) five-year-olds ultimately agree to the wisdom of the social-inclusion–inspiring discipline "You can't say you can't play" on their practices of imaginative play as they live with the children of different races and social classes in their classroom, while in pictures and captions Cowhey's six and seven-year-olds challenge Thomas Jefferson about the contradiction slave-owning represents to his noble ideas about the rights of all human beings (2006, p. 131). Again, these practices are rare, and especially once our broader culture perceives schooling as about learning subject matter (beginning in the second half of elementary school), the confusion that sets in around the importance of rightness-wrongness is universal. Likewise, the fear of error, deconstructed the most clearly by psychoanalysis as typically entangled with even normal-neurotic energies, dominates the work of education, even through college.

Britzman's interpretation of psychoanalysis for education teaches us the parallel truths out of which the abundant material emerges: "Unexpectedly, new experiences conjure old ones" (1996, p. 117). Here she reminds us of the reality of the unconscious and the tensions in human life created by love and its continual (mis)placements and transference relationships. Writers focused more specifically on inequitable distributions of wealth and power clearly complicate these tensions. They direct our inquiry to how attitudes about authority are acquired: who deserves what kinds of it when? In the context of this inquiry it is useful to consider how our earliest informal education can mis-educate us along lines that play out politically, not just personally. Ernest Becker further illuminates how all forms of internalized media reinforce what he names the "hero systems" that characterize the historically patterned defenses with which we, as individuals, collude, in order to deal with our constant human anxiety about how to behave socially in a world of fragile egos bumping up against other fragile egos. He makes a powerful case for the dominance in our evolving conceptions of our place in the world of what he calls "hero systems," with the "commercial-industrial hero system" operative at the time he wrote this classic text, *The Birth and Death of Meaning*. In keeping with the hero systems framework, Christopher Lasch defined as "the culture of narcissism" the era following, leading me to speculate with my students that we have moved into a "private wealth-technology hero system."

Clearly, though, a downside of psychoanalysis is dependence on the authority of the therapist, which Britzman extends not quite metaphorically (yet not with total identification) to the teacher, the fallible human being who, like Freud or Jung in relation to Spielrein (see Chapter 3), may have her/his own stakes in squelching imagination. Here, I am inspired to ask/caution my student teachers: "When might you want to squelch the imagination of the learners in your care?"

A paradoxical challenge related to the work of educating autobiographical knowledge in the classroom is its endless resources; as Britzman points out and we have emphasized, the opening of the inner life affords an abundance of material: so when does the preoccupation with this material become narcissistic—too focused on the self—replicating the problems of subjective autonomy? When does it remove too much attention from the possibilities for Dewey's charge to us of "[putting an emphasis on] whatever binds people together in cooperative pursuits and results" (1916, p. 98)? With regard to this worry, I can report marvellous conversations with my students about the phenomenon of narcissism inspired by Jean Anyon's (1981) essay, "Social Class and School Knowledge" (see Chapter 4). In our efforts to define "excessive individualism" or "narcissism," we have played with the possible relationships between distribution of narcissism and distribution of wealth and power (see also Chapter 5). Again, the active navigation of these tensions created by the imperfect theories of depth, Marxism and psychoanalysis (via Freud) through the reading, discussing and writing of our own life stories, with this critical focus on our narcissism placed front and center, represents a hope for moving the curriculum away from the preoccupation with rightness and error that is so destructive for education. We must continue to play with tensions in practice, articulating with our students these tensions as we co-create the questions and assignments that drive our courses.

WHAT IMAGINATIVE LITERATURE OFFERS

I remember taking an existentialism course during my sophomore year of college at the University of Rochester and, quite suddenly one day, thinking that I was responsible for my own life and would need to give up the clarity about rightness-wrongness I perceived myself as having inherited. Adding to the immediacy of this realization was a dramatic sense that I understood what freedom was for the first time. Looking back, what made the course particularly useful to me was that the professor espoused Sartrean existentialism and had us brainstorm what factors would make it more possible for some individuals (rather than others) to take responsibility for the choices they made in their lives. It was a different era, and the possibility that seizure of this freedom to be responsible was not evenly available to everybody was not news to my peers and myself to the extent that it is to our contemporary students. Our students need multiple examples of the way Gordon's complex personhood, in great part a function of wildness, plays out in the context of power manifesting itself in many different and sometimes contorted ways. These examples will likely be more potent when they come from multicultural imaginative literature as opposed to theory, even though that might seem counterintuitive.

What such literature uniquely provides is a structured environment for the examination of characters whose lives, through this gift of the necessary interdisciplinarity of life-text provided by whole life stories, play out the social and economic inequalities of capitalist culture, with the complicating factors of wildness. The second time I taught *This Side of Brightness*, for instance, my students developed sensitivity to dynamics of what we collectively named the cross-cultural transmission of trauma. We came to the realization that politically induced trauma (that is, trauma induced by political realities like racist violence) can be taught unintentionally to children as wild education, just as politically motivated, useful hopefulness can be taught to children as wild education. Then the reality of helping to heal trauma becomes a part of what a democratic society must do, making the global egalitarian project that much more clearly a mission of education. The division between education that is therapeutic and education that is intellectually rigorous is exposed as a false dichotomy, especially as work in affect theory increasingly teaches us that what Raymond Williams (1977) names "structures of feeling" (which are certainly present in the lives of all social classes and groups) are being unconsciously reinforced and/or derided in all teaching. Consequently, efforts to make this project conscious would certainly provide more honest education. We need to make real-life experiences, different from their own, visible to our students; we need to support their experiences of empathy and their ability to appreciate an array of characters playing out their lives as loveable, or once loveable, and as having wildness parallel to the students own, but often impacting their behavior differently, partly on account of being situated in different relationships to power.

Related to the above notion of situatedness, Avery Gordon proposes an assignment that seems more promising for my contemporary students than the challenge offered to me more than forty years ago about whom was positioned as more or less likely to be able to take responsibility for our/their own lives: "One day, the students in my undergraduate course on American culture and I made a thorough list of every possible explanation Toni Morrison has given in *The Bluest Eye* (1970) for why dreams die" (p. 3). A teacher of mostly privileged students comes to realize that at least as important as the students' willingness to consider the unearned gifts that privilege bestows is their grasp of the consequences of error that privilege buffers, and related, the extent to which privileged access to everything the world has to offer can keep dreams, in the best inspiring sense, alive.

TEACHING *THIS SIDE OF BRIGHTNESS*

This last realization provides rationale for the teaching of my favorite selection of imaginative literature. Colum McCann's 1998 novel *This Side of Brightness* features four generations of a bi-racial African American family whose sympathetic patriarch, Nathan Walker, is a tunnel digger when his story opens in 1916. Walker's story is situated in his job in a crew of sandhogs, the diggers who shoveled out the New York City subway tunnels. The novel is structured so that alternating chapters are presented from the limited omniscient narrative perspective of Walker's historically evolving story, and that of a character introduced to readers as Treefrog, who lives in the present in an elevated cave he has appropriated in a city subway station above the tracks. Near the end of the novel, we learn that Treefrog is Walker's grandson, and that Treefrog's self-imprisonment above the subway tracks is punishment for his insanity that represents the internalization process of what my students and I named the cross-generational transmission of trauma. The highest goal of my teaching of this text is collective recognition that to love Treefrog is to agree to be haunted by the way racism constructed his life chances, including becoming aware of Gordon's something(s)-to-be-done, always movement in the direction of commitment to the global egalitarian project.

The book works in relation to these complex teaching challenges precisely because Treefrog (real name, Clarence Nathan), the grandson of the sandhog, Nathan Walker, literally loses the intimate-to-broader social supports that make him able to function in what we characterize as society over the course of the novel. We, as readers and students who are prospective teachers, experience the reality that being targeted by oppression, and the patterns developed by one's parents to survive oppression, can literally make a person crazy; there are limits to the amount of trauma from which human beings can recover. This novel offers our students intimation of the frequency and magnitude of experience of trauma as related to the dynamics of oppression. Clarence Nathan creates his cave-like nest above the subway platform in order to remove himself from society after his drug-addled effort to, in his conception, pull his beloved grandfather, Nathan Walker, out of the body of the teenage daughter he adores; the effort results in sexual abuse. Both Treefrog's drug addiction and the abuse follow his unsuccessful effort to literally save his grandfather's life by lifting Walker out of a subway tunnel before an oncoming train eviscerates him.

Yet, the oppressive and paradoxically exhilarating circumstances of the building of that very subway tunnel, and the private domestic life constructed around commitment to that work, are traceable in the "weird abundance" of Walker's complex personhood, and the complex personhoods of the other characters as well. At the same time, we Deweyan readers can appreciate John Dewey's positing of a "surplusage of value" in the work generated by life immersed in the playing out of collective human ingenuity. Even the exceptionally oppressive circumstances of the lives of the sandhogs in this specific and virulently racist era of rapid capitalist "development" do not extinguish the inspiration provided to African-American Walker, his fellow southern European and "shanty" Irish sandhogs, and to some extent Walker's family, by immersion in a project representing the playing out of human ingenuity.

To teach this novel is to repeatedly ask students to name the multiple social contradictions in the lives it makes accessible to us, even as we continually return to the question "What makes us most human, and what challenges our humanity?" The sandhogs, the men who dug the New York City subway tunnels, lived lives so extreme in the physical (bodily) sacrifice demanded of them, as they shared an intimacy that "pierced a hole in the knowledge" of white supremacy and its value-ranking according to color and class. Yet their own underground pro-democratic culture, resonant with some moving snapshots of loving family life, was not reflected in their more public lives above ground, except in their social life in a particular bar whose white owner owed his life to Walker's intervention, and in a few of the novel's most exceptional moments. And even when the Civil Rights Movement became a reality, it apparently had no direct impact on this novel's characters. (Many years earlier, in 1934, Walker had "a policeman's billy club mashed into his head" when he had "gone alongside the protesters silently and stoically," who "were shouting about job losses and low wages" (p. 89).)

As a black man in the context of the 1930s, Nathan Walker could (at least within their "earthy" circle) marry Eleanor, the Irish daughter of Maura O'Leary. Maura O'Leary had been widowed by an accident narrated at the beginning of the book in which her husband, Con O'Leary, beloved by Walker and the other sandhogs, was literally spewed out of the river on account of an explosion of the massive displacement of earth for the underground steel rails which would carry generations of manual and white collar workers to the companies that typically produced alienating work conditions (as well elaborated by Marx). Yet this alienation was often contradicted in the experience of the sandhogs. The sandhogs' love of the tunnels had a quality of artful, haunted passion about it; their digging was, paradoxically, a labor of love, mirrored in the masculinist, often sexual imagery reflected by McCann:

> At the head of the tunnel they reach the Greathead Shield, the last safety precaution, a giant piece of metal that is pushed through the river by hydraulic jacks. If there is an accident, the shield will hold the mud back like a lid on a cylinder. But the four men must go even further. They each take a deep breath and then stoop to enter the door in the shield. It is like entering a tiny room at the end of the world: seventy-five square feet, all darkness and damp and danger. Here the riverbed is propped up with long breast boards and huge metal jacks. Above the men's heads a steel ceiling juts out to protect them from falling rock and sliding mud. Right in front of their eyes hangs a wire-caged bulb, revealing mounds of dirt and puddles of filthy water. The bulb has a pulse to it, the electricity not constant. Sloshing through the water on the floor of the room, Nathan Walker and Con O'Leary reach out and touch the planks for good luck. (p. 11)

Students tend to agree that the sexual starkness of that imagery is peculiar in its romantic quality. Its weight is consonant with the extreme danger of the work that will soon kill Con O'Leary, and opposite (in weight of) the paltry returns in wages; the social disrespect afforded the sandhogs is so extreme that it periodically erupts in violence between the workers, normalized—and literally stabilized—by the codes of race hatred ("[Walker] was [once] coming out early from the hog-house showers and was set upon by four drunken welders. They used the handles of pickaxes as weapons. The blows rained down on the top of his skull, and he fell. One of the welders leaned over and whispered the word 'nigger' in his ear, as if he had just invented it" (p. 27).

In class, we co-constructed in small groups and then edited in our whole group the following paragraph in response to my assignment to the class to convey in writing, as poetically as McCann does, the parallel nature of the "earth's potential anger" and the violent quality of the lives of the sandhogs, using the description to introduce and situate Maura's life following O'Leary's accident:

> *The social ugliness is mirrored by the angry, pulsing, pressurized earth, the possibilities of the bowels of it erupting back to announce the weight of that jealous density of nature's matter threatened by removal for the near future delivery of men to alienated labor. In exchange for her husband's loss Maura is offered (and rejects) a hundred dollars from the company man, Randall, come in a motorcar. "The body might emerge; then we can pay for the funeral too. We'll pay for the funeral anyway. Are you going to have a funeral? Ma'am? Mrs. O'Leary? I believe in looking after my workers." (p. 25)*
>
> *... [Maura] tells her neighbors that her husband has already become a fossil, and some of them wonder what the word means, but they nod their heads anyway and let it hang on the edge of their lips: "fossil." Afterward, Maura "... curses herself for offering Randall some tea." (p. 26)*

The type of reading-writing assignment that generated the above represents an effort to develop with my students a vision of radical interdisciplinarity informed by Gordon's conception of haunting. As we practice this vision of radical interdisciplinarity, more ideas emerge about how to allow it to influence our reading, and related, our thinking about pedagogy. We might stop and consider Maura's poetic allusion to the dead body of her husband as already fossilized, already a part of the very earth he moved as an act of the development of the economic system that would never benefit him; even more specifically, Con O'Leary is earth under pressure, and as a result of the weight of that physical pressure, transformed into a marker of his existence. Yet the image of the fossil points to his expendability as well; Con is already irrelevant to the moving present—a fossil, unable to effect any changes. We consider in class the metaphor of the most expendable human beings—the most exploited class of workers—as the lowest fossil layers: the bone matter of humans sacrificed to mining, tunnel-building, pipe-laying accidents before unions or after racist unions. This is a fine subject for poetry craft, especially if we took the time to study the formation of fossils and then captured the science in the poems. And then we might examine an actual burial site by introducing, for instance, historian Robin Fleming's article, "Bones for Historians: Putting the Body Back into Biography" (2006) in which

Fleming traces the oppression of women in the middle ages based on analysis of the bones in an eighth century Cambridgeshire cemetery. I share this thinking with the class: My students are momentarily excited about the idea of a future course with only one complex work of imaginative literature on the syllabus, and the requirement to co-construct the rest of the course their collaborative responsibility, shared with the professor.

Later in our study of this text the second time I taught it, I crafted the following and distributed it to the class, a composite product of the students' individual construction as "homework notes" of the assignment to "trace evidence of the cross-generational transmission of trauma in the novel." Again, the same directive was offered in class to use as much poetic imagery as possible, but this handout also attempted to replicate the pacing of the novel's accreting social horrors as they, like a tornado, swept up detail related to the wildness of the characters:

> *Later it is Walker's grandson, Clarence Nathan, uncannily talented in the art of balancing who, although African American at a time when construction unions are still practicing racist exclusion, and despite his mother's hopeless drug addiction following his father's/her husband's brutal murder by the police, gets a good job working on skyscrapers, marries the beautiful African American Dancesca and begets a beloved daughter, Lenora. Clarence Nathan's grandfather, Walker, empowered to hold onto life by a jazz recording and his love of Clarence Nathan's family, although crippled with rheumatism but uncannily full of energy, one day at age eighty-nine insists that he and Clarence Nathan walk the subway tunnel under the river. This was the tunnel dug by himself, Walker, Con O'Leary, and Sean Power (now dead of cirrhosis of the liver), the tunnel into which Maura O'Leary, mother of Clarence Nathan's now dead grandmother, Eleanor, threw, at the time of the celebration of the tunnel's opening, long after her husband's death, the wedding ring which Walker now insists on retrieving.*
>
> *Eleanor, Walker's wife, had been killed on the way home from the laundromat by the car driven by the same alcoholic, demented racist McAuliffe, who had years earlier threatened their young daughters, Clarence Nathan's aunts, with a long lecherous tongue. McAuliffe, in turn, is killed in a rage along with the racist policeman who fails to arrest him by Clarence, son of Nathan Walker, father of Clarence Nathan, after which Clarence is brutally murdered by the police. Years later, Clarence Nathan will have his famous balance assaulted when he can't lift his grandfather, Nathan Walker, out of the subway train's path; he will lose his mental balance after his grandfather is struck by the subway train and he will look to the drugs that killed his mother for escape when he feels compelled "to kill his hands." In his drug-addicted state he will unwittingly molest his daughter in a perverted act of love, lose his family, and then imprison himself in a morbid, yet peculiarly creative life in a social underworld above the tracks.*

It is significant that the term "the cross-generational transmission of trauma" had emerged in a classroom conversation in which we were collectively groping for a way of describing how people damaged through their experiences of being targeted by (and, one student insisted, being targeters of!) oppression sometimes unwittingly and sometimes purposefully passed on to their children resonances of their own trauma. Such "cross-generational transmission of trauma" was repeatedly reinforced by the different racisms experienced by each succeeding generation. The next time I taught *This Side of Brightness*, one student's autobiographical knowledge of damage inflicted by an affluent family gave her and us the phrase, in this student's words, "prized achievement in a way that made love unavailable." We examined, after my suggestion, images of the genital clamps wealthy Edwardian families regularly affixed to the penises of their young adolescent sons as part of a bedtime ritual; erections caused the clamp to sting the skin with sharp metal prongs. Certainly, we agreed, we might anticipate later psychosexual disturbance emerging in the class of grown up "privileged" children so tortured every night. In this context, it proved very helpful to briefly return attention in class to Britzman's claim about the gift of psychoanalysis: a means for analyzing social life [that] lends a weird abundance to the work of trying to understand humanly created events such as war, art, group psychology, religion, and education" (p. 59).

With regard to encouraging hauntedness in my students, another specific hope for the teaching of *This Side of Brightness* is that it might legitimate and expand our exploration of the theme of *wild* education, offering especially white and privileged students in liberal arts schools access to an abundance of material with which to counteract their feelings of wrongness and blame whenever the subject of racism is on the table. Based on the autobiographical connections they record as we navigate this weirdly abundant text, my students do make realizations about their own social construction, deepening their typical analysis with an understanding that the impact of political and cultural realities have shaped "who their parents are," affecting "who their parents raise them to be." Psychology turns out to be, at least in part, internalized politics, as it appears Freud may have understood more than he shared. We know that John Dewey charged that parents raised their children to "get on" as opposed to raising them towards the "promotion of the best possible realization of humanity as humanity" (1916, p. 95).

Indeed, I now believe that articulation of the reality, "the mix-up of love and education begins life" (Britzman, 2011, p. 59), is a possibly universal approach for diffusing blame and beginning to conceive of how to take responsibility for the global egalitarian project with any group of students/human beings. We are born into misunderstandings, and our continual rebirth through education will mean that we will encounter new misunderstandings, as we re-evaluate old ones. The point is the unveiling of the something-to-be-done as we unearth our haunted reality.

When I positioned this very complex novel in a course titled Global Philosophies of Democratic Education, we primarily studied educational philosophers who were heavily influenced by, or offered similar thinking to, that of John Dewey; the key conceit being that the classroom is the site for promotion of individual growth in the context of a community to which one has obligations. *This Side of Brightness* turns out to be a hopeful text for using students' emerging awareness of their own wildness to unearth and examine haunted sites for information about the something-to-be-done. Paradoxically, the burial of such sites is partly accomplished by the typically well-intended, but mostly disembodied, theoretical teaching about racism and classism deconstructed by Gordon.

Certainly, feminist theorists in educational studies have sought to correct the disembodied quality of foundational theory we teach our students in teacher education, making the specific reading by Nel Noddings (featured in Chapter 3) especially appropriate in this course for its suggestion of a something-to-be-done. In her plea for teachers to allow feminist discoveries to influence their approach to social studies and math curriculum, educational philosopher Noddings points to the typically ignored peacemaking work of women, including Emily Greene Balch, winner of the 1946 Nobel Peace Prize (1992, p. 60). Coinciding with a focus on the patriotically documented wars that frequently name my social studies student teachers' unit plans, the study of anti-war movements often initiated by women (as well as the practices of home-making, child-rearing, and the rules, rituals, and exceptional expressions of love and romance) can fill the serious gap of the day-to-day material and cultural realities in the historical record, especially as represented in high school history texts. To require our students to teach about the anti-war movements that emerged in the lead-up to, or during, every war they are required to teach is a something-to-be-done. To establish the legitimacy of anti-war movements, to help our students understand that no wars are inevitable, is the social studies curriculum to which we teacher educators must attach our efforts.

A return to that early long quotation at the beginning of *This Side of Brightness*, after study of the Noddings text, initiated in this particular rendition of the course a delighted examination of the construction of masculinity, with students noting the paradox that Clarence Nathan cannot effectively grab Walker to save him from the oncoming train because Walker is preoccupied with the rescue of a tea cosy he comically, perhaps ridiculously, wears as a hat, ostensibly in memory of his beloved wife, Eleanor. One older and extremely wise graduate student, Jennifer McDowall, proposed an alternative thematic construction for our examination of the novel when I expressed the intention to tie our study to the theme I have already discussed, unearthed by a former class, the "cross-generational transmission of trauma." Jennifer proposed that the quest for domesticity as an escape from continual racist assaults and humiliation led to the downfall of the characters, and that we might speculate that the characters sought to escape into domesticity in proportion to the pain of the oppressive (and humiliating) experiences they had suffered. This idea, once inserted into our discussions, led to a conception of political struggle and domesticity as potentially oppositional, even as Noddings offered us an alternative and believable argument about women's special stake in peace-making. Then, a discussion about the public invisibility of important female actors in the Civil Rights Movement actually carried over into an unplanned addition of a focus on women in the Civil Rights Movement in a Women and Education course I taught the following term, another something-to-be-done organically pursued.

The conception of the potential contradiction between the pull of an escapist private sphere and the desperately needed investment in a revitalized public sphere for which beloved educational philosopher Maxine Greene continually advocates became the context for a quite heated discussion later in this class. This heated discussion concerned a central event in the text that features a teenaged Clarence, the son of the African-American Walker and the Irish-American Eleanor, making a surprise visit to the factory where Eleanor works, intending to share with his mother his delight at earning an "A" in a science course. In tearfully recounting the incident to her husband, Eleanor explains how a proud Clarence stood before her, calling her "Momma," and she, about to be revealed as the mother of a bi-racial son, pretended that she was not his mother but merely his neighbor:

> And O'Leary [the boss] was staring at me and his eyes all wide. And Clarence he's just staring too. Clarence has got this report card in his hand. I looked at the boss and I said it again, "It's [Momma's] just a term of speech, you know, how people talk." And Clarence, he's got this look on his face like the whole world has just tumbled in on him. Like something went in and just collapsed his face right down. He says to me, "Momma." I think I'm gonna hear that word forever, the way he said it. Momma. Momma. Momma. Like it's just the most important thing he ever said. And O'Leary, he takes Clarence by the scruff of the neck, "What're you wasting this lady's time for?" he says. And Clarence says, "I just wanted to tell her that I got an A in science." And O'Leary he swells up real big like and he coughs and he looks around the warehouse. "An A in science!" he shouts. "It musta been in evolution." (p. 138)

Already haunted by Clarence's way of calling her "Momma," Eleanor continues explaining to Walker her uncontrollable failure to recognize her son, even as her boss physically removed him from the factory:

> He's got these big tears coming down his face. And he says to me again, "Momma." And I didn't say a word to him. I just didn't say a word. I didn't even say well done. Well done for the A in science. I was just dumbstruck and I didn't mean it, I didn't mean to be that way, it just happened to me, Nathan, I swear I didn't mean it; oh, God in heaven, believe me that I never meant to ignore him like that. I just sat there and watched O'Leary drag Clarence out of the warehouse, and I've never felt a sorrier thing ever in my life. (p. 139)

Eleanor then recalls how, as soon as Clarence was ejected from the factory, she ran out past her co-workers to search for him. Even as she is telling her husband the story, she still hasn't found Clarence, and she begs Walker to go find their son.

When we unpack this scene as a class, the more obvious context for such devastating behavior on Eleanor's part—which she regrets and attempts to reverse immediately—is, according to our reconstruction in class, the weight of her suffering, especially related to the violent public rhetoric (and actions) in response to "mixing of the races" at this time in history. In Eleanor's limited and isolated life, she has experienced multiple humiliations related to her cross-racial marriage and bi-racial son. Readers early on witnessed, for instance, Walker's inability to protect her from a policeman's lechery. Then, as newlyweds, the couple experiences bricks thrown through their windows with glass landing on their bed; the only relief is a higher-floor tenement apartment. We know that O'Leary, Eleanor's Irish boss, who does not know of her marriage to Walker, is one of the few people outside of her private family life who has ever treated her humanely. And of course, there's the issue of her keeping the job on which her family's livelihood is clearly dependent.

Yet for some students, Eleanor's behavior is unforgivable: this incident reduces her to an "unlovable," unfit mother. A student named Alex, for example, argues the position that Eleanor's denial of her son in that moment at the factory constitutes child abuse. Amber, however, calculates the weight of Eleanor's crippling insecurity and says, as an aside to another student, "You can't know the level of Eleanor's unsafety." At this point, it is evident that there are no easy racial alliances to support us in either making each student's contribution *count* or *discount:* biracial Moana agrees with white Amber, and Mexican-American Wendy asserts that a mother's alliance with her child is what all basic security rests on. From Wendy's perspective, a mother cannot disown her child, ever. In assessing these initial responses, it is clear that Eleanor's behavior is unforgivable to white and affluent Alex, as it is equally unforgivable to working-class and first-generation Mexican-American Wendy.

Interestingly, after one less-comfortable class session, a kind of softening ensued around an agreement that, as a group, we would not reach consensus in our classroom community; two students were able to articulate the reality that we had been shaped by different life experience, raised in different families. My sense was that had the disagreement played out along strict race or social class lines, the experience could have been more destructive of the sense of classroom community that made this particular class so generally engaged and engaging.

It was in the third iteration of teaching this text in a Philosophy of Education class taught to Colgate students last year as part of my leadership of our Manchester (U.K.) Study Group that a student raised the issue of the isolation of this family from any early anti-racist consciousness of the time, a connection she had made from having studied DuBois's *The Souls of Black Folk* in the mandated Challenges of Modernity course that is part of Colgate's now-unusual required core curriculum (note reference in Chapter 1). This added complexity to our conversation, as students had to grapple not only with a nascent awareness that political movements can affect the consciousness of individuals, but also with other complicating realities, including the likely middle-classness of DuBois's most publicized activities, his preoccupation with the white audience to which he was appealing.

Teaching *This Side of Brightness* in Manchester added a different sort of contextual depth to the study group's analysis of and reactions to the novel, as Manchester is the city that inspired *The Communist Manifesto* and, as a city, has done a remarkable job of preserving as museum installations the history of the

Industrial Revolution. This preservation includes not just models of its ingenious technological triumphs, but also records of both the costs to the human beings who were attached to and mangled by that technology, and the social protest and advocacy movements those people gave birth to. The presence of the sprawling People's History Museum on prime downtown real estate further affirms a kind of plea for forgiveness that is palpable in the air of Manchester. My students and I visited mills, museums, aqueducts, iron bridges, and mines throughout the United Kingdom during a two-week fieldtrip-based course on the history of the Industrial Revolution that preceded their other coursework, including my own Democratic Educational Philosophies course. We were encouraged by the retired engineer who taught the fieldtrip-based course to revel in the ingenuity of the civil engineers and inventors, yet the suffering of the workers and the social movement–building that was the response to that suffering were always part of the subtext, whether explicitly presented or not.

In this setting, which contrasts greatly to the quaint, upper-middle-class rural village where Colgate is located, the conversation regarding Eleanor's denial of her son completely eclipsed any consideration of her blame-worthiness as a mother who denied her child, even though this class appeared united in the view that this denial of him was the beginning of the end for Clarence. Collectively, the study group saw this incident as the beginning of the degree of heightened internalized oppression and its concomitant rage that would lead to Clarence's murder of the racist and lecherous McAuliffe, and then of the policeman who failed to arrest him after McAuliffe kills (Clarence's mother) Eleanor in a hit-and-run accident.

This particular group of students, with its much-more balanced racial and social class diversity than is typical at Colgate, was apparently not invested in an essentialist construction of motherhood, and could hold in their consciousness two realities: that white Eleanor could deeply love her black son and could simultaneously deny her relationship to him, a particularly vulnerable child, in a way that would poison his life. As well, a student did offer insight about a less-obvious context for Eleanor's behavior in this scene, and that was the wildness implicit in her marriage to Walker, a man not only old enough to be her father, but a man who also served the function of father during Sunday visits throughout Eleanor's childhood. "What if Eleanor relied on Walker to be the father figure with regard to questions of race?" this student asked. Eleanor then, although she has been shunned and disrespected when publicly visible as mother to a son of color in numerous interactions narrated in the text, has never really processed being parent to a child of color, except passively, as a victim. In the first circumstance where she, a white woman, must stand up as a parent-ally to her own child of color she cannot do so; she has not processed the pain-for-him of his identity, the very pain that her active alliance, could, to some extent, mitigate. This discussion represented one of those remarkable moments that confirm for me my belief in the study of imaginative literature, as opposed to much research in psychology, for its education in emotional intelligence.

Here we are returned to the paradox of some level of actual "impossibility" in terms of the consideration of teaching as a profession, as exposed by Britzman. I could not have "taught" in the previous iteration of my Philosophy of Education course "the social construction of Eleanor's inability to claim her son" in that scene in the factory, because for some students, a kind of maternal essentialism overrides effects of social construction. What I conceive of as the more powerful reception of my most recent class in Manchester to the depth of this text was determined by a difference in transference relationships. The "old relationships [which] conjured new ones" in this case allowed far-deeper meditation on the weight of racism and especially on the weight of internalized oppression on a family isolated from any emancipatory knowledge and protection related to the virulent racism that circumscribed their lives. Yet these different transference relationships are also explained by the reality of having more students of color and more students of working-class families in the class I taught with my Colgate students in Manchester. And their responses were, in turn, shaped by a something-to-be-done, the articulation of a reality: the cross-generational transmission of trauma, that emerged in previously haunted classes who studied this text.

What seems clear is only that our charge as educators is to do for our students what Paul Ricoeur (1998) proposes for history writ large and public, and for history internal and individual, lived as memory:

> I am thinking of what Raymond Aron said in his 1938 thesis on the limits of historical objectivity, when he proposed that the task of the historian was to "defatalize" the past, in other words, to place oneself in the situation of the protagonists, who, themselves, had a future; to place oneself back in the situation of uncertainty in which they found themselves when they were waiting for, fearing, hoping for, and in any case lacking knowledge of, what would come after. (p. 124)

As conveyed by Ricoeur, Aron's conception of defatalizing the past suggests the necessity of bringing imagination to the presentation of history, and by extension, literature—an approach to the teaching of text discouraged by the current test-driven curriculum, with its valuing of the certain and the conclusive. Similarly, the Common Core English standards very specifically privilege the teaching of non-fiction over fiction, suggesting a preference for "the facts" as in conventionally navigated history and literature, over interpreted, and/or interpretation-driven presentations of life as lived by a set of historical and/or imaginatively constructed characters. Parallel to this shift is the change in rules for the evaluation of research in the social sciences, where qualitative studies are no longer funded by the federal government. Related, too, we note that art and music classes are the first to be defunded when the budget cuts take their tolls. Imagination, closely associated with creativity, is presented as something frivolous that we can no longer afford.

Never has the capacity to imagine been so shamelessly starved in the public sphere where "the suffocating reality principle whose distillate is the economy" prevails. It is the right time to remind ourselves that Dewey conceived of imagination as that which young people bring to social challenges. Britzman invokes Julia Kristeva, who corrects for Dewey's idealism, in her recognition that the freedom to play with ideas is modeled (or not) first in the family and then in schools; clearly in both places a combination of the operative hero system, dynamics of oppression, and the complex personhood of family members and teachers can constrain or make available this freedom of play.

Dewey actually shares with most educational philosophers a fairly limited notion of play with ideas for all of the detailed attention he pays to method in thinking. In his emphasis on the function of schooling to teach against war, for instance, he points out the limitations of teaching only "the horrors of war and to avoid everything which would stimulate international jealousy and animosity," calling instead for a *positive* emphasis in the curriculum on "whatever binds people together in cooperative human pursuits and results, apart from geographic limitations" (1916, p. 98). It is not his work to detail the psychological constraints (perhaps the political internalized) that play out as failure of imagination, perpetuating the "stimulations of international jealousy and animosity" that characterize the teaching of wars I observe regularly in classrooms. Beyond the focus on "occupations" and artifact based social studies education, Dewey tends to assume a certain well-behavedness on the part of appropriately directed learners and their teachers which oversimplifies the process of transmission of knowledge. His learners are without wildness. Speaking more generally of applied learning theory also intended for well-behaved learners, Britzman identifies how

> education founders when it mindlessly repeats idealizations of cooperative learning, role models, and socialization. One of the implicit tensions these approaches to emotional ties bury is that individuals are educated in groups but urged to think for the self, to create one's own mind, and to overcome the fear, prejudice, and acting out that suture group life but destroy the capacity to think. Yet, the dominant and taken-for-granted discourse on learning only magnifies one aspect of this world: that students should behave and that identifications are only conscious. (2011, p. 117)

We might add that in an era like the present, when schools are gripped by "a suffocating reality principle whose distillate is the economy," the necessary openness to misunderstanding that might allow for play with ideas, is likewise more generally suffocated. Further, testing for rightness and wrongness will increasingly determine who will experience any Kristevian freedom to play in their futures. Thinking of our time as an era for the very well-behaved, perhaps for those who are paralyzed by fear of error and unable to play, we might want to recall our doubts about people we'd describe that way.

Indeed, considering the reality that a particular historical era can leave all of us more afraid than previously tends to add weight to the proposition that we human beings have an awful lot in common. Again, we must recognize the tensions in practice of teaching between a focus on what we share as human beings, versus the cultural (most broadly construed) variations that shape our different beliefs and needs. Perhaps the only truth that can drive our work is Gordon's assertion, borrowed from Patricia Williams, that "life is complicated" (p. 3). We want to keep in mind that complex personhood is always rubbing up against the infinite ways that power can assert itself, skew the opportunity structure, and distort the curiosity and ingenuity we share when that power plays out in ways over which we have no control, don't know our control, or whose control we have not yet built the appropriate resistance to counteract.

With regard to building such resistance, my students have proposed something(s)-to-be-done at levels of both individual and collective response. Many have made commitments to love "the Treefrogs" they encounter, assuming and projecting backstories they cannot know, agreeing to attempt to offer others the allowances they offer themselves. We have had productive conversations about our capacity and need to protect ourselves; we can acknowledge that Treefrog, drug-addled and desperate in the scene where he assaults the clerk in the pharmacy, could have been dangerous to us as workers or patrons of that store. We have agreed that it's possible to offer love to someone from whom we are aware of a rational need to protect ourselves. We've also agreed that there is a kind of "allowance" that is no easier for narcissistic people to come by than others, and that is genuine self-forgiveness. I find students ready and willing to grapple with the seeming paradox that we, the relatively affluent, can be thoughtless about our own genuine needs, the needs that emerge when we agree to disrespect the "suffocating reality principle whose distillate is the economy," even as we are often unaware of our own privilege and disregarding of the obligations to others we cannot know. It is important, though, to give students opportunities to play with this paradox. The following assignment has proven promising in this regard:

> *Assignment: Note the sentence that ends "with the knowledge of those who might be dead in just a few hours," on the very first page of chapter two. Appreciate how close the circumstances of living a life of extreme oppression and pain bring one to death, and then how that closeness to death makes the liveliness of life of the "mind-body in wholeness of operation" as identified by John Dewey, glow in relief. Thinking of this book as one long, exhilaratingly painful poem about lives lived on the edge as a result of race, class, and gender domination rubbing up against the wildness of the complex personhood that defines each of the characters, consider the complex personhood that defines you as a reader. Select a memory whose meaning has been destabilized during our study of this text. Using the computer program Final Cut Pro, construct a digital story with a 350-word or less voice-over, that explores how any thinking or rethinking that this novel has inspired on your part makes a memory mean something different than it has in the past. Allow yourself to be influenced by the conceptions of complex personhood, social contradiction, oppression, and/or wildness as we considered them while reading this novel. The commitment that drives this assignment is your commitment to love Treefrog, meaning that you believe him to be worthy of the same level of material, educational, psychological, and spiritual resources that nurture you, and that you recognize your interdependence with all human beings on this planet. That includes that you, like they, deserve forgiveness, but that doesn't let you off the hook.*

The hope is that our students and we as teachers can begin to appreciate resonances between love and the challenge to view all human beings as worthy of the same weight of material and spiritual resources as we are. I would argue that healthy child and adolescent development is nurtured by such resonances, and that they define the joy in classrooms like Mary Cowhey's and Vivian Paley's. Further, to extend this recognition of worthiness to even the most tormented lives made available to us in imaginative literature like *This Side of Brightness* is to potentially refine us as readers, thinkers, and philosophers of education, perhaps even turn us into poets. The reality that *This Side of Brightness* does often read like poetry has been alluded to, but not systematically examined in this chapter. Certainly the text opens us to the post-modern sense that words evoked in the description of lives lived so precariously help to construct particular complex personhoods. Such complex personhoods in turn project the reality of having lived with so little margin for error. These words will return in other contexts, and they'll have a haunted quality, reverberating with a potential something-to-be-done. Most inspiring for us teachers is the reality that the capacity to grasp a something-to-be-done emerges out of whatever spaciousness can be made for readers with a new willingness to face their uncertain obligations to others. In my experience, the book becomes a significant milestone in the lives of many students who read it, and for some it provokes greater interest in creative writing and poetry.

HAUNTEDNESS, FORGIVENESS, AND INEVITABLE NEW ERROR

I have periodically urged students to try to experience the hauntedness of our own language—to become more conscious of sensual reverberations in the words we use. The words have been with other people in other places, and both the people and places can take up residence in our souls, lessening our perception of the differences between our worth, needs, and desires, versus those of others. Helpfully, there is the discovery in the artists' records of analysis Britzman examines that "there is a double difficulty conceptualizing the poetics and promise of the imagination; all at once we are reminded of our dependency to others and to the unknown world" (2009, p. 105). Further, and more optimistically:

> We glimpse a counterdepressive force against intolerance. After all, when the field of education encounters the failure of imagination, it confronts both its own crisis of responsibility and its relation to others… We can stay on the side of the failure of imagination and its repetitive grammar by insisting that we know in advance what is important and unimportant or we can try again to encounter the unknown. (p. 105)

Here I add that the freedom to play with ideas, open to encounter with the unknown is, after all, the only hope for Dewey's "bind[ing] people together in cooperative human pursuits and results" (1916, p. 98), perhaps another way of understanding Badiou's global egalitarian project.

What becomes evident in our work of attaching our students to the global egalitarian project in this historical era is that we have a contradictory dual mission intimated by Britzman above. We must bring our students to recognize the depth of social injustice whose denials haunt their/our aspirations and possibilities. This is the unknown world on which we are dependent. But we must also forgive the ones who came before us for having assimilated the layers of hero systems that have shaped the haunted education passed on to us, creating their ghosts mostly out of fear of error themselves. We teachers and our students must forgive ourselves as we agree to take responsibility for the inheritance that has in large part determined the haunted terrain of our own lives and education. We encounter the new from our situatedness in the old, dependent on Hannah Arendt's phrase "those already here" (as cited in Britzman, 2009, p. 56). Freud's analogy of building our lives on the rubble of ancient Roman cities is an apt one; what emerges as the something-to-be-done, always a product of defatalizing the past, shares the same problem: It will inevitably generate new error.

CHAPTER 7

ON PERSONAL AND POLITICAL GHOST STORIES

Hauntagogy, *Nurturance, and Investment in the Pretend*

> To exorcise not in order to chase away the ghosts, but this time to grant them the right … to … a hospitable memory … out of a concern for justice.
>
> —Jacques Derrida, *Specters of Marx*

Is it becoming a ghost story, this vision of education as nurture of selves in the interest of the public good—education as the playing out of our unknowable obligations to others? The ideologies of the individualism that serve capitalism—meritocracy, competition, both knowledge and technology in commoditized form, and the distorted notion of accountability shaped by these—increasingly shape our students' understandings of themselves as disconnected from politics and, increasingly, as a set of measurable and technical competencies to be rewarded by consumption. These obstacles bar their attachment to the global egalitarian project; therefore they present pedagogical challenges.

To what extent might hauntagogy, which squarely faces the more tangled complexities of personhood and power, confirm the continued validity of pursuit of the global egalitarian project as teacher education, indeed as a reason to live? With its dependence on respect for educative stories, as well as its appealing creepiness in an era hooked on vampires, might hauntagogy also help us reconnect our students to that empowering understanding, certainly supportive of commitment to the global egalitarian project, that the "personal is political?"

PRELUDE: THE VAMPIRIC NATURE OF CAPITALISM

Terrell Carver's *Postmodern Marx* (1998) provides hope for a meaningful revival of the understanding that the "personal is political," as it responds to Derrida's flawed effort to deconstruct *Capital* in his Spectres of Marx (1994). Carver mocks what he describes as the convoluted and indirect arguments, clarifying why and how Derrida both misses and obscures the primary message of *Capital*. Instead of what he characterizes as a too-dense spinning from Marx's use of the word "spectre," Carver concentrates on the obvious: *Capital*, the text that has been wrongly dismissed as too technically economic and materialist to be of interest to most political philosophers (and by extension, although not stated by Carver, educational philosophers), is the one in which Marx is poetically lyrical on the theme of the vampiric quality of capitalism. Carver traces the specific appearances of the word "vampire" and its derivatives in Marx's text, where capitalism is described as a "blood-sucking" institution, deadly for most of its victims, yet powerful enough to construct a good deal of what we have come to consider human nature.

Carver is motivated by the desire to make *Capital* both accessible and accessed by political philosophers and a wide array of readers because of what he believes is its most important (and currently marginalized) message: Capitalism constructs our understanding of what we consider to be human nature, shaped by this image of the vampire who takes what it needs from others, willing to bleed others dry for a profit.

Many of our students respond with similar characterizations of human nature, especially in Colgate's required core course Challenges of Modernity when faced with paradigms that suggest a need for cooperation and a willingness to be moved by the wants and needs of others. "It's not human nature," is a line I increasingly associate with the relatively recent erosion of what Jean Anyon characterizes as K-12 "affluent professional" education with its focus on issues of social inequality and often, the study of labor movements, the Civil Rights struggles, and the continually contested nature of domestic robber baron and global colonizing cultures (see Chapter 5 where I discuss this erosion in more detail). Carver's attention to the social construction of human nature in the context of the vampiric nature of capitalism offers us a window to introduce socially critical historical knowledge that our students have increasingly not been asked to personalize in their previous education. It is also significant in its literariness, its appeal to metaphoric and associative thought, especially when I consider that the only (now classic) television series for which every student in my last spring's curriculum theory course and I shared intimate knowledge and appreciation was *Buffy the Vampire Slayer*. Despite the problems and potential excesses of post-modern deconstruction which Carver delightedly ascribes to Derrida's *Spectres of Marx*, acts of deconstruction can call up in our students the promising leaps in thinking that implicate their *wild* autobiographies; deconstruction helps us understand the myths that underlie our values, habits, and institutions, including the ones that miseducate and possibly misshape our children.

INTRODUCTION

Befitting an ethnographic inquiry into a haunted educational philosophy, I am framing this chapter's inquiry through three ghost stories from the overlapping realms of the personal and the political: the personal, usefully complicated by Avery Gordon's conceptualization of complex personhood, characterized by the non-rational nature of self, including its sometimes self-defeating thoughts and actions, and the political, made richer by her assertion: "the power relations that characterize any historically embedded society are never as transparently clear as the names we give them imply" (Gordon, 2008, p. 3). The three numbered stories are interwoven between and among their tellings by the usual cast of characters inhabiting this book: all are philosopher-teachers—some emphasizing philosophy more than teaching, and some teaching more than philosophy: Dewey, Badiou,

Greene, Paley, Ruddick, Grumet, Readings, and Britzman, with Avery Gordon finally pulling together the refrain of this chorus.

The first story is about a miseducative interaction in the life of a child, one who seeks to make sense of an early experience with death by asserting his own agency as a storyteller and writer. The second features educational philosopher Donna Kerr as a soon-to-be mother in which she pleads for recognition of the nurture of childhood agency as the point of education. She is supported by early childhood teacher Vivian Paley, who serves as both storyteller and theorist. The third relies on the essay of Yup'ik community elder, activist, and social servant Harold Napoleon, written from prison at the time of his sentence for alcoholism-related violence. In his essay, Napoleon seeks to interpret and heal the alcoholism of his Alaskan Native people, recognizing that the denial of "The Great Death" as an unfortunate "survival" strategy proved so emotionally devastating that it compelled chronic intoxication. This last essay came to me by way of an observation visit to the Arctic Class taught by my educational studies colleague Melissa Kagle, who grounded her lesson in deconstruction of a range of Yup'ik words that contained the root for "pretend." All three of my "storytellers" encounter a resistance to their stories that speaks to issues of power and complex personhood. How might Gordon's conception of haunting, activated for use by teachers in Stern's conception of hauntagogy, point us to a something-to-be-done related to the parallel resistances encountered by the child, the educational philosopher-mother, and the Yup'ik elder? How might it make the something-to-be-done more available and attractive to our students to conceive of our critical reading work with them as exorcising ghosts? Finally, how do/might the stories resolve, and what do we teachers learn from their resolutions?

THE FIRST STORY: MY DAVID TRIES TO WRITE THE GHOST

The first, the personal story, was recently told to me by my beloved husband, David, in the course of a powerfully emotional dialogue between us about the state of our growth and continuing challenges as life partners of thirty years. Here is David's story, mostly in his own words:

> During the summer when I was seven years old, my Nana, my mother's mother, was dying in our house in the room upstairs right next door to mine. She was in constant physical pain and probably deep emotional pain as well; once her illness was diagnosed terminal, she was abandoned by her narcissistic husband, my grandfather. So she had come 'home' to her daughter's family to die; the late fifties was not a time of good public dissemination of information about end-of-life pain management, nor about death and dying; certainly nobody in my family talked about dying with dignity. Nobody ever talked about dying at all, so my grandmother was resuscitated by emergency visits from police and other rescue workers numerous times during that summer. My mother was completely identified with her mother, having experienced what was then called a "nervous breakdown" earlier in her life. I was over-identified with her, and we lived in

> a continual state of denial, depression, and panic. My grandmother periodically moaned audibly for my mother and in my memory these moans included a wailing of my mother's name, which was particularly painful for me as a child.
>
> My grandmother died at the end of that summer. Shortly after her death, one evening I approached my mother, who was washing dishes at the kitchen sink. I was delighted about an idea I had. I told her I wanted to write a ghost story involving my grandmother. I remember that it was going to be a good ghost story, a happy ghost story; I don't know if I had time to convey to her the intended happy quality of the story before her reaction silenced me. My mother's face was distorted by rage when she turned to me and railed, "Whatever gave you an awful idea like that?" I felt obliterated at that moment. I remember that I went off alone, and I knew that there was nobody with whom I could ever talk about what happened.

I am naming David's idea a "deferred ghost story," and imagine that, had it been welcomed then, when he was seven years old, it would have revealed a something-to-be-done as conceptualized by Avery Gordon, a something connected to a child finding inspiration to fuel his own growth and happiness in a painful time, while offering a challenge to our limited Western reception of dying. The deferred ghost story held all of the imaginative promise of a literate child's first encounter with death: the desire to make some positive sense of his confusing experience, including his own and his family's suffering in the face of the profound loss of a beloved family member, to offer a community of potential readers—including his mother—his own creative response to finitude, to grapple in retrospect with the loneliness of that long summer with no adults in charge. This is the brilliant use of imaginative response that grows the self's resilience and the self's ability to keep generating energy to create new presentations of understanding.

I appreciate how Maxine Greene's words in *Releasing the Imagination* (1995) capture and interpret the joyful surprise conveyed by David in that brief awareness of his story's possibility:

> The surprise comes along with becoming different—consciously different as one finds ways of acting on envisaged possibility. It comes along with hearing different words and music, seeing from unaccustomed angles, realizing that the world perceived from one place is not *the* world. (p. 20)

In my reading of my husband's life, that unwritten happy ghost story has been a profound absence, a haunted place that has marked his life-long ambivalent relationship to his own creative agencies, to his art, including music, and particularly, to his own writing.

I am not interested in contributing to the significant literature and popular culture stereotypes that blame mothers for the world's ills, nor am I intending to present David's mother as a monster, which she clearly was not. She was a gifted children's librarian during the many years when anguish did not limit her ability to participate fully in the life of her community. She was not only a woman who appreciated, remembered, and told some wonderful stories, she was also finely attuned to David's appreciation of the natural world—a mother always happy to stop on walks to allow him to examine insects and leavings like fossils and shells, all of which supported the depth of spirituality and intellect that have characterized him as a life partner to me and father to our children.

Avery Gordon (2008) helps us hold empathy for David's mother too, jogging our periodic remembering of what we like to forget with this segment of her reflections about complex personhood:

> Complex personhood means that all people (albeit in specific forms whose specificity is sometimes everything) remember and forget, are beset by contradiction, and recognize and misrecognize themselves and others. Complex personhood means that people suffer graciously and selfishly too, get stuck in the symptoms of their troubles, and also transform themselves. (p. 4)

This is not to deny the damaging nature of that highly charged interaction with David as a seven-year-old, especially as it was typical of the playing out of family patterns that would repeatedly teach him to mistrust his most powerful creative instincts.

THE SECOND STORY: A FIERCE MATERNAL PHILOSOPHER AND HER TEACHER ALLY DEMAND NURTURE AS EDUCATION

Yet educational philosopher Donna Kerr (1996), supporting Gordon's conception of negative realities featured in complex personhood, suggests that damaging family patterns are the norm and not the exception, contrary to the contemporary right-wing rhetoric that valorizes the family as the only place where nurture and the construction of responsible citizens can happen. Kerr reminds us of the cruelty often visited by families and homogeneous communities: "Adults using children for their own purposes, compulsions, and other private or domestic forms of domination can just as surely visit harm near the hearth as can tyrants at large in the state and market" (p. 39). In her use of the words "compulsion," "domination," and "evil," she invites the interpretation that parent-child relationships are haunted by the complex personhood of the adults in charge.

Pregnant at the time the inspiration for her article came to her, Kerr pursues an inquiry into "the moral significance and power of the soul or self as it can be cultivated through relationships of unfailing respect and trust" (p. 51). She is not naïve, nor does she suggest that the public sphere can absorb all personal distress and transform it. Kerr invokes the words of Anthony Giddens who supports my contention in this book that (family) psychology can represent politics internalized; Yet Giddens argues, interestingly, with an emphasis on the personal pole of "the personal as political" whereas I argue with an emphasis on the political pole. He contends that "if we are to transform our public world in ways that provide for this necessary nurture of the self, we shall have to import democracy, a heretofore public form, into the family" (as cited in Kerr, 1996, p. 53). Giddens helps us understand political oppression internalized by the family as a kind of ghost. Without naming them, he identifies adultism, the oppression that damages the appropriate agency of children, and sexism, the oppression that damages the agency of women and girl children, as the oppressive psychologies that will be challenged by "family democracy." Completing Gordon's ideal trajectory of haunting recognition, Giddens proposes the importing of democracy into the family as a something-to-be-done.

Equally interesting, we have the potential to translate into the private family context Badiou's conception of education as a piercing a hole in knowledge. In this case, the "import [of] democracy, a heretofore public form, into the family," *educates* the "knowledge" that is (limited and conventional) psychology. Yet Kerr also identifies the potential for an expanded civic sector that might bring together the strengths of both home and the public sphere associated with government, mitigating the negative complexities of both. She calls for a lively civic culture supporting public schools as sites of personal nurture, and rails against the current obsession with technology that has narrowly rationalized the curriculum.

Kerr also recognizes the complicatedness in what she advocates, the personal clarity involved in the commitment to nurture, which she nearly equates with education. "Nurture has something to do with listening carefully to each other's stories, but how can we even begin to listen through the noise of our own narratives, which are born in part of our not having been nurtured so well ourselves: Are we even capable of not wreaking evil as we attempt to nurture others?" she asks (Kerr, 1996, p. 41).

Kerr finds a positive model, a writer whose depth unfortunately frequently eludes my students, in the work of early childhood educator Vivian Paley. Paley bases her teaching on the children's dictation to her of their own stories, and enactment of them with their peers. Her most beloved book, *The Boy Who Would Be a Helicopter* (1990), famously features Jason, a child whose preoccupation with helicopters provides a window into his soul's confusion about how to connect with others. Paley's capacity to listen in the role of teacher allows her to weave together into her own equally compelling "stories" the insights of Jason and his peers. She and the children, standing in for all of us, are made to feel useful through the unique insights they contribute to the sense-making operation that is life in this classroom. The book is a study of how we are made to feel loved by one another, versus how hurtful exclusions can lead to the opposite: feeling like one's resources are wasted, feeling unappreciated, feeling invisible. Paley's later book *You Can't Say You Can't Play* (1992) is considered more overtly political, as it features the reality of patterns of construction and exclusion of social "others" even in early childhood classrooms. The book models the gifts and challenges in building a classroom community, even possibly a school community with the most significant operative rule: "You can't say 'you can't play.'" I have often thought that this book would generate more vital dialogue in high school, where students might feel gratified to be invited to debate the implications of the rule for their own school community, as Paley does when she reports in the book on her conversations with older elementary children about the rule she enacts in her kindergarten.

THEORIZING NURTURE IN THE PUBLIC SPHERE

I want to assert that I am not interested in producing more theory that can be commodified for the economy of calculation in which the university of excellence functions when I insert the haunting metaphor here. I believe that Paley knows that patterns of construction and exclusion of social others haunt her classroom and lead to the revelation of the "you can't say you can't play" rule as the something-to-be-done. Like Gordon, I am preoccupied by how to inspire attachment of my students to the global egalitarian project in this historical era.

I was lucky enough to teach early elementary school during the era that nurtured Paley's genius, and my dissertation and first book featured similar classroom storytelling. I found inspiration in the central focus of the "maternal thinking" of philosopher Sarah Ruddick (which I repeat here from the introduction) who captured a reality of mothers' stories that clearly drive the stories elicited by Paley as well:

> As she pieces her children's days together, a mother creates for herself and her children the confidence that the children have a life, very much their own and inextricably connected with others. (Ruddick, 1995, p. 98)

Only now in writing this book have I grown the confidence to speculate about why our students frequently complain that they don't understand how Paley figures out what to say to the children in her classroom, and how she elicits the stories she does. I literally had a student say last year, "It feels like she is hearing the children say things I can't hear, or mean things that I can't figure out how she knew they meant!" I believe that my students' problem is in identifying with the specific confidence that Ruddick and Paley reinforce in order to make education possible—the very terms of Ruddick's proposition: that they (the children, the students) do have "a life very much their own," and that they are "inextricably connected with others."

Alain Badiou clarifies the reality of my privileged students' socialization: "What is being inflicted on us today…is the conviction that the will, dominated by a suffocating reality principle whose distillate is the economy, should behave with extraordinary circumspection—lest it expose the world to grave disasters…" (cited in Peterson, 2010, p. 162). Badiou has wisdom, too, about this second part of the sacrifice of confidence imposed (especially) on the affluent children who grew up to be my/our students. Educational philosopher Thomas Peterson contextualizes Badiou's thinking in philosophy to guide curriculum-making, examining Badiou's contention that the ideology which includes this suffocating "reality principle" has already succeeded in adulterating the ideals associated with the French Revolution: freedom, equality, and fraternity. As he quotes from Badiou: "Formal freedom means a freedom that is neither articulated to a global egalitarian project nor practiced subjectively as fraternity" (p. 162). Here, Badiou echoes Maxine Greene (1988) in her claim that we idealize spectacularly ungratifying "freedom from" incursions on our time and attention, freedom from "distractions" in the way of our pursuit of the prize: ever-elusive financial security that will drive lives organized around consumption (p. 1). Such a pursuit stands in opposition to the freedom to negotiate with others the actual realities of our collective lives as global citizens. Badiou continues: "As for fraternity, it is the real itself, pure and simple, the sole subjective guarantee of the novelty of experiences, since equality remains programmatic and liberty instrumental" (Badiou as cited in Peterson, 2010). So the genuine freedom that is "articulated to the global egalitarian project," that is "practiced subjectively as fraternity," finds itself unthinkable by those who live inside of the "suffocating reality principle." Unfortunately, Badiou fails to develop the feminist implications of his recognition of the devaluation of connection.

It is instructive that John Dewey noted a similar problem as the one identified by Badiou when he was writing educational philosophy during the "gilded age," another era during which robber barons dominated public life. As early as 1916 in *Democracy and Education*, Dewey asserted that while teachers are "men striving to educate their successors not for the existing state of affairs but so as to make possible a future better humanity," parents are typically obstacles in that they "educate their children so that they may get on; princes educate their subjects as instruments of their own purposes" (p. 95).

It is interesting to speculate on this question at a time when robber barons have returned to us in a degraded context: whereas in Dewey's era they harnessed productive labor, however exploitative the relationships, now the One Percent manipulates financial markets in order to accrue a far greater concentration of wealth for "investing" in those same financial markets to accrue still more private wealth. We need green building and re-building; we need the schooling that will grow the citizens ready to develop clean energy sources and outlaw war; yet we choose (long-term) non-profitable fracking, destructive to the earth and our health, while our brightest college graduates design cell phone apps or support further concentration of wealth that threatens the global economy on Wall Street. Was Dewey delineating the likely choices of two different social classes of parents: those who will educate for a modest "getting on," possibly accruing minimal material security, and those, like royalty, who must specifically manipulate their children in order to maintain their unearned privilege against the claims of other princes? However unclear Dewey's meaning, there is an implication here of the desire of parents to achieve or maintain higher social class status for their children, robbing them of both the gratifying independence to make their own life and the empowering confidence that nurturing ties to others—opportunity to play out their unknowable obligations—will offer their lives meaningful depth, including joy.

When we complain that our students are "too conservative" this is what we mean. They appear to be conserving what they understand as their life force embedded as they are in a "suffocating reality principle," which narrows their expectation of what is possible and therefore limits the connections they make. They are used to believing that capitalism is the substrate of life and that the need to become a certain very limited and prescribed something in order to compete successfully for the jobs available to their social class, for the life trajectory that is advertised to their social class, requires that in all of their important decisions they conform to the advice of mom and dad who, especially if they are privileged or seek greater privilege, are likely to have internalized this reality principle. We teachers and teacher educators are ever more embarrassingly dependent on the few students in our classes, who, are erratically—and sometimes strategically—refusing "suffocation," which ironically means that they sometimes refuse us.

"Getting on," then, is the opposite of having a Deweyan social vision. Significantly, this era invites the morphing of Dewey's "getting on," which allows for a certain hopeful indeterminacy, into the contemporary common expression "get with the program." Listen to the intensification of the process of imposing limits on social vision, and perhaps invoking Badiou's terminology to point to the "suffocation" of vision altogether. Because of her continual focus on story, Kerr has a good deal to contribute to our understanding of how far from Dewey's vision the contemporary global educational program has deviated.

We can appreciate similarities between David's mother's obliteration of his profound literate impulse of a happy ghost story, and the non-nurturing treatment of young people's creative sense-making capacities in schools as described by Kerr, especially in the current technocratic era of enforced standardization and testing. Translating the personal into the political here for my purposes would mean translating the personal family life in the home for the school, and David's individual creative response presented to his mother, to "school curriculum," with the teacher as mother/leader. As mentioned in the introduction, an early personal mentor and important feminist philosopher of education, Madeleine Grumet, popularized the idea that mothering is the prototype for teaching in *Bitter Milk* (1988). In such a translation, David would be trying to co-construct the curriculum as John Dewey insisted children could and should do. A Deweyan teacher would accommodate David's growth by "spiraling curriculum." Where might a curriculum go once the writing of David's ghost story spiraled into it?

STORY #2 CONTINUES

Kerr understands that such Deweyan pedagogy is seriously endangered. As a lioness of a new mother, she is angry, and confirms Gordon's thesis that theory cannot do the work she wants to do. Her philosopher's tools are not adequate to convey the "prickly things" she must say: "The topic is too fundamental, too important, too laden with moral meaning, too uncharted, too rich to fit on my old legal pad. Instead, [she] must resort to stories and metaphors" (Kerr, 1996, p. 37). Again we hear from an academic about the limitations of theory when we are considering moral meaning; again we hear that only stories and metaphors can unearth certain kinds of depth.

The story she tells centers on the wake-up call delivered with the birth of her first child, the recognition that the nurture of this child was the first project she could not put aside, re-prioritize, renegotiate, or put on hold. Arguing for the particularity of any situation in which a human being nurtures another, she insists: "It can take place only in the concreteness, the immediacy, of a particular time and place, in a particular moment of a particular life, within particular human relationships" (Kerr, 1996, p. 38). She argues that "if schools are to have moral meaning, they can do so only as instruments for the nurture of our children" (p. 40).

Kerr's view of nurture as constructing the very integrity of the child advances her critique of the broader school curriculum. This critique deepens when she uses an "instructional package" for science teaching as stand-in for the increasingly technocratic K-12 curriculum. This kit, directing the dissection of a dogfish, has apparently removed from its course of study any consideration of the life of a dogfish. A series of existential questions haunt her inquiry about this curriculum on behalf of the young people who will move through its paces: "But could one perhaps take a few minutes to observe a dogfish in the water, or even to just encounter one washed onto a beach? Could one just watch for a time? Could one just mess around with it? Could one allow oneself to be curious, to somehow experience the dogfish? Dare a student poke around at the dead, split fish upon the beach, marveling at how things connect and trying to surmise why?" (p. 42).

"No," "No," "No," "No," "No," chorused the exemplary but demoralized local experienced teachers on our Colgate teacher education program's Teacher Advisory Council in response to each of Kerr's questions. We were studying this article with them the week before they were to administer full days in succession of standardized tests. They laughed in emotional relief at the universality of their fear, anger, and embarrassment, combined with the absurd humor in the situation. They were seated sometimes across from, sometimes next to, the student teachers of whom they expected an enlivening, as opposed to deadly, experience with the "dogfish" of the day for the students in their classrooms.

Kerr leaps to what she identifies as the "main point":

> If science must (no thoughtful researcher would countenance such tunnel vision) be conducted in denial of the self, then it is inherently immoral and should be banished. Morally, nothing is so primitive as acknowledging and respecting the self that has experiences; morally, nothing is so important as nurturing the self. Without a self, there can be no agency, hence no morality. (p. 43)

From this stance Kerr offers a critique of technology resonant with that of Martha Nussbaum and many contemporary social philosophers: "There may be no harder place to see, to comprehend this thing called the self or the soul, than in a society in which the computer metaphor, instrumental thinking, and consumerism prevail" (p. 43). Kerr argues that the literal treatment of the metaphor of "the mind processing information, about how the mind can be programmed" bespeaks tragedy; we are already seeing that tragedy play out in public education where "[a] mournful bell tolls when language forecloses consideration of 'acts of meaning' or of the self that would shape, texture, and color the world in its own way" (p. 43). Martha Nussbaum is shocked when her own similar thinking, which she characterizes as "mainstream humanism," is met with the following from the dean of a prestigious American college of education: "How surprising, says she, no one else I've talked to has mentioned any of these things at all. We have been talking only about how X University can contribute to the scientific and technical progress around the world, and that's the thing that our President is really interested in. But what you say is really interesting and I really want to think about it" (p. 54). Nussbaum's response to her readers:

> I start imagining the future of education in my country and in the world: initiatives focusing narrowly on scientific and technical training, producing many generations of useful engineers who haven't a clue about how to criticize the propaganda of their politicians, and who have even less of a clue about how to imagine the pain of a person who has been excluded and subordinated. (Nussbaum, 2009, p. 54)

Here is a plea for Ruddick's maternal stories and the Deweyan classrooms of Mary Cowhey and Vivian Paley. Kerr and Nussbaum confirm that the generative education we are rapidly sacrificing to instrumental conceptions of schooling would allow the individual student to shape the meaning of her life in the context of a classroom of equally worthy other shapers. I increasingly observe that my college students, even those who attended private schools with mission statements promising both individual nurture and "excellence," were not typically nurtured in ways that promoted the point of education, the point of living, that is a sense of their own "art of shaping … the world" along with their peers.. They were not directed to negotiate with these multiple "shapings" of their own and their peers to emphasize our "desire to extend the reference of 'us' as far as we can" (Rorty, cited in Greene, 1995). I interpret Rorty's words as describing a translation of Ruddick's maternal stories into initiation in the global egalitarian project, a translation that is especially useful for guidance in teacher education and of course, resonant with the visions of John Dewey, Maxine Greene, Mary Cowhey, and Vivian Paley. I hope I am making it clear here that we have a powerful chorus behind our inquiry.

Rapidly increasing concentration of wealth in the hands of the few has led the majority of my students to experience social segregation in housing as they were growing up. These housing patterns mean that the one or two non-upper–middle-class children of color who best articulate wisdom about exclusion, like those in Paley's research, are increasingly likely to be excluded at admissions. These are the very students who support her to educate the white and upper-middle-class majority about why, in fact, "You can't say you can't play." The same is true of children like Jason in *The Boy Who Would Be a Helicopter*. For good reason Paley avoids labeling Jason as "on the autism spectrum." Yet in this era of increasing standardization of curriculum, we know that poor and working-class parents of neurologically challenged children are not likely to find a teacher who has the support to remain as wide awake as Paley does. Her imagination, skill, and knowledge are nourished by expensive resources in the form of small class size, generous planning time, and her own continuing professional education. She loves Jason because she can see him, and in turn, can teach her students how to see him. Such teaching mirrors the perspective of parents who have the material and/or spiritual resources to appreciate their reality: This child is just another complex person deserving love like all the rest of us. When appropriately understood, his special challenges (and they can be demanding, sometimes exhausting challenges, even to the wide-awake Paleys of this world) illuminate a spirit that imagines differently. For any of us lucky enough to be in his life, he also *models* imagining differently, and such modeling will be key to making the global egalitarian project imaginable to the majority.

Paradoxically, re-segregation and certain labeling of children like Jason in classrooms where tests are administered differently and scores reported separately (in "fairness" to teachers), have deprived, and will continue to deprive "typical" children, like my students, of the most empowering education possible: that "typical" young people, too, are complex persons who deserve respect for their differences. My current Colgate students have been deprived of practice with the "you can't say you can't play" rule. Reading Paley's book, we, the college teachers and some of our students, watch that rule remind us of the rewards and mostly rewarding challenges of our own invitations into expanded boundaries. We observe that her young students' imaginations are enriched by thinking differently, challenging the "suffocating reality principle" that had already begun to constrain them. Had they experienced childhood with Paley as their teacher, our students might have found that their own classroom community helped create models for the global community. In this global community, we must learn to live with one another as, in Clifford Geertz's words, a "disorderly crowd of not wholly commensurable visions" (cited in Greene, 1995, p. 185). To seriously entertain Geertz's vision, we must eliminate war and the gross imbalances of power that lead to disinvestment in protection of the earth's non-renewable resources, including all of us and every member of our families.

But, admittedly, in the Dewey labschool where she teaches Paley might not have the same worries about the effect of Jason's standardized test scores on her job security and pay as do contemporary public school teachers. Yet even if Paley functions in less-constrained circumstances than those of typical public school teachers, the lesser level of constraint does not reflect negatively on Paley, nor on her inspiring and important books. Few teacher-writers can illustrate to our students what is possible should they choose to "awaken" as teachers, and push the world's inhabitants to share this awakening.

Those of us who intend to usefully enact the "you can't say you can't play" rule in our college classrooms face related challenges to those of teachers in re-segregated public schools: the problem of the low numbers of non-affluent students in increasingly financially nervous private colleges. A certain cynicism in the higher education "diversity mission" can exclude promising African American, Latina, Chicana, white working-class students, and students who have lived in poverty in the United States in favor of relatively wealthy and well-educated international students. My comments are in no way intended to suggest that we should not be welcoming international students, nor that their presence in our classrooms is not beneficial to us; I am simply trying to place their admissions in the competitive and often cynical context of the present functioning of the corporate university. Because students educated in increasingly under-resourced school districts graduate from high school needing academic and social supports in order to succeed at academically demanding public and private colleges, colleges facing financial pressures and conservative about spending their endowments will cut such supportive services and still appear "multicultural" by selecting better prepared international students.

I am familiar with the theory of those who have advocated for teaching to the empty seats of the underrepresented (while simultaneously moving forward the global egalitarian project's agenda for greater equity in education in both what they teach and in the political activism they pursue outside of the classroom). But as we become more clear that the work of hauntagogy unites the personal with the social, I doubt that we can accomplish it without the presence of working-class and U.S.-born students of color in our classrooms. Further, I am pained by continued teaching to and from empty seats; the knowledge that the students missing are precisely those most needed and most needing to be there is the constant reminder to those of us teaching in elite private colleges of our undeniable complicity with a grossly inequitable system.

STORY #1 CONTINUED

It would be a mistake to leave the reader feeling that only a perfect synergy of suddenly available resources can support the probability of our students' identification with the global egalitarian project. Returning to David's experience, might we find a hopeful resolution of his deferred ghost story that speaks to our skepticism?

As a middle-class child with access to what Jean Anyon (1981) characterized as "affluent professional" education, David was usefully connected to what public schools had to offer. His "dogfish lessons" erratically included consideration of some of Kerr's existential questions. His relatively privileged affluent professional public school education offered him inconsistent-yet-continual opportunities to question authority, and to critique some of the inherited certainties that come with socialization in families and relatively homogeneous communities.

Interestingly, examination of an area where his formal education failed him allows me to highlight the general effectiveness of David's public school education, and to find inspiration in it. David was schooled in Teaneck, New Jersey, at the time when African American students were bussed into the high school with no forums on racism, no conception of white privilege articulated in classrooms, and one Black History course in which David was the only white student. (Eventually, he was encouraged by the African American teacher to take it as an independent study "to avoid discomfort to himself and the other students.") We know from the writing of educational studies professor and powerful pro-democratic activist Michelle Fine that nearby Montclair, New Jersey, did learn something from the combination of aware and unaware racism that characterized Teaneck's mistakes of that era. Though there is no denying that David cannot stand in for all students, given his relative privilege and the anti-racist education he sought out, the promise of his education does offer hope of what public education, when appropriately well-funded and resistant to excesses of standardization, can offer. We have models for this education, now, and the Mary Cowheys to inspire us to improve it. We could even fund it with the relatively non-controversial billionaire's tax proposed by Warren Buffett.

David did continue to seek meaning in history and imaginative literature's exploration of life's powerful questions. He also remained preoccupied by a search for answers that led him briefly back to an exploration of one of his family's contributions to his foundational knowledge: Judaism. In other words, he too sought a spiritual dimension for his path in life. Just after we married he began rabbinical school.

During his years of rabbinical training, David was able to tell a "ghost story" after all, this again after the death of a beloved family member. At the time of that telling, an adult and recent father himself, he gave a sermon in the chapel of Hebrew Union College, Cincinnati, shortly after his father's death in 1987. American culture had changed since his childhood in the late Fifties and early Sixties with regard to openness to public consideration of available discussion about death itself as well as end-of-life philosophies. In his sermon, David argued that the conventional medical practices that had comprised the treatment of his father's fully metastasized and terminal cancer were not only irrational and materially wasteful, but were also morally offensive in that they constituted a war against the aspect of life that is death. (The treatment of his grandmother in the original deferred ghost story had constituted the same kind of war.) As a child, David had needed to restore dignity to his grandmother in the form of the good ghost story about her, and now, as an adult, he had the opportunity to restore dignity to all dying people through this sermon in honor of his father.

Through at last telling a good ghost story about the questions still haunting his family after his father's death, a story that deeply resonated for him with the hauntedness surrounding his experience as a child of his grandmother's dying, David addressed the something-to-be-done. He was fortunate in that he could tell the story to a well-targeted and politically responsive audience of fellow rabbinical students and their teachers. Maybe it was the positive reception of that sermon that supported a shy man to commit to periodically coming together with others in an effort to demand political change. In 1995, on the insistence of our then–nine-year-old son, Ben, our family traveled with six other members of David's congregation and a student of mine from my Social Action as Curriculum course to participate in a church rebuilding project in Greensboro, Alabama, following a Ku Klux Klan firebombing. Then, when our children were in high school, he accompanied them and a number of their friends to four out of the five major New York City and Washington, D.C., anti-war demonstrations against the impending war against Iraq. David has written two novels, both of which consider the potential of Jews and Muslims to coexist in relative peace. He believes today that the confrontation on his part with the "war against the aspect of life that is death" both motivated him to write these books and led to his serious interest in Buddhism. His current commitment to American Zen Buddhist meditation practices has freed him from a certain number of ghosts, and convinced him, more or less, of his right to exist in his own complex personhood.

THE THIRD STORY: THE GREAT DEATH AND DENIAL

Nearing the end of my work on this book, I wanted to close this last chapter with some reflection on the haunted experience of a community very different from that of both my husband, David, and the educational philosopher, Donna Kerr. My hope was to continue to reinforce the specific challenge to the closely related fields of cultural studies and educational studies this book intends to represent—that is, their tendency to privilege difference over universal claims about what it means to be human. While powerfully respecting difference, and invested in the elimination of all oppressions, I want us, in the contemporary neoliberal era, to focus more on the realities that bind all of us; these emerge from our unknowable obligations to one another—obligations I view as dangerously denied or minimized in the parallel work of contemporary public schools and the corporate university of excellence. Both of these are situated in the market relations that dominate our reality and impose on all of us "the suffocating reality principle whose distillate is the economy."

With such challenges for the end of the last chapter of this book in mind, I had the honor of observing the teaching by my educational studies colleague Melissa Kagle in her Core: Arctic class, a lesson that included study of the article "Yuuyaraq: The Way of the Human Being" by Alaska Native lay scholar, Yup'ik community civil servant, and eventual controversial elder, Harold Napoleon (1996). He begins his remarkably accessible and moving essay:

> For the past four years I have repeatedly tried to write letters and papers addressing the problem of alcoholism and alcohol abuse among Alaska's Native people. Each time I have stopped or thrown the paper away because the picture was never complete. There was always something missing. My efforts were like an incomplete sentence. (p. 1)

Writing from prison following an episode of drunken violence in which his son was killed, Napoleon revisits his personal history of descent into alcoholism during the years of his life that he devoted to the Yup'ik people while reclaiming his own Yup'ik identity. He attributes his recovery in prison to his intense grieving for both his son and for the Yup'ik community, as well as the research opportunity presented by incarceration with so many of his people. During this time, Napoleon recognizes precisely how "The Great Death"—particularly the final blow of the Nome influenza epidemic of 1900—not only decimated his people, but more significantly, destroyed their faith in "Yuuyaraq," the detailed oral code for living that included relationship to "the spirit world and the beings that inhabited it," "in deference to [which] Yup'ik life was lived" (p. 6).

Napoleon begins a complex example of hauntagogy with his focus on how the generations of his people who followed "The Great Death" understandably failed to unearth its ghosts, the failure of which facilitated a desperate and suicidal accommodation to Western colonization including Christianity:

> Unable to relive in their conscious minds the horror they had experienced, they did not talk about it with anyone. The survivors seem to have agreed,

> without discussing it, that they would not talk about it. It was too painful and the implications were too great to control. It was better not to talk about it, to act as if it had never happened, to "naullunguaq." To this day "nallunguaq" remains a way of dealing with problems or unpleasant occurrences in Yup'ik life. Young people are advised by elders to "nallunguarluku," "to pretend it didn't happen." (p. 12)

Of particular significance to our Western and language-based understanding of phenomena we did not personally experience, Napoleon (in his writing) and Kagle (in her teaching) offer us, their students, attention to this specific construction in the Yup'ik language introduced above by Napoleon.

Kagle grounded her lesson in the deconstruction of a range of Yup'ik words that contain the root/suffix (identified as a "post-base" in this family of languages) "uaq" meaning "made-up" or "pretend." This post-base, for instance, when added to the word denoting the small rectangular windows of the village houses, creates the word describing the geometric patterns (on typical fur-lined parkas) invoking these high windows (on the sod houses that were purposefully submerged in the earth for insulating warmth). Similarly, the same post-base added to the word for mountain identifies the geometric pattern of the textile design invoking the mountains visible through those high windows, and, when used as a border pattern on parkas, also identifies a different family lineage than that of the wearers of the window-derived pattern. A slight deviation of this post-base in the form of "(ng)uar" similarly affects verbs, so that "Calinguartuq" whose root is "Caling-" meaning to work, means "pretending to work" or "working without trying to really accomplish anything" (Jacobson, 1995, p. 282).

What speaks to us so profoundly in Napoleon's article as further interpreted with the support of Kagle's insights about the Yup'ik language is the specific focus of this deeply spiritual people, so continuous that it is recorded in the language, on *degree of removal from direct experience.* In this language, a word describing the intricate patterning of textile design on a coat refers not just to the high window of the submerged sod house that is replicated in the design, but equally to the fact of the pretense involved, even in the creation of (such culturally referential) art. It is a representation of, but not the real thing. Similarly, not all appearances, or claims of work, represent actual productive work.

This is a people so shaped by the privileging of investment in the first-order gifts of the spirit world in harmony with human agency (when such agency is respectful of the spirit world) that such consciousness is built into the language. That such a people could choose to deny its own devastation (invoking that same linguistic post-base for "pretend" conveying removal from authentic experience) that they could adopt a pretense which invalidates the possibility of rebuilding a future on an understanding of the near-historic past, constitutes a particularly poignant tragedy. Such a tragedy offers insight about a complication of haunting, which Gordon also accesses in her work: that it is not just the immediate oppressors and their allies who deny and seek to bury knowledge of the traumas and erasures for which their/our colonizations, occupations, and exploitations have been responsible: it is also the victims who have no words, no categories, and no safety for processing the trauma because the trauma is ongoing and there is no political movement correcting the victim-blaming while advocating for the sufferers. The victims are often in the position of having only disempowering non-choices, the first, the one made by the heavily alcoholic Yup'ik community to whose needs Napoleon has dedicated his adult life—to live in a traumatized non-community whose members access whatever form of oblivion is available. The other choice, to leave the community when affiliation has become traumatic, incurs a different state of suffering: wearing internalized oppression as lack of trust, making it impossible to meaningfully invest in others, and, compounding the impossibilities, continually meeting with oppressive assumptions about the sufferer's culture which the sufferer has at least in part internalized.

Yet I believe that Kagle was offering her students intimation about how these haunted choices for navigating life are different from our own more in intensity than in kind. Sara Ruddick's feminist formulation of a similar paradigm is the tension between having "lives, very much [our] own, and [being] inextricably connected to others" (1995). Bill Readings helps me understand that in our contemporary world, divorced from the Yup'ik spirit world, which was concretely alive and real for the Yup'ik people, what remains available to us as the basic sustenance of life is the reality of our unknowable obligations to others.

Thus, a people can be overwhelmed by the devastation which cannot be described in words available to their now invalidated communities of belief and practices, and, related, cannot be usefully addressed by any action that would constitute the engendering of new, more promising experience without significant re-evaluation. The point about trauma is precisely that it is paralyzing: It cuts off the humanity that is defined by our agency. The choices for a traumatized people are choices about how to live without that central aspect of humanity, the loss of which is the most profound stressor to the universal system of human flourishing that Freud (1961/1930) describes as (awareness of) the "economics of [one's] libido" (p. 28). Where will we invest and how will we distribute our diminished life energies? To what extent will we use intoxication, which in its extreme form of alcoholism and other addictions translates into the willful removal of our beings from investing in life at all, the willful evisceration of our all-too-painful humanity?

SOMETHINGS-TO-BE-DONE: THE END OF THE STORIES

In terms of the politics and spirituality of hauntedness, the experience of the alcoholism and alcohol-induced violence among his people that Napoleon seeks to redress, might be too severe and specific to spawn generalizations. Nevertheless, the thoughtful political proposals with which he responds—the somethings-to-be-done I will not consider in depth here—only magnify the resonances I experience between his people's suffering and the general crisis in the contemporary education-as-life crises I have sought to illuminate in this book. When Napoleon advocates for a return to his people of the fishing rights that have been taken over by global corporate interests, and for culturally specific approaches to alcoholism treatment, I find resonance with the contemporary situation in which we and our students find ourselves. The point about the internalizing of market relations in the current era is that it has proceeded so rapidly that "the suffocating reality principle" has come to define human nature, imposing a kind of death of the spirit. My concern is that with the absence of a discourse of "our unknowable obligations to one another," the increasing accretion of wealth in the hands of the top 10% of the One Percent is happening so rapidly that we are missing the words in circulation to process the rapid loss of democratic "mind-body in wholeness of operation" that is (Deweyan) life. I am afraid that the processes through which this is happening feel both so abstract and so overwhelming that we, as human culture, are responding by "pretend[ing] it isn't happening." Badiou's "suffocating reality principle whose distillate is the economy" purveys a kind of widespread trauma. Both aspects of what Dewey defines as life are demeaned: belief in the obligations that bind us to others, and belief that every human being has some unique contribution to make in the form expression of such obligations take, determined by our individual, complex personhoods.

Further, with fewer and fewer resources publically available for investment in sustaining (green) housing, alternatives to fossil fuels, and (non-neoliberal) public education of a quality that would challenge market relations (including war) with *thought*, the jobs available to my current students are marked by technological primacy, signaling their removal from the direct life experience of "mind-body in wholeness of operation" advocated by John Dewey, and his many allies in educational studies. We might say that our students have been deprived of fishing rights in their/our own locales. In other words many of our students have been denied the opportunity to emotionally connect to themselves and to others who are oppressed. Matthew Crawford (2009), author of *Shop Class as Soulcraft*, would argue that our graduating students who do not become *thought*ful makers, repairers, and do-ers (one model of my informal teachers) are, in the Yup'ik language, "pretending to work."

Dewey's rejection of the division of labor into thinking work and doing work as the model for education resonates with the cautions built into the Yup'ik language about degrees of movement away from direct agency and its association with the primal, with the visceral, with the spirit world, and with our unknowable obligations to others. I project onto Dewey a hope I believe Harold Napoleon would share: that pursuit of the questions Kerr raises about the dogfish must be central to the education of young people; such questions call up the reciprocity of the exchanges that encourage a more conscious balancing of our individual "economics of libido," without dependency on intoxication and addictions (including consumerism).

With the support of hauntagogy, can we move our students to appreciate how the deprivation of the very specific confidence—in Readings's terms the confidence inspired by recognition of one's unknowable obligations to others, and in Ruddick's to the twin truths of their "having lives very much their own" while also being "inextricably connected to others"—"haunts" their every presentation and reception of knowledge? If we *can* support them to identify ghosts, can we collectively grapple with the something-to-be-done beginning with Kerr's suggestion of a commitment to really listen to the stories of others in our classrooms and their surrounds, extending to the global egalitarian project? Just as significantly, might we loosen the stranglehold of "the suffocating reality principle whose distillate is the economy" on our college students by igniting renewed interest in pursuing the missed possibilities of their (haunted) "child and adolescent growth"? And might we accomplish this direction through the study with them of complex narratives like Harold Napoleon's reconstruction of not only traumatic Yu'pik history, but also of the genius of a language that asks us to notice when we depart (perhaps too far) from the direct experience, so central to the maintenance of our mind-body agency?

There is vast repair work for the global fabric intimated here, and our students can commit to any part of it, but much of the work will need to be culturally relevant and led by people whose specific needs are being addressed. This is the other importance of identity politics, yet it is Napoleon who would brilliantly build into social policy a time limitation on certain kinds of special attention to the needs of all traumatized groups, a category in which I would include the unemployed and underemployed.

As painfully poignant to me as the terms of this specific rupture experienced by the Yup'ik people are, I experience with equal weight (but on the opposite emotional pole) exhilarating joy that Bill Readings does not even intimate that our unknowable obligations to others constitute a spiritual center for us. Rather, he acknowledges that "it is easy to sound mystical when speaking of incalculable obligation or unknowable (and hence unpayable) debt, of non-finite responsibility toward the Other." He continues:

> But I am not trying to sound mystical. I am saying something rather simple: that we do not know in advance the nature of our obligations to others, obligations that have no origin except in the sheer fact of the existence of Otherness—people, animals, things other to ourselves—that comports an incalculable obligation. (pp. 188-189)

I find such a convergence of spiritual and political obviousness intimating somethings-to-be-done especially hopeful in the current era. Yet to seize such hopefulness is to loosen the linguistic boundaries between structural, post-structural, and spiritual discourses about reality and its possibilities. We teachers will need to agree to be propelled by feelings of liveliness nurtured by our unknowable obligations to others. (The now decimated and only partly recoverable Yup'ik spirit world contributed to the Yup'ik people a parallel enlivening consciousness.)

David's journey can be seen as a journey of reclaiming balance for himself after a loss of confidence in his own child's world of meaning-making. He had emotional and material resources to assist him in this journey made available by the same imperfect parents who could not appreciate his first ghost story. His community included a public school system that at least sometimes appreciated the need for children to closely observe a live dogfish—a system in which there was some recognition of the interaction between relations of power and the complex personhood of the players. (As we consider the inadequacy of one class on African American history and no attention to the history and politics of white privilege in the mid-Sixties, we must recognize that there will always be limitations in consciousness, precisely the reason to keep alive the focus on haunting.) And unlike the Yup'ik people in the time before "The Great Death," David's community explicitly held the Deweyan intention of expanding his knowledge beyond that available in his family and immediate community's private and necessarily limited culture.

Kerr pleads for an education for her child and for all children that will make available in the public sphere of schooling encouragement for ghost stories like David's, and fears, quite reasonably, that this vision of schooling is threatened by the policies of the contemporary neoliberal agenda. She recognizes the specificity and immediacy of the project of nurturing each individual child like her own, which will require not only the commitment to listen to the stories of every one of them, but also the provision of living dogfish that can be observed and wondered about in their natural habitat. Harold Napoleon translates the provision of such nurturing education to the needs of his own people, where a focus on "The Great Death" and its devastation of their world might begin the healing education promised by revisioned global history—as much needed by my own students as his. This education is part of the obligations to others that sustains life for all of us, and it will require the return of fishing rights to those most aware of the complexity of their relationship with the local fish.

With my awareness of the *personal is political* in the navigation of my own individual life, I feel a need to re-evaluate my attraction to the answers provided by Marxism, psychoanalysis, and now, a peculiar combination of both of these with Zen Buddhism, recognizing the determinism, the toughness, and the masculinity of my choices. Why not invite in more explicitly the feminist wisdom that provides the counterpoint to market relations of my earliest mentors in the field of educational studies, Madeleine Grumet (1988), Sara Ruddick (1989), and JoAnne Pagano (1995)? They argued so persuasively that the central haunting of our lives as teachers is the construction of educational philosophy on concerns of power and knowledge, as opposed to connection. Might their critique make even more accessible nourishment for the curriculum in "the mix-up of love and education [that] begins life" (Britzman, 2011, p. 59)? Might the focus on the framing of our (actual) first education by the knowledge that we have all come out of the body of a mother—that we owe our life to her—give another kind of compelling credence to Readings's claim of our obligations to others?

I believe I am coming to understand the most promising inquiry to propel me forward in the last quarter of this life of mine in which human-ness and teaching are inextricably connected: What are the fishing rights that are mine to reclaim as teacher and mother in an era of devastating pretenses, thefts, and denials? And how might the hauntagogy I practice with my students find new inspiration in a willingness to be guided by both the awareness of Readings—that "An order of knowledge and an institutional structure are now breaking down" (p. 191) and that "the university originates in the imperatives of the church of the Middle Ages … [when] knowledge becomes associated with a rejection of the body and a fear of desire"? (Schott as cited in Pagano, (1995). Readings does not need to remind us teacher educators of our need to resist when the discourse of excellence that marks this breakdown "tells teachers and students simply not to worry about how things fit together, since this is not their problem" (p. 191) or in recent times, 'on the standardized test.' We know that how things fit together is very much our problem.

How *do* things fit together, then, when we assume a human nature constructed by the knowledge that we are all born out of the body of a mother, and that we share different iterations of the mix-up of love and education that greets each of us? Both of these pieces of knowledge determine the reality that we are born in a dependent state and will always need the people who came before us, whose limited hero systems construct the challenges of our lives around both social inequalities and the divorce of mind and body recognized not only by feminists, but also by John Dewey and his allies among social reconstructionist educators. Our relationships will always be fraught with hauntedness, especially as we recognize that in some ways we have already done what Dewey proposed: We have moved beyond the places of our births to allow ourselves to realize that our local wisdom is limited—it *needs* education. So we turn our attention now from the distortions imposed by disciplinary boundaries in education, and entertain Bill Readings's proposal for "a shifting disciplinary structure that holds open the question of whether and how thoughts fit together" (p. 191). We will need to engage our students in this challenge, and to do so, they must embrace the global egalitarian project as undiminished teachers themselves, "because ultimately haunting is about how to transform a shadow of a life into an undiminished life whose shadows touch softly in the spirit of a peaceful reconciliation. In this necessarily collective undertaking, the end, which is not an ending at all, belongs to everyone" (Gordon, 2008, p. 208).

THE FEMINIST PROFESSOR'S DOUBTS

I am participating in the Great Mother Conference in Nobleboro, Maine, and we are studying the myth of Parzifal. I find excruciating the directive of the White Queen, Herzeloyde, to her courtiers to gather together and strangle the birds in the forest. This directive follows Parzifal's exhilaration with birdsong; he confides in his mother how the song of these birds lifts his heart and makes him believe anything is possible. The feeling of possibility resonates in all of us participating in our collective performance of the myth, as it does in Herzeloyde, with desire for deeper engagement with the wide world, and with her grief, held intact by virtual isolation from any community in which she might engage this grief. Yet possibilities for her son that promise engagement with the worldly pursuit of power in tournaments and knighthood mean, to her, delivery of her son to the death that met her beloved Gahmuret. Herzeloyde is responding to her desire as a mother to protect her son Parzifal from his joining up with the three knights who are urging Parzifal to return to the world.

Brilliant in this myth is the phrase "losing the ability to shudder," the description of the effect on Parzifal of the loss of birdsong. This book has grown out of my conviction that everything hangs on ours and our students' collective recovery of the ability to shudder, closely related to the ability prized by the poet Louise Gluck to intimate a wholeness that does not sacrifice the mystery of the unfinished. Writing of her attraction "to ellipsis, to the unsaid, to suggestion, to eloquent, deliberate silence," Glück likens the unsaid in a poem

> to the unseen; for example, to the power of ruins, to works of art either damaged or incomplete. Such works inevitably allude to larger contexts; they haunt because they are not whole, though wholeness is implied; another time, a world in which they were whole, or were to have been whole, is implied. (p. 378)

Glück captures the power of haunting in its reference to a wholeness that "[was] to have been," and in so doing, identifies for me the frustration of the work of teaching for social justice in the contemporary era. I am writing in response to the complicated reality that most of my students are not appropriately haunted by the unfinished, the damaged, the ruined pro-democratic curricular projects inspired by the conception of *The Educational Imagination* (as intimated by Elliot Eisner in his book of that title in 1979/2002).

I conceive the work of teaching in the contemporary era as literally to induce haunting in my students, recognizing that their lives, including their formal education, are circumscribed by the neoliberal agenda that denies hauntedness. In schools it seeks to create a closed, disconnected testable curriculum that will determine through its endless testing who deserves what in a society that increasingly has little "what" to offer and currently allows even those meager resources to slip into the possession of the ten percent of the One Percent.

I understand the curriculum to be the whole to which Louise Glück refers when she says: "The problem is to make a whole that does not forfeit this power" (p. 378). She knows, and we know, that the project is an impossibility, though the direction towards this impossibility is all we have, and in teaching, it is represented by *thought*, as defined by Readings.

When poet Michael Quam writes "these skins into which so much has been poured must give back with our voices, our gestures of gratitude" (2007, p. 54), he invokes for me an interpretation of something-to-be-done that is not entertained by Gordon's sociology of haunting, but is intimated in Britzman's psychoanalysis of teaching and in Readings's unknowable obligations to others. Gratitude is expression of the self/the skin capable of recognizing itself as carrier of poured goods, and therefore having a plenitude to afford the global egalitarian project.

A desire to end with an original poem raised the concern that including the poem would obligate me to rationalize my increasing use of poetry-writing assignments with my students; the increasing use of poetry and poetry craft in the classroom represents an extension of my growing awareness of the importance of poetry to my own continued intellectual and spiritual growth.

Yet I had to face the reality that I am not yet ready to fully articulate that rationale; I think I need more study of poetry and poetry craft myself, and more experimentation with poetry writing assignments with my students, in order to observe emerging patterns. Once patterns emerge, I will know how to angle stories related to my teaching of poetry craft and my use of specific assignments whose educative potential I can articulate. It is the case, though, that I had actually considered writing this book as a collection of poems; that is how tightly tied for me is the theme of the need to unearth ghosts with poetry craft. When I thought that I might write such a book, I searched for great quotations about or related to poetry, and the best two I found, both by Deborah Britzman, I realized I *could* use in this epilogue, both to introduce my own poem, and to suggest what I am beginning to explore and expect to write about more extensively in the future. Here is the first quotation from Britzman:

> The ego's paradox is that it is already in the world and must find a way to live there. The poet's solution is narrative revolts, an appeal to the imagination. The poet constructs an affecting story, one wherein people can see themselves anew and think about their quills. The poet revolts against the suspension of meaning that group psychology creates by giving representation to that uncanny suspension and, in doing so, must disregard real relations with others. (2011, p. 118)

Britzman captures here the reality about poetry writing that sometimes stops me in my own journey into the world of poetry. She explains why producing poetry, perhaps producing any art, is ultimately a lonely path. The paradox of people trying to learn together in a group is that in any group, each person's ego, including consciousness of specific others (which includes the parent/leader/teacher/preacher/therapist) will generate a great deal of wildness. That wildness will impede education, even as the wild transference relationships, the positive and negative effects of love restimulated, make all education possible. Learning is the way "to live in the world." Love of knowledge, love of the teacher, love of one's co-learners, is the reason people learn. This realization is not unrelated to Dewey's understanding that education is for the continual replication (with improvement) of the human race and the world humans impact, except that it adds the element of possible impossibility which Dewey did not want to consider.

The transference relationships in any classroom will prevent a distillation of meaning, and this is both the hope and curse of education. The poet will not accept any "pretend" distillation; for instance, a singular one being promoted by the teacher and/or the text, or even the "there's two sides of every story" distillations being promoted by liberalism. The poet will not accept that a classroom rebel and her allies have the whole story either. The poet "revolts" against any easy, even any hard-won narratives, and stays allied with the quills in every possible interpretation, holding out for the missing (?) truth (yes, that problematic word appears again) in suspended meaning, as opposed to making the typical accommodations to not knowing for certain: feelings of powerlessness that typically collude with anti-intellectualism and an unwillingness to act.

But the sad reality for me is that in giving representation to the suspended meaning, the poet agrees not to be identified with the life world constructed around any group's interpretation. This explains the loneliness implicit in the work. A related realization is that the desire to have my students participate in "narrative revolts" means that part of my work is helping to socialize them to tolerate more loneliness. Such a reality conflicts with our focus on identification with specific learning communities, our continual emphasis on being in community with others. It might even contradict my certainty about the pursuit of the global egalitarian project.

The suspended meaning holds all the ghosts, it turns out, and the poet wants to expose them. Britzman identifies the very pressure the poet resists:

> In any learning one feels pressure, without knowing from where it comes, to make knowledge certain and so to stabilize the object lest it escape one's efforts. This fight with knowledge meets its limits in anguish over the loss of certainty, a loss needed in order to symbolize what is new. In the dream work of education, we act without knowing in advance what becomes of our efforts and meet again ignorance and hubris, but also our passion and desire. We hope that education can help us out of this mess and worry that education is this mess. We can, with confidence, admit that because learning is always an emotional situation, the very thought of education animates our fantasies of knowledge, authority, and love. (2009, p. ix)

Even when challenging disciplinary constraints, an academic book will always forfeit some of the power that Glück elegizes, because as Britzman recognizes, that is the cost of symbolizing anything new. Poetry perhaps forfeits somewhat less the power of the unfinished, even as it seeks wholeness. I close this book with a poem, in the hopes that it will be partially redemptive, and that it will resonate with Britzman's desire to liberate the dreamwork of education, or liberate education to dreamwork:

The Feminist Professor's Doubts

In the dream, someone more decisive than myself
found the right tall staircase and unrolled a book
like a Torah scroll, from the carpeted top step,
having figured out the good boundary crossing story
between the girl who made privacy from soap scum
and the teaching of Shays' Rebellion
as the most lost battle of the Revolutionary War.

It features lessons in Deweyan imagination:
We girls arrayed against those Boston bankers,
demanding respect for boys who fought and won
while we upheld our end of the bargain.

"All teaching is interference,"
said Anna Freud, in a tongue not my mother's.
And prepared to interfere mightily:
We could storm the lecture halls:
"Those silly Brits already banned slavery!" we'd yell,
and even in the math labs:
the Mozambiquan basket weavers
now of ethno-mathematics fame—
model one seventh of a circumference
as Euclid could not

They're women, you know,
women who prefer the fixed shape.
And did you know that capitalism grew
because ancient girls left home with husbands?
Remember Rebecca at the well,
leaving Mom for that shlemazel, Isaac?

The more households, the more baskets,
the more exchange, the more books.
Books, too, are neither dreams nor poems.
They have fixed shapes.
We need to resolve if my book is
something anybody needs.

REFERENCES

Anyon, J. (1981). Social class and school knowledge. *Curriculum Inquiry, 11*(1), 3-42.

Apple, M. (1996). Education, identity and cheap French fries. In M. Apple, *Cultural politics and education* (pp. 1-21). New York, NY: Teachers College Press.

Aptheker, B. (2006). *Intimate politics: How I grew up red, fought for free speech, and became a feminist rebel.* Emeryville, CA: Seal Press.

Badiou, A. (2001). *Ethics: An essay on the understanding of evil.* Verso.

Becker, E. (1971). *The birth and death of meaning: An interdisciplinary perspective on the problem of man* (second edition). New York, NY: The Free Press.

Becker, E. (1973). *The denial of death.* New York: Free Press Paperbacks.

Brach, T. (2003). *Radical acceptance: Embracing your life with the heart of a Buddha.* New York, NY: Bantam Dell.

Britzman, D. (1996). Pedagogy and transference: Casting the past of learning into the presence of teaching. *Theory into Practice, 35*(2), 117-123.

Britzman, D. (1998). *Lost subjects, contested objects: Toward a psychoanalytic inquiry of learning.* Albany: State University of New York Press.

Britzman, D. P. (2009). *The very thought of education: Psychoanalysis and the impossible professions.* Albany: State University of New York Press.

Britzman, D. P. (2011). *Freud and education.* New York, NY, and London, England: Routledge.

Burns, K. (Director). (2001). *Jazz* [Motion picture].

Cabasso, J. (2011, June 19). US Mayors Conference considers call to end wars. Environmentalists Against War. Retrieved from http://www.envirosagainstwar.org/know/read.php?itemid=11038

Campbell, J. A. (1996). Oratory, democracy and the classroom. In R. Soder (Ed.), *Democracy, education and the schools* (pp. 211-243). San Francisco, CA: Jossey-Bass Publishers.

Carver, T. (1998). *The postmodern Marx.* Manchester, England: Manchester University Press.

Chang, I. (1997). *The rape of Nanking: The forgotten holocaust of World War II.* New York, NY: Basic Books.

Cochran-Smith, M. (1991). Learning to teach against the grain. *Harvard Educational Review, 51*(3), 279-310.

Cooper, H. (2011, June 21). Cost of wars a rising issue as Obama weighs troop levels. *The New York Times.* Retrieved from http://www.nytimes.com/2011/06/22/us/politics/22costs.html?pagewanted=all

Cowhey, M. (2006). *Black ants and Buddhists: Thinking critically and teaching differently in the primary grades.* Portland, ME: Stenhouse Publishers.

Crawford, M. B. (2009). *Shop class as soulcraft: An inquiry into the value of work.* New York, NY: Penguin Press.

Delpit, L. (1995). *Other people's children: Cultural conflict in the classroom.* New York, NY: The New Press.

Derrida, J. (1994). *Specters of Marx: The state of the debt, the work of mourning, and the new international.* New York, NY: Routledge.

Dewey, J. (1915, 2001). *The school and society & the child and the curriculum.* Mineola, NY: Dover Publications.

Dewey, J. (1916). *Democracy and education.* New York, NY: The Free Press.

Dewey, J. (1928). Body and mind. *Bulletin of the NY Academy of Medicine.*

Dewey, J. (1969-1991). Body and mind. In *The collected works of John Dewey: Later works, volume 3:1927–1928, essays, reviews, miscellany* (pp. 25-40). Carbondale: Southern Illinois University Press.

Dewey, J. (2000, May 28). *John Dewey and the F. M. Alexander Technique.* Retrieved from The Alexander Techinique Center: http://www.alexandercenter.com/jd/index.html

REFERENCES

Douglas, A. (1998). *The feminization of American culture.* New York, NY: Noonday Press.

Eisner, E. W. (1979). *The educational imagination: On the design and evaluation of school programs.* New York, NY: Macmillan.

Ellis, C., Adams, T., and Bochner, A. (January 2011). Autoethnography: An overview in the online version of the journal FQS Forum: Qualitative Social Research Volume 12, No. 1, Art. 10.

Fine, M. (1991). *Framing dropouts: Notes on the politics of an urban public high school.* Albany: State University of New York Press.

Fine, M. W. (2003). *Silenced voices and extraordinary conversations: Re-imagining schools.* New York, NY: Teachers College Press.

Fleming, R. (2006). Bones for historians: Putting the body back into biography. In D. Bates (Ed.), *Writing medieval biography: Essays in honour of Frank Barlow* (pp. 29-48). Woodbridge: Boydell & Brewer.

Finn, P. J. (1999). *Literacy with an attitude: Educating working-class children in their own self-interest.* Albany: State University of New York Press.

Freud, S. (1961). *Civilization and its discontents* (standard edition). New York, NY, and London, England: W.W. Norton & Company.

Geertz, C. (1973). Thick description: Toward an interpretive theory of culture. In C. Geertz, *The interpretation of cultures: Selected essays.* New York, NY: Basic Books.

Glück, L. (2004). Disruption, hesitation, silence (1994). In Dana Gioia, David Mason, & Meg Schoerke, with D. C. Stone (Eds.), *Twentieth-century American poetics: Poets on the art of poetry.* New York, NY: McGraw-Hill.

Gordon, A. F. (2008). *Ghostly matters: Haunting and the sociological imagination.* Minneapolis: University of Minnesota Press.

Gordon, J. W. (1946). *My country school diary: An adventure in creative teaching.* New York, NY: Harper & Brothers.

Greene, M. (1982). Public education and the public space. *Educational Researcher, 11*(6), June-July, 4-9.

Greene, M. (1988). *The dialectic of freedom.* New York, NY: Teachers College Press.

Greene, M. (1995). *Releasing the imagination: Essays on education, the arts, and social change.* San Francisco, CA: Jossey-Bass Publishers.

Grumet, M. R. (1988). *Bitter milk: Women and teaching.* Amherst: University of Massachusetts Press.

Hadley, T. (2011, June 6). Clever girl. *New Yorker.*

Harste, J. W. (1984). *Language stories & literacy lessons.* Portsmouth, NH: Heinemann Educational Books.

hooks, b. (1994). *Teaching to transgress: Education as the practice of freedom.* New York, NY, and London, England: Routledge.

Jacobson, S. A. (1995). *A practical grammar of the central Alaskan Yup'ik Eskimo language.* Fairbanks, AK: Alaska Native Language Center.

Johnston, D. K. (2006). *Education for a caring society.* New York, NY: Teachers College Press.

Kerr, D. H. (1996). Democracy, nurturance, and community. In R. Soder (Ed.), *Democracy, education and the schools* (pp. 37-68). San Francisco, CA: Jossey-Bass.

Kingsolver, B. (1990). *Animal dreams: A novel.* New York, NY: HarperCollins.

Klein, N. (2002). *No logo: No space, no choice, no jobs.* New York, NY: Picador.

Kolhi, W. (1995). Educating for emancipatory rationality. In W. Kohli, *Critical conversations in philosophy of education* (pp. 103–115). New York, NY: Routledge.

Lee, C.-R. (1999). *A gesture life.* New York, NY: Riverhead Books.

Lifton, R. J. (1993). *The protean self: Human resilience in an age of fragmentation.* New York, NY: Basic Books.

Loewen, J. W. (1995). *Lies my teacher told me: Everything your American history textbook got wrong.* New York, NY: The New Press.

Madrick, J. (2013, March). The fall and rise of Occupy Wall Street. *Harper's, 326*(1954), 9-11.

McCann, C. (1998). *This side of brightness.* New York, NY: Picador.

Napoleon, H. (1996). *Yuuyaraq: The way of the human being.* Chicago, IL: University of Chicago Press.

Neefus, C. (2008). Economic downturn hits hard for Colgate students. *Colgate Maroon-News,* September 26, p. A2.

Noddings, N. (1992). Social studies and feminism. *Theory & Research in Social Education, 20*(3), 230-241.

Nussbaum, M. (2009). Tagore, Dewey, and the imminent demise of liberal education. In H. Siegel, *The Oxford handbook of philosophy of education* (pp. 52-64). Oxford, England, and New York, NY: Oxford University Press.

Oyler, C. (2001). Extending narrative inquiry. *Curriulum Inquiry, 31*(1), 77-88.

Pagano, J. A. (1995). Matters of the mind. In W. Kohli, *Critical conversations in philosophy of education* (pp. 340-354). New York, NY: Routledge.

Paley, V. G. (1990). *The boy who would be a helicopter: The uses of storytelling in the classroom.* Cambridge, MA, and London, England: Harvard University Press.

Paley, V. G. (1992). *You can't say you can't play.* Cambridge, MA, and London, England: Harvard University Press.

Peterson, T. E. (2010). Badiou, pedagogy and the arts. *Educational Philosophy and Theory, 42*(2), 159-176.

Poppendieck, J. (1998). *Sweet charity?: Emergency food and the end of entitlement.* New York, NY: Viking.

Quam, M. (2007). "Why we sing." *Borne on swift currents* (p. 54). McKinleyville, CA: Six Rivers Press.

Readings, B. (1996). *The university in ruins.* Cambridge, MA, and London, England: Harvard University Press.

Regenspan, B. (2002). *Parallel practices: Social justice-focused teacher education and the elementary school classroom.* New York, NY: Peter Lang Publishing.

Regenspan. (2012). *Poem from Pondicherry.* Retrieved from Reflections from India: http://colgate-india-core.blogspot.com/2012/01/poem-from-pondicherry-everything.html

Ricoeur, P. (1998). *Critique and conviction.* New York, NY: Columbia University Press.

Ruddick, S. (1995). *Maternal thinking: Toward a politics of peace.* Boston, MA: Beacon Press.

Salvio, P. (2007). *Anne Sexton: Teacher of weird abundance.* Albany: State University of New York Press.

Scialabba, G. (2011). *The modern predicament.* Boston, MA: Pressed Wafer.

Smith, G. (2011). US mayors to Obama: Bring war money home! Ban the bomb! *Berkeley Daily Planet,* June 22. Retrieved from http://www.berkeleydailyplanet.com/issue/2011-06-22/article/38029

Spadola, E. (2011). Forgive me friend: Mohammed and Ibrahim. *Anthropological Quaterly, 84*(3), 737-756.

Stein, S. (2011). US mayors to push for first anti-war resolution since VietNam. *The Huffington Post,* June 15. Retrieved from http://www.huffingtonpost.com/2011/06/15/us-mayors-to-push-for-ani-war-resolution_n_877817.html

Stern, M. (2009). *Situating relation in photographic exposure: Education, ethics, and the framing of violence.* Unpublished doctoral dissertation. Syracuse University.

Stern, M. (2012). Presence, absence, and the presently absent: Ethics and the pedagogical possibilities of photographs. *Educational Studies: A Journal of the American Educational Studies Association, 48*(2), 174-198.

Torgovnick, M. D. (1994). *Crossing ocean parkway.* Chicago, IL: University of Chicago Press.

Weber Gordon, J. (1946). *My country school diary.* New York, NY: Harper & Brothers.

Williams, P. (1991). *The alchemy of race and rights.* Cambridge, MA: Harvard University Press.

Williams, R. (1977). *Marxism and literature.* Oxford, England: Oxford University Press.

INDEX

CPSIA information can be obtained at www.ICGtesting.com
Printed in the USA
BVOW08s1459170415

396643BV00002B/2/P

9 789462 098169